CITIZEN SCIE

In *Citizen Science* Alan Irwin explores the difficult relationship between science, society and the environment.

Drawing upon sociological studies of scientific knowledge and of the 'risk society', the author argues that 'sustainable development' will not be possible without attention to questions of citizenship and citizen knowledge. Having conducted a critical discussion of the relationship between science and environmental policy-making, he considers the existence of more 'contextual' forms of knowledge and understanding. Current discussions of the public understanding of science tend to dismiss these citizen expertises as uninformed or irrational. Irwin argues that such forms of expertise are essential to the processes of sustainable development – not least because of the challenge they offer to scientific institutions.

The book addresses matters of environmental threat and sustainability from the perspective of science and citizenship. For example, Irwin doesn't fall into the trap of using a simple 'pro' or 'anti' stance on science, but discusses the relationship between scientific understanding and the different ways in which people make sense of environmental concerns. In conclusion, the book considers the practical possibilities for sustainable development which emerge as a consequence.

Citizen Science provides a much needed route through the fraught relationship between science, the public and environmental threat.

Alan Irwin is Reader in Sociology at Brunel University, West London.

ENVIRONMENT AND SOCIETY
Edited by Steven Yearley

Environmental Sociology
John Hannigan

Environmentalism and Cultural Theory
Kay Milton

CITIZEN SCIENCE

A study of people, expertise and sustainable development

Alan Irwin

London and New York

First published 1995
by Routledge
11 New Fetter Lane, London EC4P 4EE

Simultaneously published in the USA and Canada
by Routledge
29 West 35th Street, New York, NY 10001

Reprinted 2001 (twice) 2002

Routledge is an imprint of the Taylor & Francis Group

© 1995 Alan Irwin

Typeset in Bembo by
Ponting–Green Publishing Services, Chesham, Bucks
Printed and bound in Great Britain by
T.J.I. Digital, Padstow, Cornwall

British Library Cataloguing in Publication Data
A catalogue record for this book is available from
the British Library

Library of Congress Cataloguing in Publication Data
A catalogue record for this book has been requested

ISBN 0–415–11548–5 (hbk)
ISBN 0–415–13010–7 (pbk)

For Doreen

CONTENTS

PREFACE

Books about 'science and its publics' typically take a number of forms. Of these, perhaps the most common is the scientist's (or the science journalist's) attempt to convince the public of either the intellectual grandeur or the practical significance of scientific research. Within this category, we can include the enormous number of 'popular science' books which deal with the more philosophical reaches of science (with quantum physics and chaos theory particular favourites here) or with various socially pressing matters within which science plays an important part (ozone depletion or 'test tube babies').

However, there has also been a steady output of books which attack science either for its 'disenchantment' of everyday life or for its linkage to troubling areas of development such as *in vitro* fertilization, advanced weapon systems or civil nuclear power. This more critical literature takes a number of forms – including the feminist debate over science and the continuing discussion over the connection between science and environmental destruction.

It follows from even this briefest of summaries of a large and expanding literature that any new book about science and its publics must at least have something original to say – a Unique Selling Proposition of some kind. So where is the USP in what follows? I want to suggest very briefly that the uniqueness of this book comes not from any single aspect but rather from its *combination* of different elements.

In the first place, *Citizen Science* tries to find a way through the usual monolithic representations of 'science' and the 'public'. Both the 'public understanding of science' and the 'scientific understanding of the public' will, therefore, be considered. In doing so, it will be important to view these categories as diverse and differentiated –

the science of quantum physics is very different from the science of epidemiology – and public groups will see it as such. Equally, the public for a science museum exhibition will have different concerns and motivations than the local public anxious about the safety of a petrochemical plant. In this book, I will try to be balanced in my treatment of both the sciences and the publics – especially in order that we can get beyond the usual sterile dichotomies.

Second, I want to suggest throughout the following chapters that social science – and especially sociology – can make an important contribution to our understanding here. In making this general claim, I will draw upon three particular areas: the sociology of scientific knowledge; theories of the risk society; empirical accounts of science and its publics in specific contexts. Of course, reference to social theory will at times make this book a little difficult for the non-specialist reader. However, my strong claim is that such literatures have a substantial relevance here and not least in offering a new and constructive way of conceptualizing the current situation. At the same time, the study of this important area can make a major contribution to our wider theoretical interpretation of the changing social structure.

In arguing this, I am aware that not all scientists – or social scientists – will agree with me. Recent encounters between these academic groups have not always been as constructive as I would have wished. Hopefully, what follows will rebalance this situation.

Third, this book will address issues of science and its publics within the context of risk and environmental matters. At one level, the selection of such a context needs no justification – risk and environmental concerns represent a pressing set of questions and also a major area of encounter between scientific institutions and citizens. However, the argument here will move beyond this so as to suggest that questions of knowledge and expertise are central to environmental response and to the very idea of sustainable development. Put simply, a sustainable society needs a sustainable way of handling science and expertise. Equally, risk and environmental matters serve as an exemplar of other areas of social and technical debate – the lessons drawn from here have applications and consequences elsewhere.

Fourth, and this has been implicit in my comments so far, this book is aimed at that point where analysis and intervention meet each other. On the one hand, I want to make some general suggestions about how policy and practice might be improved. On the other, I want to argue that such matters as policy are not merely 'applications' of academic analysis nor are they simply 'implementations' – instead the whole question of how interventions are made is a major issue in itself. For scientists and social scientists alike, the contexts within which expertise becomes applied within everyday life are important sites of reflection and discovery. Contributing to public policy is therefore far from easy – but it offers the possibility of deepening our understanding of the problems at hand.

I suspect the fifth dimension of USP is found in the rather odd book title. *Citizen Science* was chosen at one level simply because it is (for me) pleasingly alliterative. More importantly, I chose it because it conveys both senses of the relationship between science and citizens as they will be discussed. 'Citizen Science' evokes a science which assists the needs and concerns of citizens – as the apologists of science so often claim. At the same time, 'Citizen Science' implies a form of science developed and enacted by citizens themselves – and one important strand of this book will deal with the 'contextual knowledges' which are generated outside of formal scientific institutions. In the following chapters we will pursue both of these connotations – with the earlier chapters concentrating on the former whilst the latter consider the relationship between formalized science (which often claims to be universal) and the less-systematized (and often 'local' – although not necessarily in the geographical sense) knowledges possessed and developed by citizen groups.

From the very beginning, I want to stress that these citizen knowledges are not necessarily 'better' than those of science – such a formulation assists us very little. Instead, we need to take a broader and more sceptical approach to environmental understanding than is implied by simply replacing one set of knowledge claims with another.

Of course, no sales pitch makes any sense unless there is a market for the product. What then of the intended readership for *Citizen Science*?

I think it follows from what has been said so far that this book is aimed at a number of audiences. Certainly, this should include those explicitly concerned with matters of science communication, the public understanding of science or science and its publics – an audience which spans students on the growing number of taught courses in this area but also those who through their employment or personal concerns operate in this field (which just about covers all of us). Second and given the strong risk/environmental flavour of what follows, this is a book for those concerned with environmental matters – it will push them particularly towards questions of expertise, citizenship and social sustainability. Third, I hope scientists themselves will engage with this book if only to be provoked out of 'deficit' (or 'enlightenment') models of an irrational and passively ignorant public for science. Finally, this is a book for social scientists and especially sociologists – I hope to convince them that this is a field where they can make a useful and timely contribution but also where they have a lot to learn.

In aiming to communicate with such diverse audiences I am of course taking the risk that I will actually connect with none. However, and if I can be allowed to push the marketing metaphor just a little further, it seems to me that there is a substantial 'niche' between these audiences – and one which is currently neglected. Thus, rather than participating in the demonization of either scientists or social scientists, I want to suggest that something substantial can be gained by bringing these groups together. Equally, environmental debates can benefit from an awareness of underlying questions of citizenship and expertise. If criticism of what follows leads any of these audiences to construct more adequate accounts of their own – then a major goal of *Citizen Science* will have been achieved.

It follows from this diversity of audiences that I have a diversity of acknowledgements to offer. Various parts of this research were supported by external bodies – and I am particularly grateful to the Science Policy Support Group, the Economic and Social Research Council, the Nuffield Foundation and the Commission of the European Communities (Research in social and economic aspects of the environment, DGXII/D/5) for their support. The Science Policy Support Group deserves special thanks for establishing a network of British researchers in this broad field and I am grateful for the assistance provided within that network by colleagues working on related projects.

This book was also written across various institutional locations. I would like to thank the former Department of Science and Technology Policy and the current Department of Sociology at the University of Manchester for their help and encouragement. More recently, the Department of Human Sciences and the Centre for Research into Innovation, Culture and Technology (CRICT) at Brunel University have supported and stimulated me. I also want to thank the various cohorts of students who have prodded and challenged me as numerous draft chapters were thinly disguised as lectures – such students include those at Manchester and Brunel but also at Birkbeck College.

Numerous people have helped me in numerous ways. With some hesitation lest I offend those omitted, I would like to single out Donna Baston, Simon Bennett, Alison Dale, Susse Georg, Ken Green, Paul Hooper, Don Lloyd, Tom Osborne, Janet Rachel, Sue Scott, Denis Smith, Jon Turney, Philip Vergragt, Steve Woolgar, Brian Wynne, Steve Yearley and John Ziman. Steve Yearley deserves particular thanks for his friendly but incisive editing – every time I tried busking he would catch me out. Needless to say, this book would have been greatly improved if I'd listened properly to any of these people.

One aspect of the 'risk society' concerns the process of individualization whereby we are each thrown back on our own resources and personal capacities. In many ways, the preparation of this book suggests the very opposite – it would never have been possible without the support of my family in all three of its major outposts. Thanks!

Marlow
November 1994

INTRODUCTION

Science and technology are major forces in our everyday lives. They help structure our personal and working relationships. They offer new possibilities – but also new threats. They allow opposite ends of the globe to speak to one another – simultaneously, they are linked to the possible despoliation of that globe through industrial pollution and environmental damage. Science and technology also offer new ways of understanding everyday reality – they exist both as a body of 'facts' about the world and as a framework for rational thought. Meanwhile, that form of rationality may blind us to alternative ways of valuing ourselves and the world around us.

This book is written at a time when the relationship between public groups, science and environmental challenges appears more pressing than ever. However, it is also written in the belief that an emerging body of scholarship and practical initiative is well-placed to address these challenges.

Of course, given the social significance of science and technology, it is hardly surprising that these themes have already emerged as a major concern within everyday life and social theory. Max Weber is particularly associated with the notion of the 'disenchantment of the world' through spreading bureaucracy and rationalization. Above all, Weber captured the possible contribution of science and technology both to human progress and to the undermining of human values.[1] From this perspective, the citizen both gains and loses through the spread of scientific rationality. A similar sense of gain and loss through science can be found in the writing of Marx and various social commentators since the Industrial Revolution – from Dickens and Wordsworth through to Habermas and Marcuse.

This book follows (albeit with considerable humility) in this critical tradition of examining the relationship between 'science,

1

technology and progress'. More particularly, it will be argued that this relationship has special significance with regard to issues of risk and environmental threat. Social development has reached a stage where a rethink of the linkage between science and everyday life is urgently needed.

However, it is important to emphasize from the outset that science and technology should be seen above all as *human* activities. The frequent portrayal of science and technology as an unstoppable juggernaut is not only theoretically inadequate – it is also antithetical to any practical attempt at renegotiating the relationship between science, technology and citizens. Accordingly, the following chapters will try to resist the depiction of science and technology as some alien invasion into our lives – although there are times when the relationship between science and everyday life can indeed appear in exactly that fashion (so that the relationship between science and culture becomes like a 'cigarette burning through silk' as one author vividly puts it).[2] The recognition that science does not simply fall from another planet should encourage us both to be more critical of scientific knowledge but also to be constructive about the kinds of science which will assist in dealing with pressing matters such as environmental destruction. In no sense is this book anti-scientific. Rather, it begins from the premise that the best friend is one who is prepared to offer unpalatable advice.

This book has then a number of purposes – to consider the part played by science and scientific expertise in our everyday lives, to review practical initiatives aimed at bringing the 'public' and 'science' closer together, to consider the possibilities for a more active 'scientific citizenship', to link these issues into public policy for risk and environmental threat. However, before beginning to explore these specific questions, it is important to explain something of the thematic background to this book. This is all the more important given the inevitably wide-ranging nature of the account which follows. This background can be explained through four overarching themes.

The first of these concerns contemporary science and technology and their relationship to our modern culture and way of life. Stephen Hill presents this theme as 'the tragedy of technology'.[3] He writes:

the *experience* of technology is the experience of apparent inevitability. It is the experience of being 'framed' by an immutable and 'tragic' power, even though this is power that at the same time offers continually new and enchanting means of mastering the problems humanity confronts.[4]

It is this double-edged (or Janus-faced) aspect of technological society that seems to fascinate. Information technology, for example, offers us vastly improved communication systems, greater efficiency, easy (at a price) access to databases and knowledge systems, the possibilities of more leisure time, greater productivity and a decentralized approach to decision-making. At the same time, it offers the routinization of clerical tasks, unemployment, the centralization of power and the potential (through advanced security systems and databases) for loss of freedom and autonomy. This is just the kind of impact which Weber had also considered as part of the 'disenchantment' produced by scientific rationality.

A similar account can be applied to other areas of scientific and technological 'progress' – whether we consider the biotechnology revolution, new manufacturing systems, satellite broadcasting or nuclear power. Our culture is to a large extent 'framed' by technological development – in the sense that science and technology provide many of the material possibilities for modern existence. That development can also be decidedly ambiguous in the benefits it offers to us all. This double-edged character is particularly apparent with regard to environmental issues – fast cars, energy-consuming domestic technologies, new products and processes all stimulate our consumerist tendencies even as they threaten our quality of life. The modern challenge is to find a way of avoiding this double-edged quality – is there such a thing as 'clean technology' or is this simply a contradiction in terms?

Of course, many commentators (perhaps, in our 'technological culture', the majority) present the impact of science and technology as being largely beneficial to society. Certainly, we should not be dismissive of these benefits – in particular, we need to be watchful lest a critique of modern technical development leads us into a hazy romanticism about living conditions in previous times (a cursory glance at improved life expectancies in Western societies over the last hundred and fifty years is instructive here).[5] However, and despite the claims of certain contemporary scientists that science has brought about the 'kingdom of freedom',[6] it seems that the ambiguities of scientific and technological progress represent an important subtext within our lives and a major challenge to future inter-

3

national development. Of course, it is important here to repeat that although we often feel passive in the face of new technologies, these technologies are themselves the product of socially organized production lines and R&D facilities. The 'tragedy of technology' should not imply an inevitability or immutability in the direction of science and technology.

In what follows, this first theme will be approached from a number of directions – the uses of technical advice within environmental decision-making, the problems of living with technological systems such as a petrochemical complex, the difficulties of achieving a more even balance between scientific expertise and the needs (and *knowledges*) of citizens. It will be argued that science needs to be self-critical in the face of public scepticism about its linkage to 'progress'.

At present, public groups are frequently portrayed as ignorant or irrational in the face of scientific progress. External criticism of science and scientific institutions is taken to imply a deficit of public understanding rather than a need for scientific reflection and self-appraisal. Discussion of the ambiguous benefits of science and technology thus leads us to consider the possibilities for institutional change towards a more constructive pattern of knowledge development and dissemination.

The second theme of this book deals more directly with citizenship, democracy and everyday life. If Hill's 'tragedy of technology' is emblematic of theme one, then the second belongs to Raymond Williams' dictum: 'Culture is ordinary':

> A culture is common meanings, the product of a whole people, and offered individual meanings, the product of a man's whole committed personal and social experience. It is stupid and arrogant to suppose that any of these meanings can in any way be described; they are made by living, made and remade in ways we cannot know in advance.[7]

Williams' emphasis on the depth, resilience and richness of working-class culture – together with his profound commitment to democracy and to the 'authentic diversity and complexity of any people'[8] – offer an uplifting and positive incentive to consider the relationship between citizens and scientific expertise. In addition to injecting a much-needed element of optimism into some of the starker analyses of 'technological culture', Williams' account emphasizes the need to begin this analysis from the perspective of citizens rather than (as happens so often) from the 'higher rationality' of scientists and élite groups. In that way, it becomes possible to construct a citizen's view of science rather than (as is more common – at least in the printed form) a scientist's view of citizens (as ignorant, misled or plain contrary). Williams' work, therefore, offers us a means of turning the usual accounts of the 'public understanding of science' on their head and, in so doing, of establishing a more 'symmetrical' relationship between 'public' and 'formal' expertise. That, at least, will be the endeavour of this book – to consider science from the citizen's side rather than from that of the scientific establishment.

Williams' ideas also lead us to think more carefully about the notion of 'citizenship' – a concept which is presently attracting some deserved attention from all sides of the political spectrum. Citizenship questions in this book will centre on the place of individuals and groups of individuals in the face of technical 'progress' – in what way is it possible for their voices to be heard? What obstacles currently exist? What would the consequences be for current institutions and social processes? In order to deal with such questions, we will need to unravel the concept of citizenship and the issues of knowledge, trust and identity upon which it hinges.

These two themes – of 'technological culture' and of 'citizen culture' – lead directly into the third. After the 'tragedy of technology' and 'culture is ordinary' we now have 'science for the people'; in other words, the various attempts (both practical and theoretical) to place technical expertise at the direct service of the public. This theme is no more original than the previous two. Certainly, it can claim a heritage at least back to the nineteenth century. However, it does highlight the relationship between science, technology and human values in particularly direct fashion. As Nelkin put it in 1975:

> The complexity of public decisions seems to require highly specialised and esoteric knowledge, and those who control this knowledge have considerable power. Yet democratic ideology suggests that people must be able to influence policy decisions that affect their lives.[9]

In many ways Nelkin's point is still valid in the mid-1990s – although this book will suggest that the concern for 'democratic ideology' extends beyond public decisions and into a series of wider questions about everyday understanding and control. As the next

5

chapter will argue, there have also been a number of important developments in our grasp of 'technical expertise' and its relationship to 'everyday expertise' – developments which may suggest a greater need for humility (and a willingness to accept institutional change) than was always evident among the 'science for the people' protagonists of, for example, the 1970s. In particular, earlier statements about 'scientific democracy' seem to suffer from the same flaw as many contemporary exhortations concerning the 'public understanding of science' – an implicit judgement of the superiority in every context of the scientific worldview.

The limits to science must, therefore, be assessed and acknowledged. We must also consider the possibility for constructive knowledge relations within society. As one commentator puts it following a discussion of 'Science Shops' (which will be discussed in Chapter 6):

> demystifying – which we did, by and large, do – is not enough; people won't even really accept being 'demystified' unless they have something to put in its place. So I feel that nothing much can happen unless and until we start producing knowledge which is positively relevant.[10]

This reworking and radicalizing of the 'science for the people' theme will take place especially in the latter half of this book.

The final theme represents in many ways the emerging context in which the previous three will be tested out – the socio-scientific challenges of achieving 'sustainable development'. Once again, this is a term that has been in currency for some time (at least since the early 1980s). However, it gained popular attention in 1987 with the publication of *Our Common Future*, the report of the United Nations World Commission on Environment and Development. 'Sustainable development' is defined by this report as: 'development that meets the needs of the present without compromising the ability of future generations to meet their own needs'.[11]

At first consideration, 'sustainable development' seems very far from the issues of technology, culture and democracy which have been presented so far in this Introduction. However, it will be argued that issues of environmental threat and world development cannot be successfully tackled without a full consideration of *local* as well as global initiatives and of *citizen-oriented* as well as state-led programmes.

These issues are inseparable from questions of *knowledge* and the

6

status of *science* within competing notions of social progress. There is a danger at present that the international debate over sustainability will be conducted without a critical account of science itself – and indeed that a global scientific discourse will prevent the expression of more localized understandings and expertises. A particular form of science will 'frame' the issues in a manner which may not be open to other ways of knowing and other ways of living in a sustainable fashion.

The UN Commission itself gives great priority to questions of social *equity*: 'our inability to promote the common interest in sustainable development is often a product of the relative neglect of economic and social justice within and amongst nations'.[12] Or, in more specific terms:

> Meeting essential needs requires not only a new era of economic growth for nations in which the majority are poor, but an assurance that those poor get their fair share of the resources required to sustain that growth. Such equity would be aided by political systems that secure effective citizen participation in decision making and by greater democracy in international decision making.[13]

Going further, and as the Commission's report argues, there is a strong case that groups which feel themselves lacking in social influence and restricted in their everyday options are unlikely to ponder long-term environmental consequences or to see the relevance of official advice and information. Instead, short-term matters of everyday survival become the overriding priority.

Such questions will certainly figure in the following account. More specifically, we will consider the important relationship between 'citizen science' and 'environmental citizenship' – for any kind of citizenship which neglects the knowledges held by citizen groups will be restricted in its practical possibilities. Such a limited approach to citizenship will restrict the 'social learning' between science, technology and public groups which, I will argue, is essential to the processes of sustainable development.

Thus, there will be no 'sustainability' without a greater potential for citizens to take control of their own lives, health and environment. However, success in this goal requires some careful thought about the relations between technical expertise, citizen needs and contemporary culture. This book will consider the very practical implications of such a rethinking. In particular, it will review 'social experiments' which attempt to implement these notions.

Despite this thematic introduction, the chapters which follow are only partly concerned with theoretical matters and abstract debate – they will also present a series of case-studies and specific initiatives which relate to 'Citizen Science'.

Nevertheless, it will be argued that these actual experiences and practical lessons make little sense unless presented with a wider and more theoretical framework. Equally, however, practical experiences are an important stimulus to theory. Certainly, the whole direction of what follows challenges the sterile and outmoded distinction between 'social theory' and 'empirical research'.

As can already be gathered, this book is committed both to an improved understanding of 'science, technology and citizenship' and to better social practice in this area – and especially with regard to questions of risk and the environment. Accordingly, it risks being simultaneously over-descriptive and over-conceptual – I plead guilty to both charges.

Finally, I need to offer a note about the usage of 'science' within this book. In what follows, I generally employ 'science' in the broadest sense so as to encompass a whole worldview and a set of institutions within society. At times also, 'science' encompasses areas of knowledge and application which might more properly be referred to as 'technology'. I am very aware of the distinction which can be made between 'scientific' and 'technological' forms of understanding but have at times used the former as a succinct way of describing both. For the purposes of this book, I consider that to be a reasonable approach – especially since we are mainly concerned to establish the *heterogeneity* of these forms of knowledge and understanding rather than narrowly defining either. I hope the reader will forgive the necessary blurring of categories which sometimes follows from this linguistic shorthand.

1

SCIENCE AND CITIZENSHIP

Now, what I want is, Facts . . . Facts alone are wanted in life.
Plant nothing else, and root out everything else. You can only
form the minds of reasoning animals upon Facts: nothing else
will ever be of any service to them.
(Thomas Gradgrind, Esq.)[1]

I wish I could collect all the Facts we hear so much about . . .
and all the Figures, and all the people who found them out;
and I wish I could put a thousand barrels of gunpowder under
them, and blow them all up together!
(Thomas Gradgrind, Jun.)[2]

Concern over the relationship between citizens, science and technology seems to be characteristic of contemporary society. Right now,
for example, various political and social groups (industry, government, environmentalists, scientific organizations, campaigning
bodies) are attempting to educate, propagandize or cajole the general
public into accepting their own evaluation of a series of technical –
or at least technically-related – questions (over the best means of
tackling environmental issues, the desirability of new consumer
products, the dangers of AIDS, the merits of various energy policies
and an endless array of social questions such as genetic screening,
transport safety and the implementation of new technology). In that
sense, we are all barraged with new 'information' about developments in science and technology which might affect our lives and
also, of course, with exhortations about what different social
groups would like us to do about those developments.

In such a situation, it is unsurprising that many accounts have
been put forward by scientists and others which describe (or, more
usually, lament) the linkage between science, technical knowledge

and the wider population. At present, the topic of 'public under-standing of science' – as defined by, for example, the British Royal Society – has once again focused attention on these issues.

As the first section of this chapter will discuss, there have been certain recurrent elements within these more general accounts – a concern at the 'scientific ignorance' of the populace, a consequent desire to create a 'better-informed' citizenry, an enthusiasm for making science 'more accessible' (but with strict limitations on the extent of this accessibility). Notably also, and as we will discuss, these accounts have represented a commitment to 'science as progress' and offer a decidedly 'science-centred' (or 'enlighten-ment') view of society. Frequently, the accounts offered by scientists and others reveal an anxiety lest public ignorance should get in the way of scientific/technological progress. Thus, one senior British scientist entitles his book on this subject *Is Science Necessary?* but provides the answer – before the text even begins – by citing Nehru's exhortation that the 'future belongs to science and those who make friends with science'.[3]

As this chapter will outline, the notion that the 'future belongs to science' has underpinned most accounts of the relationship between citizens and science. However, there have also been a number of more critical accounts which draw upon the 'tragedy of technology' theme (as discussed in the previous chapter) and on a notion of 'science as ideology' in order to ask starker questions about the impact of scientific dissemination on everyday life. It is also possible to portray concerns over the public understanding of science as an indicator of anxiety amongst the scientific community lest it should become marginalized in the post-Enlightenment era. This chapter will begin with a brief historical excursion into these differing accounts of the 'public understanding of science' before presenting three case-studies of the contemporary interaction between citizens, science and technology.

Discussion of the role of 'ordinary citizens' in 'technical progress' extends back to the beginnings of the Industrial Revolution. In nineteenth-century Britain, for example, there was a lively debate about the general level of science education – which was seen by many as holding back industrial and technical development.[4] Just as in the late twentieth century, public indifference was viewed as an obstacle to scientific progress. Of special relevance to the themes of this book was the establishment of institutions such as the Mechanics Institutes which represented one attempt to build a bridge between formalized scientific knowledge and working-class people (although, as we shall see, there are differing interpretations of whether the Mechanics Institutes were an attempt to enlighten – or to indoctrinate – the working classes). The Mechanics Institute movement spread across Britain in the 1820s and 1830s and offered a training in science and technology to the skilled working classes.

In the twentieth century, the need for a greater awareness of science became a major theme of the 'visible college' of scientists and writers who adopted a socialist perspective on scientific progress.[5] As J.B.S. Haldane put it in the Preface to his 1939 book, *Science and Everyday Life*:

> I am convinced that it is the duty of those scientists who have a gift for writing to make their subject intelligible to the ordinary man and woman. Without a much broader knowledge of science, democracy cannot be effective in an age when science affects all our lives continually.[6]

Writing immediately after the Second World War, the Association of Scientific Workers expressed similar sentiments. In so doing, they outlined the three most regular justifications – both of that time and since – for an enhanced 'public understanding':

- that a technically-literate population is essential for future workforce requirements ('the present inadequate standards of the available labour').[7] This argument had also been important within nineteenth-century debates over working-class technical education;
- that science is now an essential part of our cultural understanding ('In this age no man can be considered to be cultured who makes no serious attempt to understand and appreciate the broad principles of science');[8]
- that, as Haldane argued above, greater public understanding of science is essential for democratic reasons.

The Association of Scientific Workers made various recommendations for improving public understanding through further education classes and also such media as exhibitions and museums, film, the press and the radio. They also stressed the need for working scientists to become more involved in public activities and in the dissemination of science – a challenge to which scientists such as Haldane and Hogben had already responded through popular publications on science and mathematics.[9]

11

The Association of Scientific Workers thus offered a model of 'progress through science' which resonates strongly with many contemporary statements of the need for both greater public understanding and public acceptance of science: 'Science offers means to use unprecedented powers with which a finer, more beautiful and happier world then ever before can be built. With mankind using a vigorously developing science for social ends, the future can be bright and inspiring'.[10]

However, unusually for a group of scientists, the Association recognized that this new world would require scientists to adopt an explicitly *political* role in society. The Association was highly critical of those who simply stood on the sidelines of social change. Important decisions needed to be made about the social control of science and industry – it was the responsibility of every citizen to get involved. Meanwhile, science itself is: 'neither good nor bad; it is organized knowledge and a method, a tool or weapon, which society can use for good or evil. It can confer the highest benefits and it can be used to destroy'.[11] Again, this notion of science as value-free has been a regular feature of scientific statements concerning the relationship between citizens and technical change.

Some forty years later, the prestigious Royal Society was to revive these debates in its 1985 report on the 'public understanding of science' – suggesting the durability of these concerns but also a perceived absence of real progress. The Royal Society took a distinctly less 'political' perspective than the Association of Scientific Workers – its recommendations emanate from a more liberal concern with the well-being of both science and society (and perhaps also from a concern that the value of scientific understanding might be neglected by society – the mid-1980s were a time of great anxiety about the future of public support for science).

Despite this difference in political perspective, the 1985 report of the Royal Society presents an argument which many members of the Association of Scientific Workers would readily have endorsed:

> better public understanding of science can be a major element in promoting national prosperity, in raising the quality of public and private decision making and in enriching the life of the individual. . . . Improving the public understanding of science is an investment in the future, not a luxury to be indulged in if and when resources allow.[12]

The report goes on to cite a number of specific areas where an 'improved understanding' would be of personal and national value:

- in terms of *national prosperity*, a better informed citizenry could appreciate the opportunities offered by new technologies and could provide a better trained workforce;
- in terms of *economic performance*, wider scientific awareness would reduce 'hostility, or even indifference' to science and technology and so aid in the rapid innovation of such product and process changes. There would also be a 'considerable competitive advantage' if those in 'positions of responsibility' were better informed;
- in terms of *public policy*, science and technology should be major considerations – for the Royal Society there is a strong case that these decisions would be improved by 'better understanding' (we will examine this assumption very closely in Chapters 2 and 3);
- in terms of *personal decisions*, for example regarding diet, smoking, vaccination safety – 'an uninformed public is very vulnerable to misleading ideas';
- in terms of *everyday life*, a basic scientific literacy is needed just to understand what goes on around us (e.g., how a ball point pen or a television functions);
- in terms of *risk and uncertainty* (e.g., concerning nuclear power or seat-belt wear), it is important that the public have a better appreciation of the nature of risks and of how to interpret and balance them: 'Once again it must be argued that better understanding fosters better public and personal decisions'.[13]
- in terms of *contemporary thought and culture*, any citizen without an understanding of science is cut off from the richness of this important area of human enquiry and discovery.

So far, we have briefly examined two major arguments – from the Association of Scientific Workers and from the Royal Society – for greater efforts to be made by scientists and citizens in the dissemination of technical information and understanding. A typical justification for such efforts has also emerged – generally based on a mixture of economic, political, personal and cultural arguments.

Certain assumptions about the relationship between citizens, science and technology have also started to become clear – assumptions which are implicit in the very concept of the 'public understanding of science'. Such assumptions include:

13

- the notion of contemporary 'public ignorance' in matters of science and technology;
- the notion that a better understanding of science will lead to better 'public and personal decisions';
- the notion that science is a force for human improvement;
- an explicit or implicit notion that science is itself value-free – although there are moral and political choices to be made about its *direction*;
- the notion that the life of citizens is somehow impoverished by an exclusion from scientific thought;
- the notion that wider exposure to scientific thinking will lead to greater acceptance and support for science and technology.

Of course, there are differences between the accounts offered by these two groups of concerned scientists – with the Association of Scientific Workers offering, for example, a more 'political' programme (linked to the aspirations of the postwar Labour Government). However, what the two accounts share is a fundamental belief in the centrality of scientific development to the future of society – and a belief (whether as part of a social democratic or more vaguely liberal ideology) that a better informed citizenry can play a crucial (but essentially reactive) role in this development. The future should indeed belong to science.

There is no suggestion in the Royal Society report that the organization of science is open to change or that it should incorporate citizen views within research policy. The goal is to make the public better informed about science but not to encourage a critical evaluation of scientific institutions. For the Royal Society and most of the contemporary apologists of science, *science* itself is not the problem – the problem is gaining public understanding and hence *acceptance* of science.

This worldview can be characterized as 'science-centred' or (perhaps more accurately) 'enlightenment' in its assumptions about science, technology and the wider public. This is not to suggest that all working scientists hold this worldview. However, it does provide a powerful and frequently reiterated case for the centrality of scientific reasoning to social development. Within such a worldview, any problematic relationship between science and citizens must be a consequence of either public ignorance or public irrationality.

This book will argue that a critical perspective on these issues is required and that there are new developments and ways of thinking which suggest that *change* is indeed occurring. We can begin by contrasting the notions expressed so far of 'science as progress' with one account of a nineteenth-century experiment in the 'public understanding of science' – the Mechanics Institute movement as discussed by Maxine Berg and others.[14] Berg's more critical analysis of this movement sets the debates so far concerning citizens and science into a much-needed social and political context.

As already suggested, the Mechanics Institutes appear to offer an excellent example of a highly localized and responsive 'continuing education' (to use the modern jargon) for one section of the working-class community. Institutes were established across Britain and offered technical training at a time when demand seemed to be high – this demand linked, of course, to the rapid progress of indus-trialization. Berg's account suggests, however, a less attractive ideological purpose to this movement – essentially the Institutes were not philanthropic in orientation but were instead one part of the legitimation of the emerging capitalist order. The underlying philosophy of 'self improvement' was designed to divide working-class communities by creating a 'labour aristocracy'. The basis of the movement was to evangelize the harmony between science and industry. The Institutes were largely dominated by the middle classes whose main purpose was to create a more ordered society and to prevent social unrest. Science was, therefore, an important legitimation of the social order rather than a force for liberation or active citizenship.

The discussion of Mechanics Institutes is important here not for its specific conclusions but for the wider questions which it raises about the relationship between science and citizens. The 'en-lightenment' approach – as exemplified by the Royal Society – would argue that the provision of scientific information to public groups will in itself be beneficial – if only in allowing a better appreciation of the scientific changes which are influencing society and in clarifying citizen choices. The analysis provided by Berg suggests that science can present an ideological face to citizens – so that it can be used to obstruct rather than assist understanding. In particular, the control of Mechanics Institutes by middle-class forces meant that training in science was also a propagandizing of a particular political ideology (in this case that known as 'political economy'). At this point, we could add to our discussion a number of Marxist accounts of science which generalize this point about

15

capitalist ideology and its relationship to contemporary science.[15] Thus, for example, Marcuse has argued that: 'The industrial society which makes technology and science its own is organised for the ever more effective domination of man and nature, for the ever more effective utilization of its resources'.[16]

Marx himself expressed such notions of 'technology as domination' with particular clarity:

> Labour [is] ... subsumed under the total process of the machinery itself, as itself only a link of the system, whose unity exists not in the living workforce, but rather in the living (active) machinery, which confronts his individual, insignificant doings as a mighty organism.[17]

Hill has developed such themes (particularly with reference to the work of Foucault) in *The Tragedy of Technology*:

> Employees generally see technology ... as an alienated force that stands somewhere behind their left shoulder, and which, with one new breath of change, may extinguish their means of livelihood. The aesthetic is one of externally imposed order rather than human harmony; the words of knowledge are opaque, controlled by the masters of the technological system and the variety of specialists who inform them. The technological aesthetic is unreadable to the layman, but is embodied in words of knowledge that say 'you shall adjust'.[18]

Of course, the argument here is that this relationship to technology is found also *outside* the workplace – so that people's general experience of technology fits this pattern of 'unreadability' and 'adjustment'.

It would appear, therefore, that we have reached the point of incommensurability between those accounts of science which stress its empowering and enabling role and those – drawing broadly on a notion of science as a source of legitimation (Habermas), alienation (Marx) or disenchantment (Weber) – which stress its role as a form of social control and dehumanization. One should nevertheless be wary of splitting debate in a conventionally-political fashion (the 'establishment view' versus the 'radical opposition'). Certainly, left-wing and environmental groups have been as eager to adopt a scientific mantle ('if only people knew the facts of ozone depletion, acid deposition or factory farming then they'd support us') as have the political establishment – although such groups have typically had far fewer scientific resources at their disposal. What should also be noted at this stage is that, despite the apparent incommensurability over whether science represents progress or disenchantment, all of these approaches stress the centrality of scientific rationality to the modern world. Whilst (and as we will discuss later in this book) some would argue that the modern world is being radically transformed into late (or post-) modernity, the substantial influence of science over the life of citizens seems undeniable and likely to remain so.

In later discussion we will address these themes once again at a conceptual level. For now, rather than pursuing them through a general debate, we should begin to look a little closer at actual examples of the contemporary citizen–science interaction. Is there any evidence that science is being used within society as a legitimatory rather than an empowering device? Can the lack of communication between 'science and its publics' be successfully explained by public ignorance or instead by some deeper-rooted set of causes? In order to tackle this, we need to examine questions of science and technology as they occur within people's lives. As a start to this project, we can consider the lessons from three examples of the relationship between science, technology and everyday life. These examples make no claim to representativeness. They are designed simply to illustrate and explore the issues of contemporary citizen–science relations. It should also be said at this point that these three examples will recur and be re-analysed at various points in this book.

Three stories of our time

2,4,5–T and the farmworkers

We shall continue to examine any soundly based new evidence or information. For the present, this Enquiry has strengthened us in our previous view that 2,4,5–T herbicides can safely be used in the UK in the recommended way and for the recommended purposes.

(Advisory Committee on Pesticides)[19]

It is the NUAAW's conviction, distilled from the experience of thousands of members working in forests and on farms, that the conditions envisaged by members of the [advisory

committee] (presumably used to the controlled conditions of
the laboratory) are impossible to reproduce in the field.
This single fact must be sufficient to demolish the supposi-
tion that the herbicide is safe to use.[20]

In 1980, the National Union of Agricultural and Allied Workers
(NUAAW – from here on 'the farmworkers') was engaged in a
highly public dispute with the British regulatory authorities over the
herbicide 2,4,5–T. By that date, 2,4,5–T had already been controversial for some time because of its allegedly hazardous properties
(chloracne, birth defects, spontaneous abortion, cancer) and also
for its overall impact on the natural environment. Although the
herbicide had been produced since the 1940s, perhaps its best-
known application was during the Vietnam War when it was
sprayed by US aircraft as a defoliant (and thus as a means of
removing ground cover). However, 2,4,5–T has also been used in a
number of agricultural, industrial and domestic situations (e.g., by
railway workers to keep lines clear of weeds, by forestry workers
to clear undergrowth, or by members of the public keeping their
gardens free of brambles and nettles).

Given international attention to the hazards of 2,4,5–T, a number
of countries had at that time either banned or severely restricted the
use of the herbicide: among them the United States, Canada and the
former Soviet Union. There had also been a number of national and
international campaigns against 2,4,5–T – with concern being
expressed particularly about the usage of this and the other 'dirty
dozen'[21] pesticides in developing countries. In Britain, a number of
groups had argued for the banning or strict control of 2,4,5–T.

This campaign had some success; many local authorities had by
1980 agreed to cease spraying as also had major users such as
British Rail, the National Coal Board, and the electricity generators.
However, the British regulatory authorities had historically been
resistant to a ban on 2,4,5–T. In this section, and as an illustration
of one interlinkage between citizens, science and technical decision-
making, we will look briefly at one episode in the history of 2,4,5–
T: the confrontation between the farmworkers and the regulatory
authorities (or, more precisely, their advisory body – the Advisory
Committee on Pesticides (ACP)) in just one year – 1980.

Of course, there are a number of ways in which such a story could
be told: as a review of the technical evidence (i.e., the 'facts' of the
case), as a clash between 'expertise' and 'trade union pressure', as

an example of the 'uncaring' nature of modern agro-business or of the use of science as an ideology to oppose workers' rights. For now, it is enough to look at the *kinds* of argument which the farmworkers and the ACP put forward to support their case and to consider the immediate lessons concerning the uses of 'scientific expertise' in such social and technical decision-making. More specifically, does this case suggest any disparity between 'scientific' (as represented by the advisory committee) and 'citizen' (i.e., in this case farmworker) perspectives?

In 1980, the farmworkers presented the ACP with their latest 'dossier' on the herbicide.[22] By that date, the question of the pesticide's safety had been referred to the ACP no fewer than eight times – with the committee standing firm on its contention that 2,4,5–T 'offers no hazard' to users or the general environment 'provided that the product is used as directed'. In their evidence to the ACP, the farmworkers discuss what they consider to be the 'realities' of pesticide use, they present the alternatives to the pesticide, they criticize previous ACP reports, and they offer a number of cases where health damage is allegedly linked to 2,4,5–T exposure.

These cases – which largely represented the 'new' evidence to the ACP – were drawn from a questionnaire which the NUAAW had circulated to its members through its newspaper, *Landworker*.[23] Questions in the survey covered the usage of 'weedkiller 2,4,5–T' (when did you last use a weedkiller containing 2,4,5–T? Are you ever given instructions on how to use protective gear? Are you given any information about the hazards relating to weedkillers containing 2,4,5–T?) but also sought out medical information (have you ever had any of the following symptoms after using weedkillers containing 2,4,5–T? Do you suffer from any of the following . . . ? Have you or your partner ever had a spontaneous (unplanned) abortion or a miscarriage?). In all, some forty questions were asked on a 'voluntary response' basis.

The questionnaire eventually provided a series of case-studies (involving fourteen individuals) for submission to the ACP. To take a typical case, one 'victim' is described as having had 'a miscarriage in 1977 and later the same year gave birth to a daughter . . . who has a cleft palate and a hare lip. Her husband had been using 2,4,5–T when he worked for the Forestry Commission'.

This information was then presented to the ACP. The overall conclusion of the farmworker submission was that:

19

Considering the additional evidence which has not been evaluated by the ACP, the existence of alternative weed killers and the overall lack of information about the effects on users of 2,4,5-T ... it becomes absolutely incomprehensible that workers, their families and the general public can remain subject to the risks for one minute longer.[24]

The advisory committee's published response to this evidence appeared later in 1980 as the *Further Review of the Safety for Use in the UK of Herbicide 2,4,5-T.*[25] This review is considerably longer than the farmworker dossier – it presented, for example, a thorough review of major scientific developments since the ACP's previous report. It appraised all the evidence in some detail and included a series of appendices on topics ranging from environmental effects and operator exposure to the consideration of alternative pesticides.

As regards the specific matters raised by the farmworkers, the ACP devoted one section of its report to a consideration of the case-studies put forward by the NUAAW. For each case the committee concluded that insufficient evidence existed to correlate the medical condition with 2,4,5-T – or at least that it seemed highly improbable that such a correlation could exist. In the above case of miscarriage/birth deformity, for example, the employment records of the father were first of all checked. Following this, the parents and the family doctor were interviewed in order to establish the level of exposure involved and the scale of alleged effects. The ACP's specific conclusion was:

The type of deformity occurring in this case is common genetically. Mrs K's only possible contact with 2,4,5-T was through handling her husband's working clothes; and the likelihood of her having absorbed sufficient to have produced any toxic effect is remote in the extreme.[26]

In overall conclusion, the ACP argued forcefully that 'there are no grounds to suggest a causal relationship with the stated effects'. The argument is further elaborated during a discussion of the linkage between 2,4,5-T and miscarriage/birth deformity. The committee suggested that the farmworker cases 'neither implicate nor absolve' the pesticide:

The reality is that some women who have been in contact with such an agent are likely to miscarry, and that some are likely to bear malformed children; but this in itself does not add up to cause and effect. Indeed, statistically it would be remarkable if families in contact with particular products such as 2,4,5–T were spared from these misfortunes.[27]

Not surprisingly perhaps, this scientific rationale did not serve to change the opinion of the farmworkers – and during at least one stormy meeting the two sides struggled to communicate their concerns about the issue. As the leader of the farmworkers stated after the meeting:

We are alarmed at the approach taken by the Committee. In their eyes scientific evidence proving the hazards of a chemical has to be absolutely watertight. In our view the decision has to be made on the balance of probabilities . . . where lives are at stake a responsible body cannot wait, as was the case with asbestos, until there is a sufficiently impressive death toll.[28]

The farmworkers vowed to fight on – both to get a ban on the chemical and to change the regulatory structure for future decisions.

Mad cows and the consumers

As the Chief Medical Officer has confirmed, British beef can continue to be eaten safely by everyone, adults and children.
(John Gummer, Minister of Agriculture, Fisheries and Food)[29]

Eating British beef is completely safe. There is no evidence of any threat to human health caused by this animal health problem (BSE).
This is the view of independent British and European scientists and not just the meat industry.
This view has been endorsed by the Department of Health.[30]
(Advertisement placed by the Meat and Livestock Commission)

Scientists do not automatically command public trust.
(House of Commons Agriculture Select Committee)[31]

In 1990, one technical issue held an especially prominent place in the British mass media: do cows make you mad? The Ministry of Agriculture, Fisheries and Food (MAFF) – and especially its Minister, John Gummer – was under widespread attack for its handling of the issue. The meat industry was greatly concerned at the impact of the scare on meat sales. Consumer groups such as the

21

Consumers' Association and Parents for Safe Food registered their low confidence in both the meat industry and MAFF. British newspapers featured photographs of Gummer feeding a beefburger to his daughter – apparently in an attempt to reassure the public. Various scientific groups stated their concern over the issue – Professor Richard Lacey was quoted as fearing that 'a whole generation would be lost' if the worst anxieties over BSE (Bovine Spongiform Encephalopathy) came true. Other scientific figures dismissed 'public hysteria' over the issue. Professor Sir Richard Southwood claimed that: 'we have more reason to be concerned about being struck by lightning than catching BSE from eating beef and other products from cattle'.[32]

Quite clearly, therefore, the 'mad cow' issue represented a major public controversy. BSE is a fatal disease which causes degeneration of the brain. It develops over several years and infected cattle, mostly dairy cows, show no symptoms until the final weeks when they become nervous and uncoordinated. The first case of BSE was reported in Britain in 1985 – by April 1990 some 290 cases a week were being confirmed. The issue which exercised the public was, of course, whether BSE – or 'mad cow disease' as it became more dramatically known – could be a threat to the human population.

As with 2,4,5–T, there are a number of ways in which this story can be told (and, indeed, already has been told) – as a struggle between scientists armed with 'the facts' and an irrational group of citizens (in this case, not farmworkers but consumers), as an example of industrial corruption of both regulatory authorities and scientists, as a use of scientific authority to legitimize an exploitative and inherently dangerous mode of food production. However, as with the 2,4,5–T story, it is instructive to look at the broad characteristics of the arguments made by both sides.

If we take those consumer and allied groups which were most critical of government action and the activities of the meat industry, then a number of features of their argument can be identified. First of all, critical groups tended to highlight certain meat industry practices – particularly the feeding of offal to animals. Second, critical groups took the line of emphasizing the uncertainties concerning BSE transmission – so that, for example, when a Siamese cat developed BSE in 1990 this was seized upon as yet more evidence that the disease could travel across species boundaries. Third, these groups could take advantage of the divided scientific opinion over the issue; Professor Lacey became a particularly public

22

figure on this basis. Accordingly, oppositional groups could make it clear that there was no scientific consensus. Fourth, consumer groups found it relatively easy to capitalize on the inconsistencies and weaknesses in MAFF's handling of the debate. As one report put it: 'Knowledge of BSE is as full of holes as an infected cow's brain . . . while the science of BSE is arguable, much more is known about the handling of crisis to contain risk, limit damage and maintain public confidence'.[33]

However, this report argued that the Government had succeeded in breaking every rule of public relations. Between them, MAFF and its Minister had:

• failed to err on the side of caution;
• acted slowly at every stage;
• attempted to score debating points rather than enlisting support (Gummer, for example, was widely quoted as labelling vegetarians 'wholly unnatural');
• created confusion by refusing to speak openly – thus also losing both the confidence of consumers and the food industry;
• opted for publicity gimmicks (e.g., photo opportunities with Gummer's daughter and a beefburger) rather than discussing the issues;
• failed to establish a system for dealing with public enquiries.

As the report concluded: 'The grotesque image of the tottering cow thus brands not only an incompetent bureaucracy but a rickety and self-serving information regime'.[34]

Quite clearly, therefore, the BSE issue became the focus for a whole series of criticisms and concerns – about food industry practices, about the independence and competence of the government ministry, about the limits to scientific understanding in such a complex and under-researched area. Despite this broad critique, the typical 'official' response was to present the issue as a challenge to the 'facts'. In statement after statement, the Minister repeated his claim that: 'We have taken action to deal with the public health concerns and the animal health aspect of BSE on the basis of the best independent scientific advice'.[35]

In April 1990, the Royal Society and the Association of British Science Writers called their own press conference on the grounds that: 'the public remains confused about its (BSE's) dangers'.[36]

The meeting was designed to 'enable journalists to write and broadcast accurately' and heard testimony from 'five experts'. The views of these experts differed slightly – from the view that there is a 'very low risk' to the human population to that the 'risks of humans contracting the disease through eating beef are non-existent'. Overall, however, the opinion seemed to be that the dangers of BSE were not great. Nevertheless, public anxiety continued – suggesting, as the House of Commons Agriculture Select Committee concluded in July 1990, that expert statements alone were unlikely to reassure the public.[37]

As 1990 progressed, BSE slowly slipped away from popular concern only to be revived periodically as new reports emerged. For example, 1994 brought another peak of concern with the action this time focusing on European attempts to control the import of British beef. Meanwhile, the divisions over the governmental response to the issue showed no signs of disappearing. Instead, many consumer groups are set for further battles with the authorities over food safety issues.

Major hazards and the residents

> Your premises are situated in an area that could possibly be affected if a major accident should occur . . . The Control of Industrial Major Accident Hazards Regulations (1984) requires [sic] to inform you of the emergency procedures that you should follow in the unlikely event of a major accident.[38]

> The industry recognizes . . . that accidents are inevitable. . . . In recognizing this, the industry is moving more towards crisis communications, crisis management and evacuation planning. At the same time it increases reassurance operations, beefs up its risk analyses and induces the wider community to share not only in the experience of risk, but also in its management.[39]

In 1982, due to accidents at chemical sites in Europe during the preceding decade – and notably at Flixborough in 1974 and Seveso in 1976 – the European Community adopted a directive for the control of major hazard installations.[40] This is commonly known as the 'Seveso Directive'.

Simultaneously, the EC took the then unprecedented step of building into the directive a 'public information' requirement. Article 8 thus specifies that members of the public liable to be affected by a major accident be informed of safety measures and of how they should behave in the event of a major accident. This requirement was then translated into national legislation so that, for example, Regulation 12 of the Control of Industrial Major Accident Hazards (CIMAH) Regulations of 1984 represents the British version of the Directive. The CIMAH regulations required that this information be provided around a fixed number of major hazard sites by January 1986.

In effect, therefore, the EEC legislation was obliging the petrochemical industry to give to the local community advice and information about the operation of hazardous installations (at least at a very limited number of sites). In contrast to the previous examples of 'citizen–science interaction', here we have technical information being given out largely *in advance* of public concern. By way of contrast also, rather than being a *workplace* (2,4,5–T) or *consumer* (BSE) interaction, this case allows us to look at a *community* matter. As before, however, this interaction is open to a number of interpretations – of communities being totally uninterested in 'technical' matters, of communities being 'co-opted' by industry (as the second quotation at the beginning of this section suggests), of a more complex pattern of local and technical knowledges in juxtaposition.

The information provision requirement of the new legislation certainly caused British industry great concern (greater apparently than the other, more engineering-oriented, requirements). The fear was that the public would react with alarm and hysteria to the information that there were hazards associated with the local chemical works. Debate also centred on the number of sites at which information should be distributed, the extent of information distribution at each site, what information route should be followed (leaflet, newspaper announcement, public meetings) and the amount of detail which should be provided.

The 'information' when it eventually appeared in Britain generally took the form of a simple leaflet giving very brief information about:

- activities undertaken on site;
- names of the hazardous substances used and their principal harmful properties;
- details of emergency warning systems;
- reference to emergency planning and/or advice on what action to take in the event of an emergency.

Despite the prior industrial concern that this would create an emotional public reaction, there is very little evidence of any outcry – with anecdotal evidence suggesting that certain companies which had been braced for public criticism actually received no phone calls at all from local residents. A more systematic social survey of one information site found no evidence of local anxiety and only a small proportion of residents claiming that the leaflet had changed their opinion of the site. Less reassuringly, however, the same survey suggested that the leaflet had only a small impact in terms of informing residents about the 'correct' emergency procedures.[41] Thus, many residents anticipated that their response to an emergency would be to 'get out of the area' – despite the leaflet's specific advice to 'stay indoors'.

It would appear, therefore, that whilst the information distribution exercise may have been successful in avoiding public outcry, it had only limited success as a preparation for a real emergency. Accordingly, the linkage between this information exercise and 'active and informed citizenship' seems somewhat less than satisfactory. More particularly, this example seems to reinforce the notion of public indifference to technical advice. Here we have specific, carefully prepared and well-distributed advice to an 'at risk' group which is then apparently ignored. Why should any further efforts be made at dissemination? In Chapter 4, we will look at the case more carefully and suggest a re-working of this analysis.

Science, technology and everyday life

In many ways, these three 'stories' have very little in common – a sustained trade union campaign to outlaw a pesticide, a sudden consumer outcry about the hazards of British beef, a public information campaign which was successful in avoiding backlash but less satisfactory as preparation for a petrochemical disaster. What themes and concerns underlie these apparently disparate cases? If we, first of all, return to the 'science-centred' worldview with which this chapter began, several characteristic notions have already been identified. These concerned the notion of *public ignorance*, that science improves the *decision-making process*, that science is a *force for human improvement*, that it is *value-free*, that citizens are impoverished by their *exclusion*, and that *greater scientific understanding* amongst the public will lead to *greater acceptance and support* for science and technology. To what extent can evidence be found in the three case-studies to substantiate this general conceptualization?

From the 'science-centred' perspective, all three cases represent the problems of public ignorance – with each case demonstrating the resistance of public groups to the well-balanced testimony of expert bodies (whether the Advisory Committee on Pesticides, MAFF or the chemical industry and local planning authority backed up by the Health and Safety Executive). Of course, whilst the major hazard case seems to represent a kind of dumb apathy among residents (and, in that sense, a sin of omission – although see Chapter 4), the other two cases represent a more active form of resistance to technical advice (and, therefore, the much greater sin of commission). Discussions in the science-centred mode tend to move from this analysis to a discussion of either how to enact decision-making apart from the ignorant/irrational public (see Chapter 3) or of how to be more energetic in disseminating technical information (e.g., the recommendations of the Royal Society). Either way, the view is that the public forms a barrier to intelligent and constructive debate.

These representations of the public became most visible in the BSE case – with numerous references to 'public hysteria' and 'media hype'. For the 'science-centred' view, continued public concern *after* scientifically-based reassurances had been given could only be the product of an emotional and badly informed public.

Equally, the three cases suggest something of the notion that science can be an impartial and 'value-free' agent in such public cases – certainly, the 'official' parties involved would reject vehemently (and be highly offended by) any suggestion that the information which they were presenting was in some way 'biased'. Their claim to authority was based precisely upon the impartiality and neutrality of the expertise which they proffered (and also upon the 'good will' and 'fair play' of the decision-making structures within which they operate). This became an issue especially in the BSE case with numerous allegations of 'false experts' on the 'opposing' side. Thus John Gummer was quoted in the House of Commons as stressing the significance of 'true' expertise:

> He hoped the BBC, ITV and others would ask before inter-
> viewing people as 'experts' whether they had published in
> journals which their peers could check or if they had sub-
> mitted evidence to the Tyrrel Committee. If they had not, he

hoped they would not be introduced as experts but merely as people with an idea or two.[42]

Particular criticism was made of Professor Richard Lacey, the Leeds University microbiologist who repeatedly expressed great anxiety over the human implications of BSE. One Commons report stated that his views 'seemed to lose touch with reality'. Lacey replied to these charges with equal vehemence: 'From a medical point of view ... it is normal to assume the worst and act accordingly. That is the difference between farmers and doctors'.[43]

This disputed territory over expertise was also manifest in the 2,4,5–T case where the farmworkers' 'dossier' was dismissed by the advisory committee for its anecdotal and unscientific methodology. From the viewpoint of a working scientist (especially, but not solely, in areas such as toxicology and epidemiology) this certainty over risk and safety may seem quite perplexing – the science is typically open to major doubt and uncertainty. The 'official' message filtered out the inevitable technical uncertainties so as to offer an apparently authoritative and self-confident message – suggesting an important difference between 'doing science' (with all its messiness, conjecture and tacit assumptions) and 'the public face of science' (where such provisionality has apparently been lost so as to offer a 'clear' voice). However, as we will see in later chapters, this 'filtering' may no longer enjoy easy success as the official presentations of scientific evidence become open to challenge.

Throughout these challenges, nevertheless, official bodies in both the 2,4,5–T and BSE cases have clung to the notion of their own superior understanding. Their task has been to cope with the peculiarities of 'public perception' (meaning *mis*perception) rather than to reconsider their own authority in these matters. In the case of major hazards (the low profile of which may be more typical of citizen–science encounters) that authority has been able to rest unchallenged when no critical voices or counter-expertises have emerged.

If we turn now to those accounts of science which stress its *ideological and legitimatory* nature, then a very different picture emerges. Such an analysis can be conducted at two important levels. First, in terms of the *use* of science to defend certain industrial and political practices. Second, in terms of the relationship between the *development* of scientific thinking and underlying social assumptions. This distinction is open to question since the two levels are inseparable – nevertheless, their presentation in this form assists discussion at this stage.

A broad line of argument can be proposed which links the official use of scientific argument to the defence of the prevailing social order. Thus, the technical language of the public information over major hazards aims to reassure the public and to avoid any larger social debate over the location of hazardous industry. It permits the *appearance* of openness (and so helps 'incorporate' local people in the *status quo*) but without engaging in discussion over competing assessments of the risk of major accident. Science thus serves to reinforce one social standpoint and to put local groups at a disadvantage – feelings of anxiety and concerns over safety seem trivial when contrasted with the powerful argumentation of quantitative risk analysis. In Habermas' term, debates over community safety are subjected to a process of 'scientization'.[44] Thus, for Jones, debates over 'risk assessment' are an obscuring of the real (i.e., class) issues:

> there is nothing natural about the fact that those who face the immediate risks of chemical production are generally poor, working class and marginal. Chemical executives do not generally live next door to their plants. . . . Risk may be seen as a mystification which attempts to hide the reality of risk as a class relation, another example of the power of capital over our lives.[45]

When local concerns *do* become a focus of attention, e.g., during a planning inquiry, citizens often feel alienated from the mixture of technical and legalistic procedure being followed. Similar points could be made with regard to 2,4,5–T or BSE – references to public hysteria and irrationality serve, from this perspective, the distinctly ideological purpose of downgrading public concerns and reinforcing the authority of existing decision-makers. Science is the servant of power – its investigations claim to open up the possibilities for policy-making but instead serve to reinforce the existing social order.

At a second level, a tradition has developed in the post-Kuhnian sociology of scientific knowledge[46] which links the development of scientific understanding to broader social influences. Of particular relevance to this discussion is the work of Wynne. In an analysis, for example, of several risk issues Wynne identifies a series of social assumptions which underpin scientific risk analyses. In the case of 2,4,5–T, Wynne draws attention to the disagreement between the

29

farmworkers and the advisory committee surrounding what consti-
tutes 'normal conditions of use':

> different parties – the scientists and the workers – defined
> different actual risk systems ... because they built upon
> different models of the social practices creating or controlling
> the risks. The scientists' implicit assumptions were of idealised
> worlds of herbicide production and use; and the validity and
> credibility of their 'objective' risk analysis was committed to
> this naive sociology embedded in their technical analysis.
> Conversely the workers, whose risk perceptions were for a
> long time dismissed as overactive imaginings of side effects,
> had real empirical experience, indeed expertise, that was
> directly relevant to an objective risk analysis.[47]

Analysis of this kind stresses the judgemental and unavoidably
social nature of expertise as offered within the decision-making
process. Certainly, Wynne's analysis could readily be extended to
the area of major hazards (where the risk analytical techniques
employed inevitably involve 'professional judgement') and to the
BSE case (how much fallibility do we assume in abattoir methods
or BSE identification when establishing new regulations?). In both
areas, assumptions must be made about whether the world of
everyday practice will differ from the controlled world of the
laboratory. Equally, of course, the 'sociology' discussed by Wynne
may not always be naïve. There is also, as Bauman has noted, a
potential for deliberate manipulation in this area.[48]

Science from this perspective cannot remain aloof from external
concerns but must itself offer a reflection of certain social assumptions and taken-for-granted practices – including, of course, those
of science itself: 'The assumptions which analysts make are often
an unconsciously expressed function of their own social values and
relationships within the system'.[49] Despite the rhetoric to the
contrary, therefore, scientific analyses must reflect the ideological
and institutional assumptions of the 'experts' who conduct them –
although these assumptions are not necessarily consciously made
and indeed their existence may be strongly denied by those who
hold them. In the case of 2,4,5–T, it is also possible to see certain
institutional assumptions at work with regard to the 'burden of
proof' required by the advisory committee and the farmworkers.
Thus, whilst the farmworkers felt that there were sufficient doubts
about the pesticide to justify its withdrawal, the advisory commit-

tee argued that it was inappropriate to act until the case was proven 'beyond all reasonable doubt'. As one trade union participant put it:

> Here a crucial difference between our two approaches emerges. 'We will rescind its clearance if the union can prove to us that 2,4,5–T is harmful' was in effect what the ACP told the union delegation. 'No', we responded, we cannot supply proof 'beyond all reasonable doubt'. Our yardstick is to estimate the hazard on the basis of what we know, and if 'on the balance of probabilities', the substance appears dangerous, then it should clearly be taken off the market.[50]

One important dimension of these assumptions will relate to the credibility and legitimacy of the institutions within which scientists operate. External criticisms of key institutions are likely to be met by those within them with incomprehension, anger and (very often) allegations of public hysteria and media irresponsibility. The powerful image of science as 'value-free' serves, of course, to reinforce these notions. Such a process can, in turn, exacerbate the problems of communication between scientists and the wider public – encouraging further the idea that the public are irrational but also fostering public doubts about the value of scientific assessments and damaging the credibility of scientific institutions. When scientists then find themselves in public *disagreement* (as appears such a regular feature of policy debates),[51] the science-centred model struggles to maintain its credibility whilst more critical voices seize upon the apparent confusion in order to stress the limitations and uncertainties of scientific analysis. In such situations, as we will see in later chapters, scientific institutions tend to become victims of their own over-inflated promises. Equally, important policy decisions must be made on a poorly understood foundation.

Towards a citizen science?

So far in this chapter, I have offered a polarization between 'enlightenment' and 'critical' views of the relationship between science and the general public. Whilst the former emphasizes the positive contribution of science to everyday life and defines the problem as being how to carry (or push) the public towards 'scientific enlightenment',[52] the latter approach is distinctly wary of such an ideology and stresses the negative consequences of much of contemporary science for everyday life. In making this argument, the critical account closely links the physical manifestations of science and technology (production systems, products, environmental impacts) with the intellectual processes of scientific production. Meanwhile, the 'enlightenment' approach stresses those manifestations which it sees as progressive and argues that the best antidote to any negative elements is further support for science. Of course, both of these approaches acknowledge the centrality of science and technology within everyday existence. They highlight the 'success' of the scientific worldview – but profoundly disagree about the consequences of this for our happiness and social progress.

These matters take on special significance given the current high level of environmental concern. Can science lead us out of the current crisis or is it the very rationality which creates an exploitative and short-sighted approach to the natural world? Should we be blaming science for environmental problems or looking to it for salvation? One other response to this apparent impasse is to dismiss the application of science in this area and to turn to more romantic (or obscurantist) alternatives – for example, the potpourri of beliefs, rationalities and self-improvement techniques which together form the 'New Age'. Whilst the science-centred approach would, inevitably, criticize such belief structures as a 'retreat from the rational', there is no doubt that they can provide a sense of order and understanding which, for whatever reason, the scientific worldview does not provide to all of society. Once again, accusations of 'irrationality' seem to compound rather than resolve the problems.

Phrased in this manner, the prognosis for science, democracy and citizenship seems extremely gloomy. Whilst the 'enlightenment' perspective hopes to re-educate a sceptical public, the critics of science and technology view attempts at 'improved public understanding' as a defensive and self-serving reaction to growing hostility and distrust. However, and as this book will argue, whilst this argument about the 'disenchantment of the world' is at least as old as the Industrial Revolution, we need also to be aware of new possibilities for renegotiation and change. Might the social and intellectual conditions of our time – where knowledge claims are increasingly challenged and authority is less readily accepted – also create new possibilities in this area?

In particular, and given these emerging social and technical conditions, we need to explore whether it is possible to build constructively rather than remain entangled in a sterile 'science versus anti-science' debate. This book hopes to suggest the possibility of a move beyond the current impasse in science–citizen relations.

In these circumstances, it is clearly important that we should consider the possibilities for an approach to science and expertise which offers at least the potential for a dialogue between scientific and citizen groups. Is it possible for a 'citizen-oriented science' (or *'citizen science'* in that sense) to emerge from these debates over the relationship between science, technology and wider society? Indeed, can the basis for such an approach be found in the three case-studies presented above?

We can begin this task by considering the range of expertise and understandings possessed by citizens but which are at present downgraded by decision-making processes. Both the 'enlightenment' approach and many of the more critical accounts discussed in this chapter offer a very one-dimensional view of citizens. Typically, they present the 'public' as homogeneous in character and also as essentially *passive* in the face of these contested technical messages. And yet, as we have already suggested, there is both a considerable diversity in public responses (and in the nature of the publics themselves) and also a rich pattern of knowledges and understandings. We will further develop this argument in Chapter 4. As we shift to a citizen-oriented perspective in these questions, we will also consider a radically different perspective on the perceived *need for* and *relevance* of science and technology within everyday life.

The notion of bringing closer together the concerns of citizens and the understandings of science is not in itself new – many of the same preoccupations can be discerned in the 'science for the people' movement of the 1960s and 1970s or various attempts at 'public participation' such as the Dutch 'broad energy debate' of the 1980s. Nevertheless, this book will argue that both our practical experience and also our understanding of science and technology have 'moved on' in such a way as to make a re-evaluation especially timely. Two further developments add to the significance of these themes:

- the special importance given to these issues by the current will to tackle environmental problems and to achieve some form of 'sustainable development';
- the availability of fresh research into these issues which attempts

33

not to reaffirm the 'public ignorance' model but instead to capture the needs and understandings of lay groups.

In line with the issues and concerns discussed so far, Chapter 2 highlights the significance of risk and environmental issues as a pressing area of science–citizen interactions. Given this significance, one important test of 'enlightenment' (or, as we can now consider them, 'modernist') perspectives will be their ability to come up with adequate responses to the social tensions of this area. How well has scientific rationality faced up to the environmental challenge?

Chapter 2 introduces two areas of debate in order to develop a new framework for the consideration of these issues. The first of these is linked to the recent work of Ulrich Beck and Anthony Giddens and concerns the notion of a 'risk society'. These social theoretical arguments provide a context for the consideration of science and citizenship. The second theoretical strand draws upon the contemporary sociology of scientific knowledge in such a way as to problematize conventional presentations of science as consensual and 'objective' knowledge.

These questions will be explored through a series of case-studies – including the three examples offered in Chapter 1 but also that of acid rain. Whilst science has indeed played a substantial role within discussions about the environment, it will be seen that this has also exposed science to considerable criticism – not least in terms of the social assumptions which have been embedded in apparently objective analysis. This chapter gives an insight into the operation and application of science in this context.

Chapter 3 builds on the previous discussion by examining the authority which scientific appraisal has retained despite the characteristics outlined in Chapter 2. Again within the context of risk/ environmental debates, the main policy responses are examined. These are categorized as 'expert', 'democratic' and 'pragmatic'. In each case, the reliance on 'enlightenment' perspectives (at least by way of legitimation) is emphasized. However, it is also noted that a series of social challenges to this policy mode is now being made – this has taken the form of environmentalist critique and a wider public scepticism. These two chapters (i.e., 2 and 3), therefore, trace the influence of enlightenment perspectives and also the rise of social threats to their hegemony.

Discussion now turns explicitly towards the existence of citizen-based knowledges and understandings which are currently excluded from decision-making and indeed from even being recognized as valid contributors to social debate. This important step in the argument is made by contrasting official advice on emergency planning with the assessments and insights of affected citizens. Chapter 4, therefore, represents an extended case-study of one social and technical context. In particular, it is argued that the failure of communication occurred in this case not because of a lack of energy on the part of disseminators but because they were operating with a fundamentally unrealistic notion of public knowledge and, indeed, of the emergency situation which they claimed to understand. The limitations of official knowledge are then contrasted with the richness and diversity of understandings within a local community.

Chapter 5 offers further analysis of the application of science within specific social contexts and presents wider evidence of 'lay knowledge' – beginning with the main cases presented in Chapter 1 and then moving into a discussion of other examples (e.g., campaigns around toxic waste, health and the workplace). All of these examples suggest a problematic relationship between the formalized language of science and the contextually generated understandings presented by particular social groups. At the very least, this disparity suggests the need to re-work the notion of 'public understanding of science' and to move to a more 'symmetrical' notion of different knowledge relations and legitimate areas of expertise. Such a shift is deeply challenging for the activities of science. This chapter seeks to generalize from the case-study outlined in Chapter 4.

In advocating this approach to science and knowledge relations, it is also important to be aware of various attempts to establish improved science–citizen relations – what we can term 'social experiments in citizen science'. In this way also, discussion can consider the practical possibilities for new social forms (or 'mediating institutions') and the obstacles which exist. On this basis, Chapter 6 covers a range of initiatives within the broad area of risk and the environment; these include major public inquiries (e.g., at Windscale or Mackenzie Valley), attempts at encouraging wider social debate (for example, the Dutch notion of 'constructive technology assessment' or the 'broad energy debate') and at including new groups in the direction of technical change. A particular case-study of 'Science Shops' is then presented in order to highlight the practical and conceptual issues involved.

Discussion in Chapter 7 is directed towards pulling together the various strands from the previous discussion. How widely applicable is this 'contextual' form of analysis to non-hazard situations? Is such an approach contradictory or complementary to more conventional analyses? Where does science fit within this framework? Discussion here moves back to the wider analytical level and to the themes set out in the Introduction. It is argued that the 'new times' of late modernity raise fundamental questions for our ideas of knowledge, citizenship and environmental response. We move, therefore, to new institutional possibilities and their implications for future knowledge relations and for the management of technical change.

These new possibilities are particularly important with regard to notions of sustainable development. The insufficient attention to questions of science and citizenship within most accounts of sustainable development (or rather their determinedly modernistic framework) – as evidenced by national responses to the Brundtland Report[53]– represents a major flaw in any attempt to produce genuine environmental response. The re-definition of 'sustainability' so as to include these elements is, therefore, one of the main objectives of *Citizen Science*.

2

SCIENCE, CITIZENS AND ENVIRONMENTAL THREAT

Understanding the nature of risks and uncertainty is an important part of the scientific understanding needed both for many public policy issues and for everyday decisions in our personal lives. . . . Once again it must be argued that better understanding fosters better public and personal decisions.[1]

The origin of risk consciousness in highly industrialised civilization is truly not a page of honour in the history of (natural) scientists. It came into being against a barrage of scientific denial, and is still suppressed by it. . . . Science has *become the protector of a global contamination of people and nature.*[2]

The main purpose of this chapter is to introduce one of the more important contexts within which citizens encounter science and technology – issues of risk and environmental threat. I will argue that, for a number of reasons, this is an especially crucial area – not least because of the high levels of public concern which it engenders but also because of the special problems encountered by science. In introducing this area, it will be important also to consider sociological arguments about the 'risk society' and the changing relationship between 'society' and 'nature' which these suggest.

Overall, this chapter will provide the background to Chapter 3's analysis of the relationship between science and the processes of policy-making in this domain. More particularly, discussion in Chapter 2 will challenge the current domination of risk and environmental debate by scientific modes of analysis. Instead, it will be argued that the social and cultural dimensions of environmental problems must be understood if we are to achieve understanding and practical action. Rather than simply presenting environmental degradation as an *external* threat, we need to ask fundamental questions about our societies and the value structures on which they currently depend.

Evidence of contemporary public concern and activity over 'green' issues is not too hard to find even if any indicator will vary over time. Such social indicators include:

- *voting patterns* – the June 1989 European Parliament elections saw strong support for the green movement in Britain, West Germany and France. Since then, the 'green vote' has wavered somewhat before falling once more in the 1994 European elections;
- attention from established *political parties* (most dramatically, the former British Prime Minister's 'conversion').[3] Again, since the late 1980s there may have been a shift away from 'mainstream' political attention to this issue – but there does appear to be an underlying awareness nevertheless;
- discussions and activity at the *inter-governmental* level as demonstrated above all at the United Nations Conference on Environment and Development (usually known as the 'Earth Summit') held in Rio de Janeiro during June 1992;
- *media attention* – environmental issues make good stories and the mass media have over the last decade maintained a steady stream of single issue exposés and environmental campaigns;[4]
- *public campaigns* – often generated by environmentalist groups (over whaling, global warming, acid rain, tropical rain forests);
- *specific local campaigns* (for example, over the siting of waste incinerators or the despoliation of green belts or open land);
- the rise of *green consumerism*[5] and attention to the *greening of industry* where government and industry have attempted to overcome the generally perceived dichotomy between industrial growth and environmental protection;
- a range of *practical initiatives* by local government, educational bodies and private organizations aimed at encouraging domestic and workplace recycling and environmental enhancement – from the provision of bottle banks to the sorting of waste materials;
- a number of *citizen-led initiatives* to live and work in an environmentally harmonious manner.[6] Such initiatives across Europe include local energy schemes (often linked to windmills or improved insulation systems), waste re-use and recycling, alternative agricultural methods (typically less reliant on pesticides or other agrochemicals) and experiments in ecological communities

(where villages are designed with ecological principles firmly in mind whilst also employing new technologies – especially information technology – in an innovative and 'environmentally-friendly' way);

- a growing number of *environmental regulations and controls* – as developed, for example, by the European Union and other international bodies such as the Organization for Economic Cooperation and Development (OECD);
- membership of *environmental organizations* (in 1991, Greenpeace were claiming over 385,000 supporters in Britain alone);
- *educational initiatives* aimed at raising young people's awareness of the environment at a local and global level;
- an avalanche of new *books and publications* on 'the environment'.

Whilst the precise significance of any one of these indicators is open to challenge, together they do suggest the extent to which environmental questions have been identified and acted upon in a variety of social settings – from local campaigns to transnational corporations and from government schemes to small-scale initiatives. Equally, there is a substantial range in the kinds of environmental issues at stake – from worldwide matters of ozone depletion, global warming and acid rain to more localized questions of factory pollution, road construction or the protection of neighbourhood space.

However, and as the environmental slogan 'think globally, act locally' captures so well (even if the precise nature of the global/local link is often hard to pin down), there does appear to be an underlying commonality to these issues – a commonality which can be summarized as 'the challenge of sustainability'. How is social, economic and scientific/technological development to take place in a manner which will value and protect the natural environment?

The argument of this book is that such a challenge is as much *social* as it is technical or environmental. In other words, the challenge is to organize our lives in a manner which is indeed 'sustainable'. We also need to consider the meaning of 'sustainability'; how is this constructed and understood by different social groups? One major dimension of this will be the relationship between our ways of 'living with' and 'knowing' the environment. Put simply, the science-centred or reductionist account – which following Beck[7] and others we can portray as 'modernist' in character – places the scientific appraisal of the environment as central with social factors operating at a secondary level. Sociological accounts of the kind to be discussed in this chapter suggest that social and cultural issues may be at the very core of environmental concerns.

Awkward questions do need to be asked about the role of science within environmental response – in particular so that we can identify the social processes through which certain issues get 'chosen' over others and also the range of anxieties about societal and technological development which find expression in risk and environmental issues. Moreover, the modernist rationale prevents us from examining science itself – could it be that it is part of (rather than the solution to) the environmental problem? Conventional approaches insulate the institutions of science from public discussion or criticism.

Concern over environmental and hazard issues certainly seems to go beyond the threat of physical and natural destruction. Instead, it would appear that demands for environmental action are also a reflection of social and personal values (and a sense of threat to those values). As the literature on risk assessment suggests,[8] questions of 'risk' and 'hazard' may serve as a focus for a whole array of doubts and uncertainties about the direction of social change. Thus, to offer one example, opposition to civil nuclear power may be as much about a distrust of centralized, large-scale technologies as it is about the level of quantifiable risk. Equally, one's preference for certain kinds of technology will be a reflection of wider social, moral and ethical preferences.

An acknowledgement of this fundamental social dimension to environmental concern has important consequences for our analysis of the modernist perspective. In particular, and in opposition to the enlightenment viewpoint, social factors play a part in the formulation of environmental problems and not just in '*post hoc*' response to such threats.

One important starting point for this kind of analysis is to portray concepts like 'the environment' or 'nature' as *social* in origination – as Mary Douglas has noted, a society's view of the outside world will reflect that society's culture and underlying structure. Douglas argues with regard to pollution issues: 'the view of the universe and a particular kind of society holding this view are closely interdependent. They are a single system. Neither can exist without the other'.[9]

40

In this vein, Jenny Diski has one of her (male) protagonists argue in the novel *Rainforest*:

> There is no nature, only Nature – an imaginary state of man's own invention, a realm of concept and language. That is man's place and it is nowhere except inside his head; a mirror image of a distorted fantasy he calls Mankind. . . . Nature is a conceit: a man-made garden in which we wander to relax and preen, as we nod to one another in passing, and congratulate ourselves on being us. We created nature so that we might take pride in how far we have ventured beyond it.[10]

The assertion here is that what counts as 'environmental harm' is a product of human and social forces rather than just 'self-evident' truths about external reality. Such an assertion – if accepted – will have a profound effect on our view of environment and hazard issues and on the privileged or otherwise position we accord to science. It therefore becomes important to consider the sociological accounts which have debated this proposition.

Cotgrove, for example, has argued that environmental disputes centre on 'different moral and social orders' so that disputes over risk are actually disputes over deeply held values (economic growth vs spiritual well-being, large technologies vs 'small is beautiful').[11] If we return to the nuclear power case, this analysis suggests that one's view of the technology will at least partly (or even totally) have been decided *in advance* of acquiring any technical information about the scale of risk. Civil nuclear power seems entirely appropriate to a general worldview which emphasizes economic growth, centralized technologies, faith in science and technology and trust in large social institutions. However, the 'alternative environmental paradigm', with its emphasis on meeting essential needs, local technological systems, wariness about 'high tech' futures and a scepticism towards social institutions, will view the very notion of nuclear power with suspicion and concern.

These 'worldviews' will also possess different views of the natural environment – with the dominant paradigm seeing Nature as flexible and resilient. Meanwhile, the 'alternative' paradigm judges Nature to be delicately balanced. As with Douglas' argument, each view of the Universe depends upon a broader social and cultural assessment of the world in which we live.

Schwarz and Thompson have also drawn upon Douglas' account in order to put forward a provocative case for 'cultural theory' in this context. For them, views of the environment are linked to specific cultural groups. According to this 'cultural' approach, assessments of the fragility or otherwise of the environment are again reflections of a larger worldview.[12]

For Schwarz and Thompson, the organizations of which we are a part will lead us to assess the environment in different ways. Thus, for example, entrepreneurial cultures see the natural world as highly robust in the face of environmental pressures. Meanwhile, hierarchical institutions consider Nature to be safe only as long as such pressures are kept firmly under control. Environmentalist groups construct the environment as liable to collapse at any point due to human activities.

In similar vein, Douglas and Wildavsky portray environmental disputes as a conflict between the 'centre' and the 'border' in society.[13] Again, our view of Nature is considered to be shaped by social and institutional location. In particular, for the border, environmental concerns become a way of justifying existence and reinforcing group cohesion – the creation of external, environmental threats is a powerful means of maintaining group identity.

All of these Douglas-inspired arguments suggest an inseparability of 'social' and 'natural' elements. According to the conventional, modernist view, the natural world is *external* to the social. However, these sociological accounts view the 'natural' as a *social construction* and in that sense as internal to the social world. At one level, this constructedness is due to the all-pervasive influence of humanity on the world around us – today's 'unspoilt' countryside, for example, was created by previous generations of agricultural workers. No part of the globe seems immune from human influence – whether the tropical rainforest being hacked away for short-term gain or isolated animal colonies being affected by chemical residues.

At another level, as the previous quotation from *Rainforest* suggests, the natural world seems unavoidably 'a realm of concept and language' simply because we are *part* of the world and not separate from it. Put in that way, the notion that the 'natural' is external to us seems strange indeed. From this perspective, it seems inevitable that our assessment of the state of nature will mirror our assessment of the state of the social structure. In that sense also, the 'environmental crisis' is simultaneously and unavoidably a crisis of our worldviews and social institutions – with consequences, as we will suggest, for our views of science, knowledge and expertise.

This line of argument will shortly be developed with regard to the recent work of Beck and Giddens. For now, we can at least suggest the relevance of sociological analysis to environmental questions. Thus, Yearley has argued strongly that social theory can make a major contribution to our understanding of green issues.[14] Peter Dickens extends these points by advocating a whole new intellectual paradigm so as to incorporate both 'natural' and 'social' explanations:

> One of the most important effects of such a merger . . . would be to abandon the distinction between 'man' (more suitably, 'people') and nature. Contemporary environmentalism often suggests that people are doing things *to* nature and that nature . . . is doing things to us. Such a picture . . . can be profoundly misleading. Dissolving the distinction between science and social science means that we can start to see people and societies as, in certain respects, *part* of nature. Similarly, we see nature as a part of and integral to human species as well as to other species.[15]

This integrative perspective on 'Society' and 'Nature' is of major importance for this book – especially in its implications for our ways of *knowing* the world in which we live. At the very least, this briefly summarized literature suggests a considerably richer and more sociological picture of environmental questions than typically emerges in contemporary debate.

Rather than attempting a full literature survey – which would distract from the main direction of this book – I am going to discuss in greater detail *one* influential form of sociological account. This account – as offered by Ulrich Beck and, in a different but related analysis, by Anthony Giddens – suggests that we are now living in a 'risk society' where issues such as those already presented have become central to our everyday existence. This argument powerfully suggests the significance of risk and environmental concerns for the future development of society. Such a view also has major consequences for our understanding of the relationship between science, citizens and environmental threat.

Science, citizens and the 'risk society'

We are eye-witnesses – as subjects and objects – of a break within modernity, which is freeing itself from the contours of the classical industrial society and forging a new form – the (industrial) 'risk society'. . . . *Just as modernization dissolved the structure of feudal society in the nineteenth century and produced the industrial society modernization today is dissolving industrial society and another modernity is coming into being.*[16]

The reflexivity of modernity turns out to confound the expectations of Enlightenment Thought – although it is the very product of that thought. The original progenitors of modern science and philosophy believed themselves to be preparing the way for securely founded knowledge of the social and natural worlds: the claims of reason were due to overcome the dogmas of tradition, offering a sense of certitude in place of the arbitrary character of habit and custom. But the reflexivity of modernity actually undermines the certainty of knowledge, even in the core domains of natural science.[17]

For Giddens and Beck, the social structure is undergoing a period of change; from *modernity* – with its faith in the Enlightenment tenets of Progress, Truth and Science – to *late* (or new) modernity – where the old truths have given way to radical doubt, reflexivity and anxiety over how each of us should live. In such a situation, questions of uncertainty, self-identity (who we consider ourselves to be) and *risk* become central. Everyday life becomes 'risky' not necessarily because of any new threat to our welfare or survival but because, at least according to Giddens, 'the self' has become fragmented and exposed. The institutions and belief systems which once protected us from 'ontological insecurity' (notably science) are now open to widespread challenge. In this new context, each of us is aware of the *choices* which exist within daily life – even the decision to pursue a 'traditional' lifestyle must be made in the awareness that there are possible alternative ways of life.

For Beck, society is undergoing a phase of 'reflexive modernization'. This means that there is a changing relationship between social structures and social agents and, in particular, that people have become less constrained by existing institutions – here there is a strong linkage with the arguments of Giddens. Citizens are now in a position to *shape* the process of modernization rather than simply following pre-established patterns of behaviour. In such a situation also, our notion of the 'political' is substantially changed – traditional notions of the 'political' (as found, for example, within parliamentary activity or mainstream political parties) become

44

replaced by a diversity of citizen actions which barely relate to these decision-making structures. The environmental movement represents an excellent example of this new kind of 'social agency'. The linkage between personal action and global consequences which environmentalism offers has largely side-stepped the whole traditional infrastructure of political life.

As was suggested at the beginning of this chapter, there has been some response from political parties to green issues – and also some advance for green parties. Nevertheless, a large slice of the 'action' over environmental concerns has been at non-parliamentary levels. Such a change has consequences for our notion of *citizenship*. 'Environmental citizenship' may depend less on the ballot box (the traditional expression of citizenship in a parliamentary democracy) and more on the expression of citizen concerns at a variety of other levels – joining environmentalist groups or single-issue campaigns, making choices at the supermarket, using bottle banks and other recycling facilities, educating children to be environmentally aware.

Now these points about the changing nature of 'modernity' take on a special significance if we examine the 'risk society' in which we live. This 'risk society' possesses a number of characteristics which have emerged despite modernity's presentation of social and technological progress as steady and unproblematic:

- whilst in an earlier social structure the key problem was one of undersupply, we have now moved to a point where overproduction is a major issue. Put differently, rather than struggling with the external world, society is now struggling increasingly with the risks and threats which it has itself produced;
- as I have already suggested, a new relationship between 'Nature' and 'Society' has developed where the two are effectively inseparable. As Beck argues, there can no longer be an 'antithesis between nature and society', 'nature can no longer be understood *outside of* society, or society *outside of* nature'. This point is, of course, crucial for our understanding of environmental issues;
- a consequence of this changed relationship between 'Society' and 'Nature' is that the positions adopted by different groups about risk issues are inevitably *social* in character. Judgements about risk and safety will reflect one's position in the social structure – and also one's degree of trust in the social institutions which currently decide about these questions on others' behalf;
- a key point for Beck concerns the role of *science* within the risk

45

society. If 'primary scientization' saw science as a liberation from the constraints of Nature, then *'secondary scientization'* now sees science as both the creator of risk and as the claimed antidote and solution. In such a situation – as the second quotation at the beginning of this chapter suggests – science emerges as the form of understanding which has created environmental destruction. In late modernity, the inherent limitations of science become increasingly visible.

For most citizens, science has become an obstacle to the expression of concerns. Typically, at least for Beck, science is used to silence concerns about the world in which we live rather than to enable and empower those concerns. Fears over the environment are met with scientifically-based reassurances that all is well – even though citizen experiences may suggest the opposite.

Science thus no longer represents 'enlightenment' but a force to be struggled against. Of course, the more science loses its special status as the 'highest' form of rationality – as Beck sees occurring within environmental disputes – the less successful it will be as a source of legitimation for powerful social institutions such as government and industry. Scientific rationality thus encounters inherent contradictions such that one can argue that the risk society threatens the very 'failure of techno-scientific rationality'.

In order to re-establish this legitimacy – and in order to serve a useful societal purpose – science needs to recognize its own role as a source of 'modernization risks' and to make institutional changes accordingly. Beck's challenge to science is to find new ways of operating within the risk society on the grounds that: 'scientific rationality without social rationality remains *empty*, but social rationality without scientific rationality remains *blind*'.[18]

We will develop this discussion of institutional and cognitive change with regard to science throughout this book. For now, the important point is to grasp the new relationships between 'science', 'citizens' and 'environmental threats' which are opened up by the 'risk society' notion. In particular, we are led to challenge the 'enlightenment' assumption that science is central to environmental response with all else as peripheral – that 'technical experts are given pole position to define agendas and impose boundary premises *a priori* on risk discourses'.[19]

This theoretical account of the 'risk society' underlines the significance of environmental issues for our understanding of science–citizen relations. However, it follows from this argument that issues of risk and the environment are not separate from wider citizen concerns around science – whether regarding the threat to civil liberties from new information and communication technologies or the fear of nuclear weapons, similar questions are likely to arise. The 'risk society' is not about physical or ecological risks alone but rather the way in which citizens feel themselves 'at risk' from social and technological development. It is this awareness of threat which makes late modernity distinctive.

In presenting these sociological arguments, however, it is also important that we note the very general and wide-ranging nature of the claims being made. Whilst both sociologists present various examples, there is little sense of a carefully-based empirical account. Thus, although these arguments may be provocative and suggestive, they must also be responded to critically and in the light of lived experience – as later chapters of *Citizen Science* will attempt to do.

At this point, it becomes necessary to draw upon the second main theoretical strand to this book – *the sociology of scientific knowledge* (SSK). At least as I will present it here, this strand is in many ways complementary to the arguments presented so far. Thus, brief reference was made to this important area of scholarship at the end of the previous chapter (specifically with regard to the work of Brian Wynne).

Nevertheless, SSK has developed quite separately from the macro-level analysis of Beck and Giddens. In particular, SSK can lead us away from the broad generalizations about science favoured by Beck and Giddens and towards a stronger sense of the heterogeneity and variety of modern scientific practice.

Above all, the sociology of scientific analysis has been rooted in the careful study of specific areas of science.[20] This 'situated' approach – often building upon the ethnographic techniques of the anthropologist – has much to recommend it as a counter-balance to more sweeping sociological statements. It also represents an attempt to learn from lived experience rather than producing externalist accounts of the workings of scientific institutions.

Moreover, the SSK analysis contrasts sharply with the 'enlightenment' view of science as homogeneous, cleanly-bounded and consensual – according to this orthodox view 'science' as a form of knowledge is value-free and objective, only its *application* is subject to social selection. The *uses* of science may be open to criticism but not the knowledge itself which remains independent of the circumstances of its development and implementation.

In contrast, a group of sociologists have successfully portrayed science as being *socially-negotiated* in character. The intellectual roots of this perspective can be traced back to various points – including the writings of Marx, Merton and Mannheim.[21] Kuhn's well-known book, *The Structure of Scientific Revolutions*[22], and its development of the 'paradigm' concept signalled that the cognitive (i.e., scientific facts, theories and ideas) as well as the institutional dimensions of science may be open to sociological enquiry. In particular, Kuhn's notion of 'normal science' and the implied relationship between scientific thinking and the processes through which scientists are trained became a pivotal insight.

No longer was sociological discussion limited to deviant science (where the pathological or mistaken must be explained) or to the reconstruction of how objective knowledge is obtained. Instead, the development and social construction of scientific 'facts' became a legitimate object of study – generally through detailed accounts of specific case-studies.[23]

According to this analysis, science is not a storehouse of 'facts' which different social groups can plunder – nor is it a prescribed 'method' for the acquisition of 'objective knowledge'. Instead, science is presented as a much more diffuse and flexible collection of social institutions. This collection includes a diversity of intellectual domains whose boundaries are constantly negotiated and renegotiated with other social institutions.

Later in this chapter, we will use the acid rain case as an illustration of these social and technical negotiations. Careful consideration of such an example suggests that there is no single science of acid rain – instead, we see a variety of different paradigms and theories being brought into play. In this case, that includes various branches of engineering, chemistry, meteorology, biology, medicine, agriculture and mathematics. These disciplines work closely with non-scientific organizations such as the electricity-generating organizations, government departments and environmentalist groups. In offering scientific evaluations of possible acidification damage, scientists must also construct a set of assumptions about the conditions of acid creation and exposure (e.g., whether stated operational conditions will be met, transport models prove accurate, other sources of pollution prove significant). In all of these areas, significant uncertainties will need to be negotiated. Science emerges as a very human and – by necessity – constrained enterprise, even if its findings are subsequently presented as canonical.

Now, there are a variety of academic perspectives within SSK and a number of sub-branches.[24] Particularly influential have been those approaches which analyse the relationship between scientific argumentation and various 'social interests'. In the case of acid deposition, obvious interests included those of the British government and electricity generators in avoiding external controls – partly for reasons of cost but also because of a broader reluctance to concede to environmentalist and international demands. Science from this perspective becomes a weapon used to further economic and political interests in a somewhat covert manner; science essentially becomes 'politics by other means'.

Whilst this 'interest' perspective can have real value in various contexts (for instance, the same line can be applied to advisory committees and their links to industrial organizations), we should not underestimate the inherent difficulty of imputing an 'interest' to complex organizations. Thus, the question of how certain interests come to dominate over others seems highly complex but also typically under-explored within this approach. Certainly, neither institutions nor indeed individuals necessarily adopt a 'rational actor' calculation of interest. This in turn raises further questions of the short- or long-term time scale against which interests are adjudged and also the balance between different forms of interest – economic, political, personal, ethical, organizational.

None of this serves to dismiss the interest approach to SSK – but rather alerts us to the complexity of analysing the social construction of science. Equally, and as we will see in the main empirical chapters, interest models may be alive and well in the general population – as when technical statements are evaluated at least partly in terms of *who* is making them.

Two other strands within contemporary SSK studies also deserve brief attention in this discussion. The former places special significance on the linguistic and discursive forms through which scientific statements are constructed and then validated.[25] Within this approach, claims to 'objectivity' and to the establishment of 'facts' are viewed as largely rhetorical devices employed by scientists to persuade others of the value of their claims. In the case of an environmental threat such as acid rain, analytical questions arise such as for whom is the hazard 'proven'? How and why did this acceptance of 'proof' occur and how is 'proof' sustained in the face of counter-claims?[26]

This sceptical approach to scientific statements and fact construction has particular value for our understanding of science in the environmental context. We are led to deconstruct and problematize the claims of scientific institutions but also public responses to this 'information'. The task for the analyst is to destabilize knowledge claims in order to assess their cultural and rhetorical underpinnings – on what basis does the scientific institution insist that we should believe its statements? Such an approach can also be adapted to the knowledge claims of non-scientific groups – whether local citizens or national organizations.

From this perspective also, scientific evidence must be skilfully marshalled and represented to particular audiences if it is to exert any persuasive power. At the same time, audiences must 'make sense' of these messages in accordance with their assumed needs and concerns – as Chapter 4 will begin to discuss.

A final source of inspiration derives from feminist debate and scholarship as it relates to science and technology. Feminist analysis is important in this context for its inter-connection of the development of science with a particularly 'masculinist' attempt to dominate the natural world and to impose a one-dimensional form of rationality on everyday reality. In the context of risk and environmental issues, this approach suggests the existence of various relevant rationalities but also a criticism of science's universalistic claims. In particular, women's knowledge and understanding can become denied by the tight inter-connection of male-dominated institutions and 'masculinist' science.[27]

Within this book, such arguments will be important for their suggestion of a dominant form of rationality which can serve to stifle alternative ways of living and thinking. The discourse of science can structure and constrain through its imposition of one form of knowledge. Meanwhile, alternative understandings become dismissed as 'non-scientific' and 'irrational'.

Taking all of these heavily summarized points about SSK together, there are a number of features which are especially relevant to *Citizen Science*:

- first of all, science emerges not as a single and authoritative account of the world but as diverse and *heterogeneous* both in terms of its knowledge structures and institutions. In that sense, we should think of the sciences rather than one science. Such a point has already been made with regard to acid deposition; we will suggest in subsequent chapters that it is more widely applicable;

- second, we become alert to the possibility that science is based upon sets of *assumptions* about the 'external world' which are *social* in their origination. This is particularly significant with regard to issues of risk and the environment where assumptions about human action and response are inevitable – but are rarely openly acknowledged;

- third, this analysis at least suggests that science can be *flexible* in the face of expressed social needs and wishes. Rather than being the inevitable product of human enquiry (a model known as 'scientific determinism'), the science we get will reflect the social priorities and audience constructions of its sponsors. This notion of scientific flexibility at least opens up the possibility of scientific reappraisal and readjustment in conjunction with new pressures and challenges;

- finally, this analysis helps to open up a constructive debate about the *limitations* to science as a way of understanding the world. This is not to deny the practical significance of science nor its intellectual potency (indeed, the SSK perspective seems to render the achievements of science all the more awesome). However, sociological discussions of science generally serve to convey the contextualized nature of scientific knowledge – both in terms of the construction of knowledge claims and of the implementation of those claims.

When confronted with the 'real-world' complexity of environmental problems (as the acid rain case again suggests), scientists struggle to eliminate uncertainty and achieve intellectual control. Equally, such problems extend beyond the accepted remit of science. Through the careful investigation of specific areas of science, sociologists have conveyed the power *and* the restrictedness of science.

Taken together, the sociological accounts of scientific knowledge and of the 'risk society' suggest a new framework for understanding 'science and its publics'. Above all, and as promised in the Preface, this framework has the possibility of being symmetrical in its treatment of both science and its publics.

This theoretical analysis can be related closely to the three examples given in Chapter 1, as we will see later. In particular, we begin to grasp something of the *challenges* to science which are created by pressing issues such as those of the environment – even if environmental debate continues to be dominated by a scientific mode of analysis. Both approaches also lead us to be critical of the conventional treatment of the 'environment' as an external threat – that threat is also conjured up and constructed through the statements of scientists. This scientific mediation is quite evident in the 'three stories of our time'. However, rather than work through all three, the case of BSE can be taken as a first illustration followed by an account of a different case – that of acid deposition.

Science, mad cows and the risk society

As noted in the previous chapter, the 'mad cow' episode can be interpreted in a number of ways; not least as a further illustration of the high significance given to risks within 'late modern' society – especially when they are embedded in wider technological concerns (in this case involving food technology and the practice of feeding animal carcasses to other animals). Within the wider analytical framework of this chapter we can now look again at the reassurance strategy of presenting 'modernist rationality' to the public. Let us reconsider for this purpose the full page advertisement of the 'Meat and Livestock Commission' which appeared in various newspapers in 1990.

> Eating British Beef is completely safe. There is no evidence of any threat to human health caused by this animal health problem (BSE).
> This is the view of independent British and European scientists and not just the meat industry.
> *This view has been endorsed by the Department of Health.*
> To protect consumers the Government has gone even further than the steps recommended by scientists.
> You can therefore eat British Beef with total confidence.
> For any further factual information contact . . .[28]

Quite obviously, this is designed as an attempt to engage with public fears and to inspire confidence. What are the major characteristics of this attempt?

1 An authority claim based on a language of *certainty* ('completely safe', 'no evidence', 'total confidence'). Quite clearly, this is intended to counteract public doubt and uncertainty. The argument behind this would seem to be that it is only by removing technical doubt that reassurance can be offered.

2 A presumption that *science* is absolutely central to the problem ('independent . . . scientists', 'further factual information'). Of course, the language of 'BSE' rather than the more popular 'mad cow disease' reinforces this point. More fundamentally, we can see that 'mad cow disease' would not *exist* as a social problem without the active involvement of scientists – how else would a citizen be aware of the issue? 'Common sense' experience seems unlikely to create the wider category of BSE. Science thus defines from the very outset the form of this risk.

3 No attempt is made to engage in any way with public concerns. Whilst there is reference to 'this animal health problem' just what it is and why there is concern does not get discussed. One scientifically-based definition of the issue is assumed from the beginning.

4 There is an implicit (perhaps explicit) hierarchical notion at work within this statement ('we are in the best position to know about these things'). Again, this claim to superiority is based partly on science but also on government and the meat industry as respected bodies.

5 There is also an implicit social model in operation – the only reference to the *audience* for this statement is 'consumers'. The statement seems to speak to individuals as consumers rather than to pressure groups, other scientists (who hold somewhat different views) or workers in the meat industry. Elsewhere, there was much reference to what 'housewives' should or should not purchase. Here, the audience seems to be constructed as atomized and isolated from one another.

In terms of the 'risk society' debate, we can describe this approach as 'modernist' in character. It presents an account of science as authoritative, consensual and 'independent'. It also presents its audience – the wider citizenship – as both unformed and un-*in*formed. The audience is constructed as passive in the face of 'rational' messages. At this stage, we can witness a tension between the modernistic presentation of science and the much more sceptical – and in that sense *late* modern – response which it actually met from public groups. In line with Beck's account, such strategies from the meat industry and others were treated by outside groups with caution and suspicion. Such suspicion significantly included the technical evidence being made available by official groups; an inclusion which is regularly portrayed as 'irrational'.

The BSE case thus offers many elements of the 'risk society' in action – the case also suggests the inseparability of risk issues from the social and technological processes which generate those risks. However, we can also gain an insight into the *struggle* which citizen groups may have to face with regard to modernistic strategies from powerful social groups.

At the same time – as the SSK perspective reminds us – we have to ask critical questions about the nature of the science which is being presented. Many laboratory scientists, for example, would not recognize the certainty with which these messages are being conveyed – the divided scientific opinions over this issue were thus being obscured in many public statements. Significant uncertainties here included whether or not BSE could cross species boundaries, whether the suggested controls would suffice, what number of animal cases might be found in the near future.

In such a case, the establishment of 'proof' becomes difficult indeed – especially given the fragility of scientific opinion. Consequently, and despite the apparent self-confidence of this public statement, a definitive account has yet to be constructed by scientists. It also follows that, rather than simply being a struggle around the use (or abuse) of science, we must also examine the very *constitution* of scientific knowledge and the assumptions which are embedded within this.

We can pursue these points about scientific understanding somewhat further through one, at times contentious, environmental issue – acid deposition. The acid rain debate is an excellent place to develop our discussion since it embodies many of the scientific difficulties raised by the 'new generation' of global environmental threats (such as acid rain but also including global warming and damage to the ozone layer). However, acid rain might also be presented as one of the more 'straightforward' of environmental issues – suggesting, if nothing else, the uncertainties found even in this relatively well-understood case. In the following section, we will consider the acid rain issue but look particularly to draw wider implications for other areas of environmental response.

Science and uncertainty: the case of acid deposition[29]

As with numerous other areas of environmental risk analysis, the acid pollution issue has throughout its history been characterized not only by heated political negotiations (e.g., between the UK and its European neighbours or the USA and Canada) but also by a series of technical disagreements over its causation and consequences. A number of areas of persistent doubt and controversy have become evident. Above all, the central question of linking *cause* (acidity levels attributable to various pollution sources) and *effect* (visible physical consequences) has been highly problematic (especially when contrasted with the common assumption that science can provide some definite 'proof' in such cases). Scientific uncertainties have surrounded:

- the *chemical complexity* of the processes under consideration. Understanding the minutiae of the photo-chemical reactions involved in the migration and interaction of pollutants has always presented substantial difficulty;
- the sheer *range of the effects* being analysed (forests, plants and crops, lakes, rivers, fish, human health, corrosion). Whilst there are common strands to the causation of all of these effects, each also presents its own individual problems for scientific analysis;
- *time-scale* problems present special difficulties for linking cause and effect. Thus, the episodic nature of acid pollution and the lag between peaks in, for example, SO_2 pollution and consequent acidity levels in (say) Scandinavian lakes add to the problem of identifying trends in the levels of international acid deposition;
- the *spatial diffusion* of effects undoubtedly represents a major area of complexity. Thus, the transboundary migration of the pollution has made it more difficult to relate a pollution effect (e.g., fish deaths) to a specific cause (e.g., British power stations);
- the *variability of cause–effect response* needs also to be considered. No two locations are identical in terms of the buffering capacity of the soil and various geological characteristics, the precise pH level, prevailing meteorological conditions, habitat, wild-life distribution;
- *intervening variables* must be taken into account. For example, the effects of other pollutants, environmental agents or 'natural' biological processes such as marine algal emissions (perhaps working synergistically) need to be incorporated in any assessment.

Taken together, these factors suggest some of the complexities and uncertainties involved in establishing the linkage between the causes and consequences of environmental degradation. Heated discussion has taken place around the 'linearity' question of whether a reduction in SO_2 and NO_x would lead to a proportional reduction in acidity levels. Equally, the precise processes of acidity damage have been open to debate – with attention increasingly being directed to the role of ozone, sunlight and the leaching of heavy metals. In all these respects, therefore, it becomes extremely difficult to link together pollutant sources, levels of acidity and observed environmental effects. Of course, it has been precisely these kinds of uncertainty which led during the 1970s and 1980s to charges from the Central Electricity Generating Board (CEGB), the British government and others that the acid deposition case is 'not proven'.

What such differences of opinion and the associated antagonisms between parties particularly reveal is the extent to which scientific assessments – and particularly scientific *uncertainties* – can become 'centre-stage' in environmental controversy. Thus, during the early 1980s CEGB resolutely defended its opposition to further pollution controls on *scientific* grounds. The same approach has been adopted by environmental groups who have repeatedly claimed to offer a 'better' scientific account than that of the 'establishment'. Once again, the bulk of society becomes a witness to a science-oriented battle between warring parties.

At the same time, 'modernist' strategies are not restricted to governmental or industrial organizations. Environmentalist groups may adopt the same approach. In that sense also, we need to be cautious about Beck's apparent recruitment of environmentalist groups to the cause of late modernity.[30]

Such employment of technical expertise as a 'resource' for different stances within environmental disputes has become commonplace over the last few decades. Certainly, parallels can be drawn with the continuing debate over civil nuclear power and also with a whole series of controversies as analysed to date by social scientists (e.g., debates over chemical toxicity, major accident hazards, mandatory seat-belt wear).[31] Going further, Cramer, in a study of the role of ecologists within environmental decision-making, has noted that a number of forms of uncertainty will affect technical experts when asked to offer policy advice.[32]

First of all, there is *pragmatic uncertainty*; scientists may be asked to offer practical advice at very short notice and without sufficient equipment or staffing resources. Whilst the field of acid deposition research has advanced substantially over the last few years, there is no doubt that many international scientists outside the main institutional laboratories have experienced this problem. This is also a common complaint by scientists drawn into other policy debates.

Second, there is *theoretical uncertainty* as occurs when there is no strong theoretical framework (or 'paradigm'[33]) which unites a scientific field but instead a disparate pattern of disciplinary approaches and academic perspectives. This seems particularly relevant in the present context since, as we have already noted, acid deposition research draws upon a large variety of backgrounds (including chemistry, meteorology, the biological sciences, physics and geology). It is to be expected that these different disciplines will each highlight different aspects of the acid deposition problem and will carry a separate 'toolkit' of analytical techniques. Such a multi-disciplinary pattern is a regular feature of research fields which have developed in a 'problem-oriented' fashion rather than emerging from a single established discipline. Thus, debates over chemical toxicity (such as over 2,4,5–T) draw upon a similar range of technical specialities (toxicology, chemistry, biology, epidemiology, public health, medical research).

Third, Cramer identifies *the uncertainty related to the complexity of the ecological predictions to be made.* Thus, ecologists are called upon to model highly complex kinds of 'real world' behaviour (i.e., 'open systems') rather than operating within the tightly controlled 'closed systems' of the laboratory. Acid deposition seems an excellent example of an 'open system' with numerous intervening variables in flux at any time, with consequently high levels of response variability and with modelling and trend identification proving extremely difficult. This move to an open system (e.g., in the case of BSE what actually happens in the abattoir or factory farm) requires a *social* as well as a straightforwardly technical judgement.

In a review of the relationship between scientific expertise and environmental issues, Yearley further notes that the fact that environmental scientists are so often working on the *margins of observability* adds considerably to these uncertainties.[34] Thus, environmental problems often involve subtle and barely tangible forms of damage, they may be difficult to monitor and their precise trends may be imperfectly understood. Once again, this applies not just to the acid rain case but also to many other hazard/environmental issues – for example, toxic chemicals or ozone layer damage. It is because of uncertainties such as these that many commentators have seen technical advice within public policy disputes as exacerbating rather than eliminating policy disagreement.[35] In a study of the role of scientific evidence in controversies over chemical toxicity, Graham et al. conclude that:

> On the one hand, when very simple questions are asked (by regulatory authorities), the conscientious scientist finds it difficult to know how to answer because of the ambiguity created by simplification. On the other hand, scientific knowledge is not adequate to answer the more elaborate questions with any measure of confidence. Our point is that scientists often seem to disagree with one another because they are caught between ambiguity and ignorance, between questions that are too hard and questions that are too simple.[36]

Within normal scientific debate such a condition of 'ambiguity and ignorance' might be entirely beneficial (perhaps as a motivation to further enquiry). However, within a policy context where highly consequential decisions need to be taken, grave difficulties can occur – especially when scientific uncertainty is concealed for essentially legitimatory purposes. In the case of acid rain and BSE it appears – although this is inevitably difficult to document – that many government scientists were ill at ease with the official positions – their doubts were filtered out in the interests of presenting a 'strong message'.

In addition to recognizing the kinds of 'structural uncertainty' discussed above, we must also be conscious of the *social assumptions* which are embedded in scientific accounts of hazard issues. As I have already presented the SSK perspective, science is constituted within particular social contexts and these will shape what eventually counts as certified knowledge. This 'institutional shaping' of science becomes particularly important in the environmental context where technical assessments are often developed in a highly loaded policy process. As was noted in Chapter 1, Wynne has argued that experts routinely draw upon social assumptions about 'risk practices' in developing their scientific risk analyses. 'The "objective" framework floats on a sea of subject commitments and assumptions which have to be more openly expressed and negotiated in risk assessment processes'.[37]

At this stage, we can return to the opening section of this chapter and its concern with 'Society' and 'Nature'. Whilst science attempts to describe the natural world it must also make social assumptions about our interaction with that world; how will a pesticide actually be put to use? What are the real conditions of factory farming? How will a chemical works actually be managed?

In the case of acid rain, such assumptions include trends in pollution emission, other human sources of environmental degradation and the extent to which we actually care about the death of fishes and trees. Equally, the problem of acidity is created by technological development and by the growing needs of our energy-dependent society. On the one hand, it is a 'natural' problem. On the other, it is created by and inextricably linked to our social system. A technical focus on pollution control rather than underlying social causation serves to define environmental problems in a very particular fashion – and also distracts from more disturbing (for certain institutions) public debates about the whole direction of technological development.

Science can, therefore, legitimate not just by the specific stances it adopts but also by framing social questions in a particular fashion. Thus, BSE becomes a problem of species transmission rather than of food production and consumption. It follows from the argument in this chapter that scientific accounts of the 'natural world' are simultaneously also statements about the social worlds in which we live.

Science and the environmental crisis

This chapter has noted that – as the enlightenment perspective would suggest – science has played a central role in discussion about environmental risk. However, and as the BSE and acid rain case studies have implied, this involvement has also raised problems for science, citizens and public policy-making. In the BSE case, consumers were the focus of official attempts at communicating reassurance. Within the acid rain discussions, citizens were further removed from the debate – represented mainly by governmental and environmentalist groups claiming to speak on their behalf.

We have seen that scientific ignorance and uncertainty has been a major characteristic of environmental discussions – linked also to science's dependence on *social* assumptions at various levels. Beck argues that the growing awareness of the limitations of science has had important consequences: 'The exposure of scientific uncertainty is the liberation of politics, law and the public sphere from their patronization by technocracy'.[38]

Thus the loss of science's status as *certain* knowledge can be seen as a severe undermining of 'enlightenment' views of the world. Instead, as Ravetz argues, we need to live with 'usable ignorance':

> now we must cope with the imperfections of science, with radical uncertainty, and even with ignorance, in forming policy decisions for the biosphere. Do we merely turn away from such problems as beneath the dignity of scientists, or do we somehow learn to make even our ignorance usable in these new conditions?[39]

The second, and closely linked, factor concerns the extent of technical disagreement and controversy. As was apparent in the acid rain case but also numerous other environmental issues, scientists cannot be expected to agree about such questions – whatever the prevailing ideology of modernism might expect. Nevertheless, as the next chapter will discuss, science continues to serve within policy debates as if it could indeed offer certainty – and thus as a wider legitimation for institutional action:

> In contrast to magic, alchemy, and other esoteric forms of instrumentalism, science and technology appear to rationalize actions with reference to a realm of observable public facts. Liberal democratic instrumentalism has tended, therefore, to encourage political actors to choose actions which are rationally and publicly justifiable in technical terms, or at least present them as such.[40]

Finally in this wide-ranging chapter, it is necessary to stress two points about the relationship between science and the wider citizenry. It is especially important that we draw attention to the changing relationship between science, society and nature such that environmental issues require a considerably broader notion of 'the experiment' than has traditionally existed. This changing relationship also offers new constructive possibilities for science and its publics. To express this in Beck's terms: 'science has itself abolished the boundary between laboratory and society'.[41]

As cases such as acid rain and 2,4,5-T clearly demonstrate, the 'laboratory' now extends to cover all those people affected by environmental threats. Put differently, we are all part of social

experiments about the environmental consequences of technological development. This seems a defining characteristic of the 'risk
society' in which we live. As such, the disassociation between the
experimenter and the experimental object can no longer apply. It
also seems to follow from this expanded notion of the laboratory
that new knowledge relations are needed – and indeed may already
be in existence. Later chapters will explore this possibility.

It also needs to be stressed that, while science is regularly
portrayed as offering possible solutions to environmental problems,
there is a perception within the cases so far examined that science
is a *cause* of those problems. This accusation generally takes two
forms. First, the argument that many contemporary environmental
threats are actually the *products* of science and technology (new
chemical formulations, production processes, energy systems).
Second, the argument that science has been antithetical to natural
processes – in its very rationality it seeks to control, dissect and
dominate the natural world ('the rape of nature'). This is perhaps
best expressed in the BSE example – hasn't modern, scientific
agriculture created such problems through its 'unnatural' methods?
How then can science possibly claim to be the saviour of the
environment? As Douglas and Wildavsky assert: 'Once the source
of safety, science and technology have become the source of risk'.[42]

Our discussion of science and the environment has led us to view
science as simultaneously a source of understanding and a source
of uncertainty and even threat. As Ravetz has suggested above,
however, the question now seems not to be whether we should
accept or reject this form of understanding but instead of how we
should draw upon it.

Science presents us with many contradictory faces – saviour,
threat, knowledge, ignorance, social, natural. In the next two
chapters, we will consider the representation of science, first, within
the processes of policy and, second, within the lives of a particular
group of citizens. How have these tensions between, on the one
hand, risk and environmental threat and, on the other, scientific
understanding actually been played out?

3

SCIENCE AND THE POLICY PROCESS

> The proposition that science-based decisions should be reviewed by independent experts strikes us today as hardly more controversial than the proposition that there is no completely risk-free society.[1]

Chapter 2 placed the relationship between science and its publics within the larger context of the 'risk society' and the sociological analysis of scientific knowledge. Taken together, these analyses open up new possibilities for our understanding of 'science' and 'citizenship' within the context of risk and the environment. 'Science' becomes a contested and negotiated area of understanding. Accordingly, citizen demands are less easily dismissed as uninformed and peripheral. Even the definition of environmental threats comes to be viewed as socially and scientifically constructed – threats such as BSE or 'acid rain' need to be mediated and identified by science and 'official' statements.

All this suggests the possibility of a fresh and innovative understanding of the relationship between science and its publics. However, as this chapter will argue, the prevailing approach to public policy-making remains firmly embedded in a much more modernistic perspective – where science does indeed construct the definition of risk issues and all other concerns, including alternative forms of understanding and different value structures, become peripheral. In this we are reminded of Habermas' account of the 'technocratic consciousness':

> Technocratic consciousness reflects not the sundering of an ethical situation but the repression of 'ethics' as such as a category of life. . . . The ideological nucleus of this con-

sciousness is *the elimination of the distinction between the practical and the technical.*[2]

Of course, there are a number of possible explanations for this science-centredness – from those which insist that science (and especially, this *reductionist* form of science) is the only rational basis for action to those which see it as a way of avoiding more fundamental issues about the relationship between science, technology and society:

> The type of reflexivity in which the public is trained by risk-assessments offered for popular knowledge and use, fends off and deflects the blows which would otherwise, perhaps, stand a better chance of aiming at the true causes of present dangers; all in all, it helps the technologically inspired strategies of efficiency-maximisation and problem-orientation to survive their unprepossessing consequences, and so to emerge from trials with their danger-producing capacity intact.[3]

However, the strength of the modernist framework lies in this conjunction of science with instrumental rationality. No conspiracy theory seems necessary to explain why dominant social institutions should be reluctant to move outside the powerful cognitive framework on which modernity was built. Of course, this in no way precludes the use at times of science for straightforwardly legitimatory purposes. Meanwhile, the underlying challenge is to construct a framework for science, citizenship and the environment which can take account of the new social, technical and environmental conditions in which we live.

In this chapter, therefore, we will explore the relationship between science and the policy-making process for risk and environmental threat. Chapter 2 established the limitations, uncertainties and social assumptions embedded within scientific accounts in this area – we can now explore the 'official' response to these in greater detail. How have these characteristics of the scientific assessment of risk been negotiated and then presented to public audiences – including, of course, the potential human victims of any threat or harm? In conducting this analysis, we will also be placing arguments about the risk society in a critical light – is there any actual evidence within decision-making structures of the kinds of social transformation identified by Beck and Giddens?

With these very broad objectives in mind, we will examine briefly three major policy responses to environmental threat. Certainly this chapter does not pretend to offer a typology of these policy modes – this is intended more as a rapid overview. Accordingly, each of these responses will be illustrated through specific examples.

The first of these responses explicitly claims to be '*expert*' in character – it is based on the assumption that only an expert assessment of the issues can produce a reasoned and objective decision-making process (put simply, 'let the facts decide'). Despite the criticisms of such an approach which were implicit in Chapter 2, and despite the implication of Beck's argument that within the 'risk society' the treatment of these issues has somehow moved on, the notion that committees of experts are uniquely well placed to 'advise' on hazard issues is prevalent. As Jasanoff has argued with regard to the US context:

> Scientific advisory committees occupy a curiously sheltered position in the landscape of American regulatory politics. . . . Advisory committees are generally perceived as an indispensable aid to policy makers across a wide range of technical decisions. They offer a flexible, low cost means for government officials to consult with knowledgeable and up-to-date practitioners. . . . Perhaps most important, they inject a much needed strain of competence and critical intelligence into a regulatory system that otherwise seems all too vulnerable to the demands of politics.[4]

However, as Jasanoff and other US-based commentators have noted, advisory committee structures in the United States have increasingly come under public challenge for their interpretation of technical evidence and for their inability to achieve policy resolution.

The main alternative approach to environmental policy-making is committed to a 'representative' or '*democratic*' structure ('let the people decide'). As McGinty and Atherley argued in 1977,[5] a fair decision-making system would give a powerful voice to the potential victims. More recently, post-Brundtland discussions concerning global issues of ecology and development have stressed the importance of democracy in this regard – both with specific reference to environmental policy but also to wider social structure. According to the Brundtland argument, only a just society can achieve 'sustainable development'.

It is difficult to identify a truly 'democratic' decision-making process in this context. However, given their greater prevalence, we will focus here on what can be more properly termed 'representative' systems of environmental regulation with special emphasis on United States experience. Certainly, we will see something of the difficulties inherent in this approach – difficulties linked at least partly to the structural limitations of technical advice as discussed in the previous chapter. In particular, it will be argued that despite the presentation of 'participatory' modes as an alternative means of achieving policy legitimation, in practice technical advice has been at the very centre of this approach to environmental decision-making. 'Democratic' approaches have, therefore, drawn on very similar 'enlightenment' models to the 'expert' approach. In other words, they pay little consideration to the expertise and understanding of citizen groups.

The third policy response considered here represents an attempt to take a non-ideological and *pragmatic* approach to decision-making (i.e., 'let common sense decide'). The example given – of British debates around the safety of petrochemical installations – suggests a combination of elements from both the 'expert' and 'participatory' approaches. It also suggests that even within this apparently incremental and 'muddled' style, the same characteristic policy assumptions can still be found.

As we will see, the Advisory Committee on Major Hazards (ACMH) appears in many ways to be a more satisfactory approach to policy-making than the previous two. However, as will be discussed, there have also been difficulties with this 'policy mode' not least in terms of its usage of particular kinds of knowledge and expertise.

The point of this chapter is not to review the effectiveness or equity of these three policy modes – nor to deny the existence of alternatives. Instead, we need to examine the assumptions concerning 'science, citizenship and environmental threat' which lie at the centre of each. As will be argued in the rest of this chapter, these assumptions are remarkably unchanging across these otherwise distinctive approaches.

Expert approaches to policy

The clearest example of the 'expert mode' as encountered so far in this book relates to the 2,4,5–T case. In common with most areas of toxic substance control in Britain, the Advisory Committee on

Pesticides is very much an 'expert' committee. Its general rationale was described by the ACP's Chair at the time of the 1980 2,4,5–T report in the following terms:

> It is independent of commercial and sectional interests alike. Its independent members bring to the Committee's work not only knowledge built up within their specialist disciplines but also the benefit of close contacts with eminent colleagues in the professions and science. . . . The Advisory Committee lays no claim to absolute mastery of everything concerning pesticides. What it can claim is that its own knowledge and experience is (sic) backed up by a valuable body of medical and scientific expertise within and beyond the machinery of government.[6]

This claim to legitimation is based upon 'expertise' of a particular scientific kind. In similar form, expert committees have become perhaps the main international response to environmental and hazard issues.

Thus, Jasanoff has carefully examined a number of areas of US policy-making – toxic chemicals, 2,4,5–T, occupational cancer – in order to demonstrate the significance of the scientific community in establishing government policy.[7] In a study of British policy for the control of cancer causing substances, an almost total reliance was found on expert advisory committees to direct policy.[8] The claimed strengths of this mode are largely as presented above by the ACP: independence, neutrality, objectivity, scientific expertise. However, a number of more critical accounts of such committees have also emerged. The main lines of *criticism* can be summarized as follows.

First of all, we need to consider the problematic nature of the expertise in this area. As the acid rain case-study suggests, the 'facts' of hazard issues do not simply 'speak for themselves'. Instead, they must be interpreted and acted upon in the light of such intangibles as professional judgement.

The uncertainties of scientific understanding in this area raise particular difficulties for expert bodies – especially when their approach tends to 'over-sell' science by stressing high levels of confidence and authority. The cost in terms of lost credibility when clear pronouncements of safety are proven mistaken can be very great – as the civil nuclear energy example may demonstrate. In that case, an initial confidence in the absolute safety of nuclear power has been forced into steady retreat – creating a public impression that all is not as it was originally presented to them.

These questions of uncertainty and expert judgement also highlight issues of the appropriate 'burden of proof' to be employed in such cases. In the 2,4,5–T example, there was a clear disparity between the level of proof demanded by the farmworkers, on the one hand, and the advisory committee on the other. The farmworkers never considered that their evidence represented 100 per cent proof of the 'guilt' of 2,4,5–T. Their argument instead was that, with so many uncertainties relating to the pesticide, the most cautious move would be to ban the substance. The ACP, however, concluded that until better evidence emerged the only justifiable policy would be to permit usage.

As one of the trade union participants described the situation, there are at least two levels of proof that can be applied: 'beyond all reasonable doubt' or 'on the balance of probabilities'. The farmworkers stressed the latter criterion, the ACP took the former. Once again, we see that expert judgements are inevitably dependent upon non-scientific factors.

Third, there is the critique drawn from the contemporary sociology of scientific knowledge. Expertise will inevitably be shaped by the social and institutional setting within which expert judgements are developed and applied. As was argued in the previous chapter, expertise in this area will depend upon a series of social assessments – including the relative credibility of different information sources (with the quotation above from the ACP Chair suggesting an orientation towards 'eminence' and high-prestige areas of science rather than marginal or informal assessments).

Whilst such contextual factors are inevitable in shaping understandings of any situation – and especially one so characterized by uncertainties – the accreditation of 'expert' status to some accounts has, at least in Britain, diminished the possibilities for open debate and appraisal. A similar account could be offered of the BSE saga. The prevailing scientific discourse in that case has tended to reduce the possibilities for a wider public debate over food safety and agricultural practice.

Building on this, there is a wider argument concerning the need for a more equitable structure to decision-making processes. The ultimate response of the farmworkers to the 2,4,5–T case was to demand a more representative policy process so that their voices could also be heard. The expert approach typically dismisses knowledge and understanding generated outside accredited scientific institutions.

Finally, and drawing particularly on US experience but also on British cases such as 2,4,5–T, there is a major legitimation problem to be considered – whilst science is undoubtedly a powerful ideology, the conclusion of an expert committee may not in itself be sufficient justification for an action. Thus, one very practical difficulty with expert advisory committees is that – once publicly challenged – they have found it difficult to maintain credibility. As Ezrahi puts the point in wider terms: 'In the closing decades of the twentieth century the intellectual and technical advance of science coincides with its visible decline as a force in the rhetoric of liberal-democratic politics'.[9]

The assumption within 'expert' committees is that they are in a unique position to appraise policy issues. However, the problems of technical assessment outlined in Chapter 2 cause major difficulties for this model. If the expert committee can operate in a relatively 'sheltered' setting then it may be able to exercise professional judgement without external challenge. Once critical demands are made upon it – as in the case of US regulatory politics or with British examples such as 2,4,5–T – then it can struggle to maintain credibility. This 'credibility struggle' is for Beck a major characteristic of the risk society.[10]

It must be stressed at this stage that these difficulties with the 'expert' mode are not necessarily a critique of scientists themselves. Rather, as we will see in later chapters, they suggest a need to look again at the institutional organization of science. Graham and colleagues, for example, have argued that attempts at 'science as legitimation' are not conducted solely in the interests of science.

> The other danger of overselling science is that the accountable political actors will not face up to the value judgements that must be made in chemical regulation. Although regulators might prefer to pass the buck by hiding behind a cloak of quantitative risk assessment, it is important for a representative democracy to deliberate explicitly about the political aspects of chemical regulation.[11]

The problem with this use of science as a legitimation device is that it obscures wider political and economic concerns. This is not necessarily an argument for the abandonment of expert advice, but instead a challenge to the notions of scientific objectivity and independence upon which it operates. One possibility, as has already been suggested, is to move towards a more 'democratic' mode.

'Democratic' approaches to policy

Awareness of the earlier problems with 'expert' approaches has led to various calls for a more 'participatory' decision-making mode. Thus the Council for Science and Society in their 1977 report concluded: 'Our single major recommendation is that those who are exposed to risks ... should have a powerful voice – expressed responsibly and on full information and sound advice – in deciding what risks they should be exposed to'.[12]

Such calls have become an almost routine aspect of British academic investigations into environmental and hazard policy. Coupled with a critique of the secrecy and 'closedness' of British decision-making, various commentators have called for a more democratic process.[13] Whilst some US-based accounts have noted a greater 'deference' to official procedures in the British system than is found in the United States,[14] there are distinct signs (as in the 2,4,5–T case but also with BSE) that expert judgements are not seen as unproblematically privileged when presented as the basis for policy-making even in Britain.

The practical question regarding this mode is, of course, which form of 'democracy' should be adopted. In principle, this mode incorporates a whole range of practices including public inquiries, judicial procedures and consultation processes. Some of the possible routes to public participation will be considered in Chapter 6. For now, several more general points will be made about practice in Britain and the United States.

In fact, British policy-making for this area has made very restricted use of 'democratic' policy-making. Public inquiries have been used in the context of planning applications (which, for example, can include hazardous installations as at Canvey Island or nuclear facilities as at the Sizewell Inquiry). For the purposes of this discussion, we can simply observe that there has been extensive criticism of the public inquiry process in Britain – Wynne, for example, has argued that the Windscale Inquiry was essentially a 'ritual' rather than an attempt at democratic decision-making.[15] One important facet of this criticism has been the argument that public groups are disadvantaged by the legalistic and technocratic manner in which technical evidence is employed. Thus, in a study of British inquiry processes linked to major hazard installations, Smith concluded that local groups were disadvantaged by the technical resources available to industry – their protests were rendered peripheral by the preponderance of 'hard science' available to more powerful social groups.[16]

Unlike the United States, in British regulatory practice there has also been only a limited amount of representation within policy processes. Thus, for example, in the area of toxic substances control the only 'representative' forum is within the structures established by the Health and Safety Commission (in particular the Advisory Committee on Toxic Substances). Here there is a 'tripartite' system for health and safety at work. The actual representatives are selected from established organizations such as the Trades Union Congress or the Confederation of British Industry. Whilst this permits a somewhat broader base for decision-making, there is a strict limit to the amount of 'participation' permitted within such a system. There are also problems here for the application of technical expertise – trade union participants have complained that it is difficult to put across their views within a committee structure which is oriented to a more technical form of analysis.

If we look at US experience of a more adversarial process of policy-making, a number of issues arise. In particular, a series of accounts of US policy published over the last decade point to the limitations of that process.[17] Whilst the restricted membership of expert committees facilitates the 'closure' of debate, the open and adversarial process offers an extensive opportunity for challenge and counter-challenge. Thus, US policy has been criticized for its slow pace, inefficiency and costliness. The possibilities for appeal and the need for an apparently infinite number of voices to be heard have rendered US policy-making extremely lengthy and inflexible.

Mendeloff portrays slow standard setting as having four underlying causes: political conflict between health/environmental lobbies and industry which leads to regular appeals to the judiciary; the effects of standards being complex and uncertain; the burden of proof lying on the agencies; agency resources being limited.[18] Accordingly, agencies engage in 'activist rhetoric' but achieve only 'cautious gains'.

However, technical expertise still plays a substantial role in these decision-making processes – even if expert advice struggles to attain consensus in such a loaded context. Jasanoff notes here that the

formal and adversarial style of US rule-making highlights uncertainties, polarizes scientific opinion and prevents conflict resolution.[19] As she concludes: 'Adversarial procedures . . . have little
to recommend them in this context, for they lead not to consensus
but to counterproductive deconstructions of competing technical
arguments'.[20]

In such a situation, commentators such as Collingridge have
argued that the contribution of science to public debate is to
exacerbate rather than diminish conflict.[21]

These points can be briefly illustrated with reference to the debate
in the United States over passive restraint systems for automobiles.[22]
Legislation in 1966 created an agency – the National Highway
Traffic Safety Administration (NHTSA) – to produce rule-making
on road traffic safety matters. One of the new agency's first moves
was to commence discussion over a stricter protection standard for
vehicle occupants – with the NHTSA attempting to 'force the
technological pace' with regard to safety innovation.

The response was industry hostility and a concerted campaign to
delay or block implementation of the standard. Techniques such as
court challenge and White House lobbying were employed to defer
rule-making. The technologies themselves came under critical
scrutiny (with attention focusing on the controversial air bag).
Technical doubts became central to the dispute: was there sufficient
data on the new restraint systems? How did the air bag compare
with seat-belts? Would the chemical propellant cause cancer? What
about the protection for children? What lead time would be
required? These technical disagreements were battled over in the
media, in committee reports, in public hearings, in the courtroom.
However, the adversarial nature of the policy process encouraged
an entrenchment of position – so that technical uncertainties
dragged on through the 1970s and into the 1980s.

In one sense, therefore, this more 'open' form of decision-making
represents a step forward in terms of citizen participation on its
British equivalent – where passive restraint systems did not figure
on the regulatory agenda and the nearest equivalent was a series of
restricted debates over the morality of seat-belt legislation.[23] It
would appear that greater openness permits a range of social and
technological options to be considered.

However, and even on the basis of this short discussion, there are
difficulties with the 'participatory' mode in the form which it has
taken in both Britain and the United States. In Britain only a limited

form of representation has occurred. In the United States, a wider public debate has taken place but a number of problems can be associated with this – not least the cost of rule-making (due to the protracted nature of the policy process) and the difficulties of actually establishing a standard.

What is important for our present discussion is that these 'participatory' modes have been highly reliant on technical expertise in the identification, construction and 'framing' of issues so that the contrast between this and the previous 'expert' mode is not so great as might first appear. Whilst the US system, for example, does permit a wider cross-examination of expertise and a broader representation of expert views, this has not fundamentally affected the reliance on expertise itself. Public hearings tend to offer a highly technical exchange – at times it would appear that only arguments expressed in technical language are credited with respectability. The question raised in this section is, therefore, to what extent these apparently democratic forms of policy-making actually encourage and empower citizen views and understandings.

In support of this suggestion that the so-called 'democratic' mode draws on a very limited range of citizen views and knowledges, we have the vivid 'insider' account of US nuclear debates provided by Meehan[24] – who actually is a strong advocate of the adversarial process in terms of the cross-examination and exploration of technical expertise. Nevertheless, the notion of 'expertise' is very much limited to the pronouncements of *scientists*. In Meehan's account, scientists become guns for hire – with citizens reduced to the status of passive audiences rather than active participants.

Of course, this point is often equally applicable to industrial, governmental and environmentalist groups. Whilst campaigning groups, for example, may claim to speak for the wider citizenry, their contribution often follows the same pattern of technical discourse.

It would appear, therefore, that 'democratic' approaches actually build upon a highly modernistic set of assumptions about both 'expertise' and 'democracy'. In that sense, most 'democratic' policy modes can be linked to an enlightenment perspective on science and scientific authority. Whilst they may represent a step forward from an entirely 'expert' policy mode, they are nevertheless handicapped by a very restricted model of the relationship between citizens and expertise. Once again, democratic discussion only begins once the issues have been identified and structured by scientific accounts. As the next chapter will argue, this seems debilitating in the area of environmental and hazard issues where other knowledges could contribute to public policy-making. Meanwhile, we need to consider one final form of policy response.

'Pragmatic' approaches to policy

Whilst the previous two decision modes are the most regularly identified and contrasted, one important approach to policy-making has been almost deliberately undramatic but nevertheless important. Thus, terminology such as 'reasonably practicable' and 'best practicable means' as applied to environmental and health and safety issues leaves maximum discretion to local regulators within specific contexts.[25] This less formalized and more flexible approach to policy-making seems to have potential for the inclusion of different voices and understandings. We need, therefore, to explore whether or not in practice it has operated with a different set of assumptions regarding 'science, risk and citizenship'.

As an illustration of this more diverse policy mode, we can consider one British rule-making exercise. The exercise in question relates to the control of major accident hazards of the type demonstrated so vividly at Seveso (July 1976), Mexico City (November 1984) and Bhopal (December 1984) – and also as briefly considered in Chapter 1.[26] The discussion here also provides a background to the case-study of major hazard control offered in the next chapter.

In Britain, the turning point (although not the beginning) for major hazard policy came in June 1974 when the Flixborough disaster occurred – killing twenty-eight people and injuring thirty-six. In the wake of great societal concern and media attention, a public inquiry was established into the cause of the accident. In November 1974, the Secretary of State for Employment announced his intention of establishing a new committee under the auspices of the Health and Safety Commission (HSC) – this became the Advisory Committee on Major Hazards (ACMH). The terms of reference of the new committee were to establish a British control policy for major hazards.[27] A typical mix of the committee's membership has been described as follows:

> Eight independents – professors, other academics and consultants; three employer nominated members with direct involvement in one of the typical industries such as petro-

73

chemicals, British Gas, the oil industry etc; and three TUC nominees, so that the workers' side of safety and their contribution to operating practices at the sharp end was fed in. There was one fire chief nominated by the Home Office and three planners or people with local authority interests nominated by the Department of the Environment.[28]

However, despite this mix, issues of technical expertise were highly important within this 'representative' committee – with implications once again for effective participation. As one member described its operation:

'Their discussions were of such a highly technical nature that TUC and LA representatives could neither fully understand nor participate in the proceedings of most of the sub-committees'.[29]

So far then the form of ACMH's response to the issue of major hazards offers a combination of 'expert' and 'participatory' modes. What distinguishes this committee from the previous description of these two modes, however, is its commitment to policy – based not on a claim to 'independence and expertise' or to 'representation and democracy' but instead to 'practicability and manageability'. As one committee member expressed the regulatory philosophy:

The overriding aim of the committee was to have a control scheme which was both workable and enforceable. We felt that it was much better to have a scheme that is relatively undemanding but which could be enforced than a strict scheme which would be impossible to enforce and which is, therefore, generally ignored.[30]

There is not the space here to itemize the full working of this pragmatic principle. However, characteristics include:

- a commitment to self-regulation rather than external standard setting or a licensing procedure. Responsibility was placed on industry rather than a government agency;
- a related commitment to flexible and negotiated controls rather than a 'rulebook' approach;
- a concern for 'practical' guidance rather than technical refinement. Thus, simple inventory levels were preferred over scientific modelling and risk analytical techniques. Equally, the historical record was seen as more persuasive than predictions of what might occur;

- the establishment of inventory levels appropriate to the available resources for inspection and control;
- in addition, the general operation of the committee must be noted. The ACMH's public reports stress a number of features of this; close cooperation with government and industry, flexibility, informality, low level of conflict, commitment to consensus rather than adversarial debate. The overall rhetoric of the ACMH must also be considered with its emphasis on 'sound judgement' and a sense of what is 'reasonable' and 'practicable'.

There are, therefore, many common elements between this mode and the two previous forms. However, the emphasis on legitimation based on 'sensible judgement' certainly distinguishes it from approaches which stress either 'let the facts decide' or 'let the people decide'.

By August 1977, the ACMH announced that it had completed consultation and was on the point of producing draft regulations. These appeared in 1978. However, post-Seveso events in the European Community overtook British discussions at that point – although it would appear that the ACMH regulations were highly influential over the eventual EEC regulation.[31]

Especially when compared to the delay and difficulty of the US policy mode, such an approach seems highly attractive. The ACMH acted with speed and confidence, the legitimacy of its operations was unchallenged, the main social groups were 'represented' but did not come into sustained conflict. Furthermore, the ACMH published three reports and invited public comment on its deliberations. Potentially at least this represents an adequate balance between 'representativeness' and 'effectiveness'.

However, a number of more critical points must also be made. The first of these is that the predilection for pragmatism may well have stifled any wider discussion of the aims, objectives and rationale of the control policy. Certainly, such a concern for pragmatism seems to have led the committee to take a very limited view of what is 'manageable' in this case. Thus, rather than choosing to highlight the resource difficulties and political constraints within which policy must operate, the committee preferred to accept these as a *fait accompli* and to build their control system around them. The regulatory philosophy of the ACMH seems, therefore, to have ruled out radical criticism of the *status quo*. From the committee's viewpoint, of course, this was the only 'sensible'

SCIENCE AND THE POLICY PROCESS

and 'manageable' approach to adopt. However, the existence of alternative perspectives on major hazards needs also to be acknowledged as does the argument that what may appear 'sensible' to one group may not appear likewise to others:

> We must . . . stress the inevitability of accidents: we must emphasize that accidents are built into the technology itself – in its widest sense, which includes the social relations built into the technology – and thus cannot be resolved by technical fixes, however elaborate and costly.[32]

This quotation from a book which attacks major hazard policy as an example of 'corporate killing' suggests at least one alternative perspective on the problems tackled by the ACMH. Translated into more political language, such a perspective suggests that major hazards are not 'manageable' without a total rethink of corporate priorities.

At this point, wider questions arise about the 'need' for major hazard sites and the possibilities of structural change in the petrochemical industry so that large quantities of highly dangerous materials are not stored close to housing. The regulatory process described here took no account of such alternative perspectives on what is most 'sensible' in this situation. As the previous quotation from Bauman suggests, the policy process appears at least partly as a means of 'fending off blows' rather than discussing the practical possibilities for change.[33]

There is also evidence as we will see in the following chapter that those who actually live around hazard sites may not always share the committee's high regard for the abilities of the chemical industry. Certainly, the current literature on risk controversies suggests very strongly that such alternative perspectives (or 'plural rationalities') are an important characteristic of environmental disputes.[34] The question must at least be raised as to whether the procedural approach of the ACMH is the best method of responding to such perspectives.

In all this, the ACMH's incrementalist approach seems to have been aided by the membership of the committee. Although the ACMH was reluctant to label itself as an *expert* body, the working groups were dominated by 'experts' drawn from either academia or the petrochemical industry itself.

The next potential area of criticism concerns the methodology employed by the committee. One consequence of the pragmatic approach is that it is very difficult to discern a coherent logic behind decision-making. Indeed, at times the committee almost seemed to pride itself on the absence of any single rationale. Instead, the whole process is based on trust and a 'steady as we go' approach. This inability to offer a legitimation (other than in terms of what appeared 'manageable' to a 'reasonable' group of individuals) leaves the committee open to charges of 'taking the easiest route out of the problem'. Certainly, there is evidence that the ACMH's notion of pragmatism led it to offer only a small-scale response to the major hazard problem.

These criticisms suggest some of the limitations of the 'pragmatic mode' adopted by the ACMH. Of most relevance, however, to the current discussion is the approach taken by the committee to the twin concerns of this chapter – 'expertise' and 'citizenship'.

Undoubtedly, the former was defined in a somewhat broader fashion than that encountered in the previous policy modes, i.e., with a stronger emphasis on 'practical experience' than on technical sophistication. Nevertheless, that breadth relied upon professional judgement rather than on citizen experiences of petrochemical safety. Those experiences and understandings will be central to our next chapter. Similarly, the approach to participation – whilst more liberal than that found within the 'expert' mode – was limited to professional and 'recognized' parties rather than those who live around major hazard sites. In that way also, the committee's assumptions about the 'limits to pragmatism' could pass un-challenged.

There are substantial differences between the 'pragmatic' mode and the previous two. However, in terms of our concerns in this book the differences are not nearly so great as the similarities. Instead, as in the other two cases, we can see an enlightenment policy paradigm in operation: a paradigm which limits 'expertise' to certain professional groups and stresses technical argumentation over alternative forms of analysis and expression.

Public policies for the environment – discussion

This chapter has highlighted environmental policy-making as an important area for citizen concerns over technological progress. Despite the structural limitations of science as discussed in the previous chapter, we have found that all three policy modes have drawn upon science as an important source of legitimation.

More fundamentally, whether in the pragmatic dealings of the ACMH, the operation of 'expert' committees or ostensibly 'democratic' (or 'participatory') approaches, scientific analysis has been presented as the 'core' of environmental and risk issues. Even when legal or citizen challenges are made to the decision process, this modernistic set of assumptions still seems to operate. Meanwhile, the bulk of the population has been reduced to an essentially 'passive' status – as *witnesses* rather than active participants. At best, the underlying policy notion has been that the public (through its representatives) is the jury for decision-making but that experts are uniquely qualified to compile the evidence for consideration and to prepare the terrain and parameters within which environmental decisions are taken. Of course, the presentation of risk issues as *technical* in nature has served as an important legitimation for this highly restricted concept of citizenship. The public is 'ignorant' and can therefore be legitimately excluded from influence.

However, general problems were also noted with these policy responses. Expert committees are under attack for their dubious claims to 'higher expertise' and for their limited base of participation. These criticisms are particularly developed in the United States but have also found echo in the UK – for example, in the BSE or 2,4,5–T cases. The so-called 'democratic' mode has been subject to probably equal critique in the USA since 'public debate' has become synonymous with dispute, delay and policy ineffectiveness.

These approaches were then contrasted with the 'pragmatic' mode which seems characteristically British in its emphasis on professional judgement, consensus and workability. However, this mode can restrict public debate and the consideration of policy alternatives. There also seem to be problems of maintaining credibility when critical questions are asked about the limits to pragmatism. In that sense, the pragmatic mode may be the weakest of the three in offering a coherent legitimation of its conclusions – 'trust us' can seem an inadequate justification in the current climate of environmental concern and social challenge. As such, the pragmatic mode may reflect a previous and more tranquil era of policy resolution.

Overall, all three modes are under challenge for reasons strongly associated with the arguments of Beck and Giddens. All three are struggling to maintain credibility for their underlying models of scientific expertise and 'citizenship'.

Of course, technical presentations also depend upon the resources and influence of certain social groups – only those who have the organizational base, the finances and the confidence are generally in a position to participate. In that sense, technical exchanges draw upon only a restricted range of social perspectives. The crucial point here is that questions of 'expertise' and 'democracy' are not separate but interlinked. Any attempt at democratizing the policy process which leaves concepts of 'knowledge' unchallenged will inevitably prove highly limited – as the case of the United States demonstrates well.

'Science-centred' accounts of policy issues remain highly influential despite the limitations described here – limitations both at the level of structural uncertainty and regarding problems of public legitimation. It would seem also that calls for greater democracy will have only limited impact if they do not consider the influence of technical experts within the decision-making process. Making the public 'ringside' in policy disputes may have some value for social equity and sustainability. However, a more radical reappraisal would examine the knowledges and understandings possessed by citizen groups which do not fit at present within the policy process. We will begin to consider these in the next chapter.

Meanwhile, 'citizenship' currently only begins when 'expertise' has set the environmental agenda. Now, it is quite clear that scientific expertise has a major role to play in these issues – but we need also to reconstruct our understanding of the science–citizen relationship in order to acknowledge the possibility of wider sources of knowledge and understanding. Part of this reconstruction must also involve an awareness of the social and institutional assumptions upon which scientific statements in this area implicitly draw.

Put more negatively, there is an indication from this review that these changes seem necessary in the face of current public concerns over risk and environmental issues. As all the examples here suggest, initially specific questions of risk and safety have moved on to become challenges to the technical and institutional structures which underpin them. Some of these citizen reactions can be seen in the next chapter where the case of major accident hazards will be explored from an explicitly 'citizen-oriented' perspective. What challenges then emerge to the modernistic assumptions of the policy process?

In order to tackle this we, first of all, need to invert the orthodox model of science–public relations. Rather than assuming the 'science-centred' approach – i.e., beginning with the assumptions embedded in current official and scientific practices – we need to start with *citizens* and their understandings of risk and environmental issues. Accordingly, in the next two chapters we will stand the general portrayal of science communication on its head. What then arises when the analytical eye belongs not to powerful social institutions but instead to the diversity of public groups who are currently the witnesses to environmental debate?

4

WITNESSES, PARTICIPANTS AND MAJOR ACCIDENT HAZARDS

To try to understand the experience of another it is necessary to dismantle the world as seen from one's own place within it, and to re-assemble it as seen from his. For example, to understand a given choice another makes, one must face in imagination the lack of choices which may confront and deny him. . . . . The world has to be dismantled and re-assembled in order to grasp, however clumsily, the experience of another. . . . The subjectivity of another does not simply constitute a different interior attitude to the same exterior facts. The constellation of facts of which he is the centre is different.[1]

The previous chapter considered a series of 'science-centred' and reductionist accounts of environmental policy-making – noting that even within more 'democratic' policy modes citizens were still taken to be devoid of legitimate expertise. Instead, the wider public was seen as a passive rather than an active force – as witnesses to a series of arguments rather than effective participants. The question of how 'legitimate' knowledge is defined thus has important consequences for the democratic involvement of citizen groups in this crucial area of policy-making.

One immediate objection to this line of argument might be to indicate the number of steps which are currently being undertaken to 'disseminate' scientific information to the general public. Especially through the mass media but also through more local initiatives (of the type which will shortly be discussed in this chapter), efforts are being made to improve the public understanding of technical issues. A strong recommendation to this effect was made in the 1985 Royal Society report:

our most direct and urgent message is for the scientists – learn to communicate with the public, be willing to do so, indeed consider it your duty to do so. . . . It is clearly a part of each scientist's professional responsibility to promote the public understanding of science.[2]

Some evidence of success in this 'professional responsibility' can be seen in the popularity of certain media accounts of science and technology (e.g., television programmes on 'popular science') and also sales of magazines and books on scientific topics. In a review of 'popular science',[3] Durant notes that the British TV programme 'Tomorrow's World' has commanded high audiences for some two decades, that *New Scientist* has weekly sales of over 100,000 and that Stephen Hawking's *A Brief History of Time* was in the top ten of best-selling books in English for the 1980s. Durant goes on to identify four different types of popular science: 'philosophical science' (the 'big questions' of the origins of life and the universe); 'practical science' (science that will change our lives); 'political science' (science that deals with pressing social or environmental issues); 'para-science' (non-orthodox or 'deviant' scientific thinking).

The popular science phenomenon can clearly not be ignored. However, in this chapter we will begin to examine everyday technical issues not from the perspective of enthusiastic science communicators but from that of citizens as part of everyday life. Equally, our concern will be less with what Durant acknowledges to be 'extraordinary science' such as the above and more with the mundane face of technological development and technical communication. In this way, it is possible to present an alternative account of the relevance and utility of science to the wider publics.

Accordingly, this chapter will deal with two studies of citizen groups and their relationship to technical understandings. In the first we will consider prevailing approaches to the public dissemination of information – approaches which draw on the 'enlightenment' perspective. From an analysis of the inherent limitations of such an approach in terms of assisting citizens with technically related problems, we will move on to consider an alternative account. This alternative shifts away from the 'public dissemination' model and towards an understanding of the place of scientific and technical issues in everyday life. No attempt will be made at this stage to 'tidy up' citizen views and assessments – instead their richness and complexity will be suggested.

Specifically, this chapter will begin with an examination of one exercise in the public dissemination of information. In this case, the exercise was a relatively small-scale and local activity aimed at informing a specific population about the risks of nearby petro-chemical production – and about the correct measures for the citizen to take in the event of an accident or emergency. This activity had been required at a limited number of European petrochemical sites as a consequence of the 'post-Seveso' EC regulations (referred to already in Chapters 1 and 3). Through this example, the 'official' processes of information assimilation and distribution will be considered – especially in the light of 'public ignorance' models of the general public. In particular, the limits to 'enthusiastic dis-semination' will be observed. We will then move on to consider an alternative perspective on citizen–science relations.

CIMAH and the provision of major hazard information: the Carrington case-study

As noted in the previous chapter, the development by the British ACMH (Advisory Committee on Major Hazards) of a regulatory system for the control of major accident hazards was overtaken (but also partly assimilated) by legislative developments at EC level following the 1976 Seveso accident. As Chapter 1 discussed briefly in the third of its 'stories of our time', the EC in 1982 adopted a directive for the control of major hazard installations.

One article of this directive – which subsequently became trans-lated into the British Control of Industrial Major Accident Hazards (CIMAH) of 1984 – specified a 'public information' requirement. Thus, for the first time, information about local hazards would be distributed to a (rather limited) number of 'publics'. As Chapter 1 suggested, despite industrial concern that this exercise might create panic, the public response seems to have been very low-key. The available evidence (scant though it is) also indicates only a moderate up-take of the relevant information.

This chapter intends to pursue this rather unpromising example by considering the issues of public dissemination which emerge. Having considered the possibilities for improving information exer-cises which fall *within* the prevailing science-centred paradigm, we will then take a closer look at the perspective of local citizens on these issues. In so doing, we will also move beyond explanations of public response in terms of public ignorance (or public apathy) and consider an alternative analysis of the situation – an analysis which suggests a rather different paradigm of citizen–science relations.

The case-study chosen for the first part of this analysis is the Carrington petrochemical complex in Greater Manchester, North-West England.[4] This site houses a considerable quantity of hazardous materials – including natural gas, flammable gases and liquids, and toxic substances such as chlorine. Under the British version of the EEC Seveso Directive, the Carrington complex was designated as a 'top-tier' site. Three installations were covered by the new regulations – Shell Chemicals UK Limited, North West Gas and British Gas. Each had to meet a number of requirements – including the production of a safety case and the preparation of an off-site emergency plan. The main interest in this chapter, however, centres on Article 8 of the original European directive:

> Member states shall ensure that persons liable to be affected by a major accident originating in a notified industrial activity ... are informed in an appropriate manner of the safety measures and the correct behaviour to adopt in the event of an accident.[5]

The British CIMAH regulations made this article somewhat more specific. CIMAH regulation 12 required that people living in the area of top-tier sites (as defined by inventory levels of the type discussed in the previous chapter) be informed by the manufacturer or the local authority of the following:

- that the industrial activity is an activity which has been notified to the Health and Safety Executive;
- of the nature of the major accident hazard;
- of the safety measures and the correct behaviour to adopt in the event of a major accident.

This was, therefore, a very specific exercise in the public provision of information. Nevertheless, it serves as an excellent example of the 'top-down' dissemination model in operation.

The first question which any dissemination exercise needs to consider is *which* public needs to be 'informed' – in this case, how large an area around the Carrington site should be specified as the 'Public Information Zone' (PIZ)? In technical terms, this specification is highly problematic; there are considerable uncertainties surrounding the behaviour of, for example, certain gases in a large-scale release. In the event, and in keeping with practice elsewhere in Britain, the PIZ was established on the basis of the pre-existing HSE Consultation Distance – a zone around certain hazardous installations drawn for planning purposes. No official explanation of this administrative choice was given to local householders.

The *form* of information dissemination is clearly important for the success of any exercise. In this case – and again in common with British practice elsewhere – a leaflet was delivered to each house in the PIZ. The contents of this were agreed between the three companies involved and the local authority – although the leaflet itself was sent out under the banner of the Metropolitan Borough of Trafford.

The information content of the leaflet was in line with the CIMAH requirement – see *Appendix 1*. As can be seen, the leaflet lists the three companies, makes reference to the CIMAH regulations, informs the residents that they are living in an area that 'could possibly be affected if a major accident should occur', and gives them an emergency procedure 'in the unlikely event' of such an accident. This 'emergency procedure' is described as follows: 'In a major accident you will be advised by the police what to do. You should first go indoors, close all doors and windows and await further instructions'.

This information is, of course, only a very *general* indication of the best emergency action. By definition, and given the enormous range of possible accident scenarios (blazing houses, toxic releases, devastation of properties) and also *'personal'* scenarios (out at the shops, playing in the fields, driving a car, attending school), it can only serve as a rough guide to accident response. Those distributing the advice chose not to 'confuse with explanation' but stick to one simple instruction.

The dissemination exercise is thus implicitly attempting to *eliminate social and technical uncertainty*. The assumption is 'keep it simple and the public will grasp the message more easily'. The technical context of this message is inseparable from its assumptions about the publics it was attempting to 'inform'. The construction of 'audience' plays an essential role in shaping the form and content of technical information. At the same time, and at least in this case, the construction is not open for discussion with that audience nor is it justified.

In addition, the leaflet gives some brief information about activities on site and offers a contact address (but not a telephone number). The emblem of the Metropolitan Borough of Trafford is prominently displayed – but it is noted that the leaflet is issued 'on behalf of and in consultation with' the three companies. Elsewhere, it is stated that 'detailed emergency plans' have been prepared 'by each site', by the local authority and by the fire, police and ambulance services. The resident is asked to keep these notes 'for reference purposes'.

Quite clearly, therefore, the distribution of this leaflet at the Carrington complex represents a somewhat low-key exercise in the public dissemination of information. However, a number of important characteristics can already be discerned:

- the treatment of scientific uncertainties within this kind of exercise has already merited our specific attention (in Chapter 2). Uncertainties surround almost every step in the exercise of assessing hazard potential and predicting actual hazard scenarios (from questions of how many people might be affected to the behaviour of toxic and flammable substances in real-world accidents). No hint of this uncertainty appears in the leaflet. The world portrayed is instead one of robust knowledge (and of robust authority);
- no real information is given about the rationale for the emergency procedure (nor for the selection of the PIZ nor the collaboration between industry and the local authority) – it is assumed that the providers of the message carry enough local credibility for their message simply to be believed without question;
- the overall tone of the leaflet seems designed to provide reassurance and also to legitimate the authority of the industrial operators;
- despite the very local and specific nature of this exercise, there was no discernible effort at encouraging debate with residents nor indeed at assessing existing knowledge of the site or its operations. Instead, discussion was restricted to a limited number of 'official' parties. The implicit model of the local public was one of ignorance. They are the *receptors* for selectively managed information.

Taken together, this exercise offers a clear case of the 'top-down' model in operation. Scientific complexities and uncertainties are filtered out in a 'clear and simple' form so as to avoid local confusion or unnecessary panic. The 'facts' are then presented in an authoritative fashion – backed by the social legitimacy of the industrial operators together with the local authority and the emergency services. No encouragement is given to debate or discussion. Nor is there any suggestion that local views, opinions or assessments would be useful. The model is one of *informing* rather than *empowering* the public. In such an exercise, residents are indeed witnesses rather than participants.[6]

This point is reinforced by the leaflet's initial consideration of regulatory matters ('The Control of Industrial Major Accident Hazards Regulations (1984) requires us to inform you...'). Essentially, this is to establish compliance with the legal requirement – and, implicitly, to establish that nothing has changed at the site. For most citizens, however, this information will simply be meaningless. They are somehow expected to absorb it even though it makes no sense to them.

What then of the public response to this exercise? Before we can deal with this, we need to know a little more about the 'public' in question.

As described by Jupp, the Carrington area has had a long (over fifty years) involvement in the chemical industry. Indeed, many of the nearby residents moved there to find work in that sector. Perhaps because of the site's sheer size, worries have inevitably been expressed about safety – although few serious accidents have occurred. However, one incident stands out in the minds of at least the older residents – an explosion in the mid-1950s at which two Shell workers were killed.[7] More recently, there have been a series of redundancies at the site – increasing local concern about employment during a period when alternative sources of work are hard to find.

In terms of housing stock, the area is reasonably mixed. Partington and Carrington existed as small rural communities prior to the site's construction – and the area still offers a combination of the semi-rural and the highly industrial. Council houses were subsequently built for Shell workers at Carrington. Council housing was also built on areas close to the site in Partington – a planning decision which would appear less straightforward today. Nearby Flixton and Sale are more middle-class in character – with private housing being the norm.

This heterogeneity – and also the size of the complex – make it difficult to identify a single 'Carrington community' and, consequently, a single 'audience' for communication. This *diversity* of publics seems an important characteristic of our contemporary social structure – as indeed Beck and Giddens argue.[8] Yet the prevailing assumption within the communication strategy is that of a homogeneous mass. A standardized approach is being adopted – especially since this particular leaflet follows a very similar format to other leaflets being designed and distributed in other hazard zones.[9]

In order to gauge public response to this exercise, a questionnaire survey was conducted during the summer of 1987. The survey was based on a random sample of 201 individuals resident in Carrington, Partington and part of Flixton. The Flixton residents – who lived outside the PIZ (but nevertheless close to the complex) – were included as a point of comparison.

In this context, it is not necessary to summarize all of the research project. Instead, two tables can be offered from Jupp's account.

In one part of the questionnaire, residents both inside the PIZ and at Flixton were asked: 'If there was an accident or an emergency at the site – how would you know it was happening?'. Table 4.1 gives the responses to this.

Table 4.1: Question 12: If there was an accident or an emergency at the site – how would you know it was happening?

Response	PIZ		Flixton	
Hear/see the explosion/fire	41	(40%)	26	(43%)
Hear the site sirens	28	(28%)	13	(22%)
Hear/see the emergency services	13	(13%)	18	(30%)
Be informed by the police	22	(22%)	4	(7%)
Radio/television/newspapers		–	8	(13%)
State of the flare (at Shell)	4	(4%)	3	(5%)
Own house affected	3	(3%)	2	(3%)
We wouldn't know	9	(9%)	6	(10%)
Other	3	(3%)	3	(5%)
Don't know	5	(5%)		–
Total Respondents	**102**		**60**	

Source: Based on Jupp, op.cit., p. 179
Note: Open responses coded by Jupp

As the table suggests, among those who received the leaflet the most common response (40 per cent of respondents) was that they would hear or see the explosion or fire. This seems to fit with the notion of an accident/emergency taking the form of a dramatic explosion – the usual analogy was with a bomb. However, in the extreme case, an incident could take the form of a gas release which would have no visual or noise warning attached to it. The second most common response of those in the PIZ was that they would hear site sirens – an equally troubling assumption given that such a system had been rejected as a warning system (mainly because of the risk of confusion with boats on the nearby canal). Responses to this question suggest, therefore, something of a disparity with the 'official' advice.

In a second question, local people were asked about their likely response to an accident or emergency at the site. Responses are indicated in Table 4.2.

Table 4.2: Question 13: If you knew that there was an accident or an emergency at the site what would you do?

Response	PIZ		Flixton	
Get out	29	(28%)	9	(15%)
Stay indoors	20	(20%)	5	(8%)
Shut doors/windows	17	(17%)	4	(7%)
Depends on accident	10	(10%)	10	(17%)
Wait to be informed by police	9	(9%)	8	(13%)
Phone police	6	(6%)	4	(7%)
See if I could help	6	(6%)	4	(7%)
Keep away	3	(3%)	6	(10%)
Nothing you could do	6	(6%)	3	(5%)
Evacuate if told to	4	(4%)	4	(7%)
Stay where I am	4	(4%)	3	(5%)
Ensure safety of family	6	(6%)	1	(2%)
Nothing – no need	2	(2%)	3	(5%)
Other	6	(6%)	7	(12%)
Don't know	7	(7%)	5	(8%)
Total Respondents	**102**		**60**	

Source: Based on Jupp, op.cit., p. 183
Note: Open responses coded by Jupp

Over a quarter of the residents stated their intention of getting out of the area – this clearly contradicts the advice of the leaflet (and might also cause a big problem for the emergency services). Nevertheless, some 'improvement' can be discerned between those within the PIZ and those in Flixton in terms of giving the 'correct' response of 'staying indoors'. A distinction can also be made between those in the PIZ who *recall* receiving the leaflet and those who do not. Of the former group, 33 per cent stated that they would stay indoors and 25 per cent intended to shut doors and windows (as opposed to 7 per cent of the latter group for each question).

Overall, this brief summary of one part of the Carrington survey suggests that – put at its most positive – the information leaflet had only partial success in improving the level of local awareness and emergency response. It should be said at this stage that local concern was *not* high – with 71 per cent of respondents within the Public Information Zone describing it as 'very safe' or 'safe'. Certainly, there is no evidence that this exercise caused local panic – instead, both its performance and the response seemed decidedly low-key.

How then are we to interpret this series of events? The Carrington exercise might indeed be described (somewhat crudely) as 'top-down' in character. What wider conclusions can we draw concerning the relations between these local publics and this specific area of scientific advice?

If we, first of all, consider this exercise from the point of view of its prime movers – in industry and the local authority – then the outcome may either be considered a disappointment (for those who seriously wished to increase awareness of emergency response) or a relief (for those who were concerned about some anti-industrial backlash). However, it must be stated that the above survey was conducted quite independently of these participants – there is no evidence of the exercise's promoters conducting their own research (either at this plant or elsewhere) in an attempt to gauge public response. Instead, the usual conclusion among industrialists and emergency planners is that such exercises have met with public indifference – thus reconfirming the notion that the public are apathetic towards technical guidance.

Of course, one positive response to this account of the dissemination exercise would be to advocate a more energetic public information campaign. Specific measures in this 'better communication' approach might include:

- the better design of public information literature (use of graphics, more explanation of advice, more durable cards);
- the repetition of information rather than relying on a 'one off' approach;
- the use of other media (local newspapers and television, public meetings, liaison bodies);
- surveys such as the one reported here to assess the level of public informedness.

Superficially at least, such a communication-based approach

seems to make good sense – and it is hard to doubt the good motives of those who advocate more energetic dissemination of emergency response information. However, as it stands, such a call serves to reinforce the notion of public ignorance and apathy ('if only we put the message across more vigorously *then* they'd listen'). What such measures significantly fail to do is to consider the underlying social dynamics of areas such as that surrounding the Carrington complex.

How then would we construct an alternative account of 'science and citizenship'? One starting point for this might be our previous conclusion concerning the treatment of social and technical uncertainty in this exercise – the leaflet's advice offered a highly simplified and idealized view of a potentially complex social and technical reality (i.e., a real-world emergency involving real people – including those who just happened to be visiting or travelling through the area).

In defence of the leaflet, it can be argued that there are an almost infinite number of possible 'scenarios'. The alternative to an en-cyclopaedic account of these (i.e., some huge document which would take hours to decipher in an emergency) is to offer a simple and suitably general guidance which can be easily remembered. If nothing else, the advice will serve until more specific instructions are available (as agreed by the appropriate industrial and technical experts). Any alternative approach would be impractical for general and public dissemination.

The *problem* with this style of 'official advice' (as with the much-parodied 'protect and survive' approach to nuclear defence or with early public information programmes aimed at controlling HIV/AIDS) is that it makes no attempt to accommodate (or even communicate with) citizen understandings and knowledges of a situation. Thus, the 'idealized' advice seems to assume that all people in the area will be near home, in family groups and that 'indoors' is indeed the safest place to be. However, questionnaire responses (see Tables 4.1 and 4.2) suggest just how 'unrealistic' these assumptions can appear. Once again, we see the significance of unchallenged social assumptions about the 'public' in framing technical messages of this kind.

More informal responses to both questions in the survey revealed a diverse understanding of what an accident might involve (why go indoors if a 'bomb' has just exploded nearby?) and also of how one how I could help). Responses also featured amused comments to the interviewer such as 'well, what would *you* do?' (particularly pertinent when 'getting indoors' could involve knocking on many different doors in pursuit of 'refuge' – so that 'getting out of the area' might indeed be a more practical action).

Questions would typically be asked as to *how* they would be informed if chaos was erupting on all sides (one's view on this appearing largely as a matter of personal faith in the emergency services). Furthermore, despite the best efforts of the leaflet's drafters to 'rationalize' the Public Information Zone (so that the PIZ was extended in order not to divide one village), residents were still left with a situation where some of those *outside* the PIZ lived closer to the site than some of those *within*. Given all these 'mismatches' with everyday experience, might it not be more logical just to fend for oneself (and one's family) in any emergency?

Thus, whilst the 'sanitized' and top-down approach has the apparent advantage of 'keeping the message simple' it does encounter major difficulties. These 'difficulties' essentially relate to the understandings of (in this case) local people whose practical experience encourages scepticism towards this kind of official advice. By failing to engage with these understandings – but rather attempting to circumnavigate them – such exercises risk being totally ignored (or perhaps provoking hostility in a more confrontational situation than that encountered at Carrington). The 'public ignorance' model thus fails because it builds 'practical' action on a flawed conceptualization of the citizen–science relationship. In this way, the assumption that local people are a mere *tabula rasa* is not only sociologically inaccurate but it also serves as an obstacle to social learning on all sides (including, very importantly, the lessons which industry might learn from critical local scrutiny).

In contrast with the dissemination model on which this exercise was based, the clear step for us now is to build upon these observations by considering an alternative to the 'public ignorance' (or 'deficit') model. In particular, we need to assess whether further investigation confirms the disparity between 'local' and 'official' worldviews as identified in this example. Accordingly, we will explore a separate case-study of people living in a hazardous local environment. If we begin with citizen voices – and with the 'constellations' referred to in the opening quotation of this chapter – where does our analysis lead?

Citizens, science and two communities

For this stage in the discussion, we move away from the Carrington area and towards two other communities living close to hazardous industry – the Clayton/Beswick area of East Manchester and Eccles within Salford (to the west of central Manchester).[10] These areas are highly urban and industrial in character – in contrast to the Carrington district which includes green fields around parts of the petrochemical complex. Instead, these two communities are crowded with hazardous industry, housing estates and busy roads. The Eccles site features older-style council housing alongside newer properties – some built close to a chemical works allegedly against the advice of the Health and Safety Executive. There is also a modern shopping centre, a hospital, a busy outdoor market, an elderly persons' home and a leisure centre situated nearby. At Clayton/Beswick, there is a similar combination of older council housing (mainly terraced) and more modern properties – all close to a number of hazardous industries. Each area contains a small amount of middle-class properties – but we can safely categorize the majority of residents (and certainly the majority close to the hazard sites across the two areas) as 'working class'.

What then of the public response to hazard information in these areas? In the first place, it must be stressed that these are not 'top-tier' hazard sites and, therefore, at the time of our study had not been the subject of any well-organized 'dissemination' campaign (although local industry in the Clayton/Beswick area had distributed some information about its activities as part of an extended public relations programme). However, what these areas did permit was an exploration of citizen views of various sources of information. Beginning with a social survey of the area (involving 358 questionnaire interviews followed by semi-structured discussion with thirty-five participants), the intention was to build up a more active account of 'citizens and science'.

One important aspect of these research areas was the generally high level of concern about factory accidents and pollution – alongside, of course, such predictable (and very real) concerns as unemployment, crime and violence and 'the rising cost of living'. Certainly, this impression was reinforced by conversations and interviews with residents in which the local works would often figure prominently. Typically, that concern would focus on noise, smell and atmospheric pollution (e.g., from the factory chimneys) and on the risk of explosion: 'there's a cornflakes smell and a blue haze, every chimney is on the go at night'; 'this place is top of the league for chest complaints'. Certainly, such chronic pollution problems figured more highly in these study areas than around Carrington.

The point, of course, about a citizen-based perspective is that issues such as pollution and major hazard threat will inevitably blend in with the wider background of other local concerns – such as those mentioned above. Put more positively, it is only within this background that issues of risk and the environment make any sense whatsoever. Thus, for example, it seems nonsensical to most local people to debate the hazards of the local chemical industry without considering the consequences of closure for local jobs. Hazards do *not* exist in some free-floating intellectual state – they are an intrinsic part of everyday social reality and of the very identity of these areas. This is clear in one characteristic exchange between two residents:

> 'I would say most people around here worry about the Aniline.'

> 'If Clayton Aniline shut down it would be a bloody ghost town around here.'

Such exchanges also reveal the complexity of risk issues for most people. Pollution is at least a sign of industrial activity – and there is little enthusiasm for a pollution-free, but socially devastated, local environment. Thus, despite the conventional notion of 'NIMBY-ism' or 'risk adversity' (a discourse which generally seems profoundly self-interested on the part of those who make such accusations), in this established industrial area urban pollution is taken to be a particular – but not defining – feature of the locality. Environmental pollution is one important characteristic of life in these localities, but it is not the *sole* characteristic.

It also follows that the statistical probability of a risk or the scientific appraisal of its consequences will be only one element in the generation of local concern. Instead, the everyday picture of living in an area will draw upon a series of other discourses and forms of evidence – generated through daily discussion and repeated (often very detailed) observation. Technical discourses are just one (not necessarily very significant) element in this complex picture.

One other consequence of the perspective adopted here is that standardized efforts at delivering 'relevant information' are likely to miss out on just these local appreciations of the area in question. As was suggested in the previous section, such efforts at technical dissemination risk being seen as either totally irrelevant to the local situation or as an attempt by interested parties to validate their existing practices. Typically, such efforts assume that 'environmental threats' can be filtered out from their everyday social context so that they are presented to the public audience as a tidy self-contained package – with the contents selected by social institutions on the basis of an assumed audience.

Despite this, what *does* stand out from discussion with local people is the significance of local industry as an information source. A strong feeling in our study areas was that, since local industry was likely to be the *source* of hazard information, then it was probably best to go 'straight to the horse's mouth'. This seems an entirely reasonable assumption since to a very large extent outside bodies such as the local authority must indeed rely on industry's own assessment of safety and pollution control. In that way, what might appear to be a wide array of potential information sources – community groups, emergency services, local authorities, councillors, members of parliament, citizens advice bureaux – actually reduces (and is seen as such) to a single dominant source of technical assessment.

This point is not lost on local people. Moreover, industry is both the source of hazard information and hazard. In such a situation, it appears logical to go there directly rather than dealing with bodies who have little direct capacity for bringing about change. In a context where 'information' may not be useful ('just what might we *do* with it?') but practical action *is*, then it seems best to tackle the institution which has it in its power to reduce environmental harm.

Together with this sense of 'knowledge for action's sake' we must also consider the generally sceptical treatment accorded to sources of information. Certainly, there is little sign from this case-study that 'information' is automatically granted a privileged – or even respected – status over other sources of advice and understanding. At one point in our social survey we asked people in the two areas to assess the 'trustworthiness' of possible 'disseminators'. A complex local picture then emerged (Table 4.3).

Now 'trustworthiness' is a very broad and multi-faceted concept in this context – it can mean 'honest and reliable', 'knowledgeable',

Table 4.3: There are various places that could provide you with information or advice about the local chemical industry. How trustworthy do you think the following would be as sources of information on such matters?

	Very trustworthy	Trustworthy	Untrustworthy	Very untrustworthy	Don't know
Local chemical companies	9 (5%)	41 (22%)	71 (39%)	34 (18%)	29 (16%)
Local community groups	20 (11%)	99 (54%)	8 (4%)	0	57 (31%)
Police	15 (8%)	97 (53%)	19 (10%)	2 (1%)	51 (28%)
Fire service	68 (37%)	91 (49%)	2 (1%)	0	23 (12%)
Local authority	8 (4%)	73 (40%)	30 (16%)	7 (4%)	66 (36%)
CAB	32 (17%)	104 (56%)	6 (3%)	0	42 (23%)
Local councillors	6 (3%)	55 (30%)	40 (22%)	12 (6%)	71 (39%)
Local MP	10 (5%)	53 (29%)	23 (12%)	8 (4%)	90 (50%)
Health and Safety Executive	36 (20%)	81 (44%)	9 (5%)	0	58 (31%)

Total Respondents = 184

Source: original research

'responsible', 'dependable'. What is interesting in this table, nevertheless, is the low 'trustworthiness score' given to local chemical companies as compared with the fire service, citizens advice bureaux (CAB) or the Health and Safety Executive. However, if we select a few comments from those made about local industry then a clearer picture starts to emerge. Independent of the actual category-decision made in response to the fixed categories of the survey question, a pattern of caution and scepticism emerges:

Very trustworthy: 'Wouldn't hide anything';

Trustworthy: 'They'd have to tell the truth but they'd hold back a bit';
'Perhaps, but probably just tell you what they want you to know';

Untrustworthy: 'Well I reckon they'd be a bit careful what they told you';
'I think they'd only tell you a load of blinding science to shut you up';
'They wouldn't give you the full view – they've got their jobs to think of';

Very untrustworthy:'Wouldn't believe a word they said';
'They'd only tell you something to put your mind at rest';

Don't know: 'They would say one thing and mean another';
'They would just let you know what they wanted you to know'.

Much more interesting for our current purposes than the obvious criticism of local industry is the overall pattern of scepticism and wariness which these quotations suggest. This pattern seems remarkably consistent across the survey categories (incidentally revealing the fundamental limitations of such questionnaire categorizations). Thus, even entries in the 'Don't know' category suggest a very cautious approach to industrially-based information and advice. The 'don't know' response certainly cannot be deemed as equivalent to ignorance or apathy on the part of respondents.

Overall, information from industry will be taken *in context*. In particular, the *source* of that information will inevitably colour response to the information itself.

What the whole 'trustworthiness' issue opens up is the very *active* manner in which new sources of information – whether technical or otherwise – will be received. There is little sense here of public groups simply soaking up free-floating or value-neutral science. Instead, we see a more critical response to science especially since, for example, it may not fit at all with practical 'lived' experience (e.g., the unrealistic assumptions we saw earlier embedded within major hazard planning).

Equally, the *source* of the information is inseparable from the information itself – in that sense, public assessments of technical messages seem to show a remarkable convergence with the 'interests' model within SSK (as briefly discussed in Chapter 2). The social position of the disseminator – in this case, industrial bodies which will inevitably wish to defend their pollution record – is seen to have a decisive effect on the framing, selection and construction of technical advice. Technical statements are 'interested' – as such they need to be treated with the same intelligent caution that one would treat the statements of a politician or neighbour. Nevertheless, arguments based on a technical legitimation can in such an established situation have a particular capacity to silence citizen groups from open discussion or disagreement.

In public fora, this silencing of public doubts could easily be misinterpreted as acceptance – as when a reassurance from a company doctor is put forward in response to a diffuse pollution concern. For unprepared citizens it is very difficult to challenge such authority directly – but this does not necessarily mean that the concern has been dissipated. Scientific authority retains an important persuasive power – but possibly at the cost of the expression of underlying fears and uncertainties. There are parallels here with Foucault's analysis of the dominance of expertise within everyday life.[11]

In particular, discourses of expertise can engender a form of self-censorship where objections will not be raised since they will be pre-defined as illegitimate. Thus, it was not unusual for public accounts of open company meetings in one of the areas to include critical reference to the information being conveyed by industrial representatives. However, to challenge that information in such a formal situation would only be to invite ridicule. How could a member of the public possibly engage in a technical dialogue? Silence in such a context is, however, very different from acquiescence.

Now it might well be objected that, whilst this 'contextualized' approach to pollution and the urban environment tells us a great deal about the local response to industry, it actually tells us very *little* about the relationship between science and citizenship. After all, there seems very little 'science' in these encounters – it was neither asked for (since the focus of a citizen enquiry was typically on practical action) nor was it given (citizens generally considered themselves to receive reassurances and self-justifications rather than technical enlightenment).

Certainly, within interviews with local people, the subject of 'science' was difficult to explore. People who could discuss the local environment and local life with great eloquence would fall silent on the topic of science and scientists – reinforcing the apparent remoteness of science from everyday existence. When asked directly, there was often a feeling that science would be of benefit – but a note of caution could often be found:

'a letter from a scientist – that would be OK . . . people would take notice. I'm not saying I'd swallow everything. I'd listen then make up my own mind. There's no point in listening to the company. Better to listen to the scientists.'

'The outside person would tell you it's dangerous, but the company might co-opt them. The company might give them money for the project, it might have got to them.'

It seems fair to conclude that 'science' as an abstract category is respected – but that this is considered very different from the more frequently encountered forms of technical advice. However, once science is imported into the everyday world it can easily be 'co-opted'. Of course, implicit in this is the notion that science is unlikely to be co-opted by local people – but only by more powerful social groups. The notion that science could work directly for citizens themselves seems outside the bounds of possibility. Of course, the apparent remoteness of science from everyday life and citizens' own sense of scientific ignorance only reinforces this assessment.

Scientists as a category thus fit into essentially the same social model as industrial representatives (albeit whilst retaining higher status). They are a possible source of information and advice but not one which can be accepted without question. Once again, we see a disparity between this line of analysis and the 'dissemination' model which simply assumes that the generally high status of science will be sufficient to win an uncritical audience.

It may also follow from these observations that only a *plurality* of information sources can respond adequately to such an active audience. Whilst the modernist worldview tends to emphasize simple, authoritative and consensual information, these residents may be better served by a more open presentation of conflicting positions in order to reach their own judgement. In that sense also, the modernist drive to 'tidy up' the risk appraisal process can lead to failing credibility.

This case-study also leads us to challenge the direct *relevance* of science to everyday concerns. Of course, the kind of science presented in the classroom (at least at the time when many of these citizens were at school) is unlikely to relate to such pressing problems. Equally, 'popular science' as discussed at the beginning of this chapter has only marginal application. Thus, whilst science has the cultural status to legitimize citizen concerns (which is why a 'letter from a scientist' might be valuable) it is not obvious to residents how its 'knowledge' can be of practical worth (at least to *them*). Meanwhile, as suggested above, its style of discourse can serve to exclude and marginalize rather than empower.

To a scientific observer, therefore, science may be central to issues of risk and environmental threat. From the perspective of local citizens, however, it tends to 'disappear'. This is partly because it is difficult from the 'citizen perspective' even to identify its presence. Science forms the general backdrop to the action (or perhaps, provides the terms of engagement) rather than being a key player. Once again we are reminded of the quotation at the beginning of this chapter. One constellation of facts, i.e., that of a science-centred perspective, may be very different from that of citizens (for whom social judgements and previous experience may be far more central). Science also disappears because 'information exchanges' are seen to contain just one powerful group's notion of 'appropriate information'. In such a situation, 'information' seems to reinforce social powerlessness rather than enable citizen action.

From this perspective, it would seem that science *does* play a major role in local debates over risk and pollution but characteristically in a manner which *opposes* rather than assists the citizen assessment of these issues – such that most citizens struggle even to see its relevance to their pollution concerns. Industry is seen as the best informed source but the information it offers serves to legitimize current practices. Residents' diffuse concerns over smells, visual pollution, health effects and everyday disturbance are undermined (to the point where it seems purposeless to express them publicly) rather than assisted by information exchanges. Whilst at the abstract level the ideal of 'pure academic science' is respected, this is largely because this ideal is defined in sharp contrast to everyday encounters with enlightenment rationale. Meanwhile, technical authority is drawn upon by industry officials in order to legitimate current practices – it is an important, but often backgrounded, element in their claim to credibility and trustworthiness.

Our account of this case-study has thus opened up a striking disparity between those enlightenment accounts of science which claim it to be of major benefit in environmental response and the views of the citizens considered here who find little use for scientific information – and indeed are likely to be the receptors for inappropriate (at least in terms of their stated needs) and legitimatory messages. This account is in many ways reminiscent of Beck's account of science and citizens in the risk society: 'A permanent experiment is being conducted ... in which people serving as laboratory animals in a self-help movement have to collect and report data on their own toxic symptoms *against* the experts sitting there with their deeply furrowed brows'.[12]

Whilst there were indeed 'self-help movements' in at least one of these areas – in the form of residents' associations and similar groups – this had only an indirect role in 'data collection'. Instead, local people compiled their own 'symptoms' generally in an informal and *ad hoc* manner – for example, when they identify night-time factory emissions as a particular problem or make a widespread connection between chest ailments and local pollution.

As Beck suggests, people may become their own resource so that contextually generated understandings are more useful at the everyday level than the legitimatory messages which originate from industry. Certainly, such data collection could be quite systematic – one resident proudly produced the binoculars with which he scans the nearby industrial site before he rings to alert them. We must nevertheless be careful to stress the incomplete and partial nature of such citizen-generated 'data' – as residents themselves are very aware and will regularly indicate. Equally, we must be cautious at this stage lest we over-generalize on the basis of one discussion.

All of these points – and especially the active knowledge constructions by citizens – will be discussed in the following chapters. Given what we have argued about the uncertainties and limitations of scientific accounts in this area, what alternative forms of knowledge and expertise are available?

Discussion

This chapter has focused on the disparity between 'top-down' efforts at dissemination and the expressed views, experiences and understandings of citizen groups. In the course of this discussion, the various limitations of the conventional dissemination approach have been noted – mainly through a consideration of citizen responses. Above all, it has been argued that the inadequate modelling of citizen understandings (e.g., the *tabula rasa* assumption that the public are 'information poor') leads to initiatives which are limited in practical terms. Instead of attempting to engage with these citizen perspectives, top-down approaches tend to assume that an authoritative and scientifically validated (even if heavily simplified) presentation will command popular attention.

The perspective adopted here has also raised problems for the 'public understanding of science'. Where scientific information is not clearly linked to practical action and where it takes little account of existing assessments of a situation, it is likely to be seen as at best an irrelevance to everyday concerns. Furthermore, whilst 'science' seemed to command the respect of our citizen groups, a similar scepticism as applied to local industry also applies to scientists (albeit to a slightly lesser degree) – they are open to being 'bought' just like the rest of us ('well, they would say that, wouldn't they?'). The provision of scientific information, therefore, is accommodated within the same critical context as other facets of everyday social life.

Contrary to notions of the public as passive and/or apathetic in the face of information campaigns, this chapter has begun to identify an alternative model for information reception. Within this model, the 'competence' of the information source will be judged alongside the perceived credibility of that source and the possibilities for practical action which are opened up by its intervention.

This final point is important given the notions of powerlessness which exist within the communities studied – what is the incentive to learn more about a chemical works when a resident's voice is insignificant (and when one feels hemmed-in by the absence of alternatives)? In such a situation, greater knowledge of, for example, chemical hazards simply creates greater frustration and raises the sense of helplessness. At its most extreme, and as informal interviews sometimes suggested, the technical nature of the official discourses can encourage public self-censorship – concerns seep out within casual conversations rather than being formally presented to those 'in control'.

The discussion of 'technical dissemination' has thus led into a discussion of the social context within which 'real-world' knowledges are received but also developed. The intention in this chapter has simply been to draw attention to these voices and to the 'constellations' on which they draw. In Chapter 5, we will begin to consider the new possibilities which are created by this perspective. In particular, we will look at the relationship between the sort of local understandings which have been discussed so far and the 'decontextualized' and formal rationalities of science.

APPENDIX 1

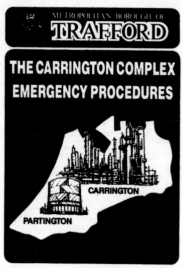

METROPOLITAN BOROUGH OF

TRAFFORD

THE CARRINGTON COMPLEX
EMERGENCY PROCEDURES

CARRINGTON

PARTINGTON

INFORMATION:

More information about these emergency procedures may be obtained from:

**The County Emergency Planning Officer,
G.M.C., P.O. Box 430,
County Hall,
Piccadilly Gardens,
Manchester M60 3HP**

Issued by Trafford Metropolitan Borough Council on behalf of and in consultation with Shell Chemicals (U.K.) Limited, British Gas Corporation and North West Gas.

PLEASE KEEP THESE NOTES FOR REFERENCE

ISSUED DECEMBER 1985

Produced by the Publicity Office, C.E. Dept., The Metropolitan Borough of Trafford. Ref. 084 12/85

THE CARRINGTON COMPLEX
EMERGENCY PROCEDURES

Your premises are situated in an area that could possibly be affected if a major accident should occur in the Carrington Complex. The Control of Industrial Major Accident Hazards Regulations (1984) requires us to inform you of the emergency procedures that you should follow in the unlikely event of a major accident at:

Shell Chemicals (U.K.) Limited, Carrington
British Gas Corporation, Heath Farm Lane, Partington
or North West Gas, Common Lane, Partington

The activities on these sites have been notified to the Health and Safety Executive.

ACTIVITIES WITHIN THE COMPLEX:

Shell Chemicals (U.K.) Limited manufacture chemicals and plastics. These are used for making detergents, packaging film, domestic and industrial plastic articles and foam insulation.

British Gas and North West Gas are involved with the bulk supply of natural gas into national and local pipelines. This includes the storage of large quantities of liquefied gases.

Flammable substances are used in these activities. In the event of a major accident it is likely that flammable vapour will be released into the atmosphere. This vapour would normally disperse safely, but if ignited could cause a fire, or in certain circumstances an explosion, within the site.

At the Shell Chemicals (U.K.) Limited site, toxic substances are used which may be released into the atmosphere in the event of a major accident. These vapours would also normally disperse safely, but in extreme cases could cross the site boundary at low concentrations sufficient to cause irritation to eyes and throat.

EMERGENCY PROCEDURES:

Detailed emergency plans to minimise the consequences of an accident have been prepared by each site, by the local authority and by the fire, police and ambulance services.

EMERGENCY ACTION:

IN A MAJOR EMERGENCY YOU WILL BE ADVISED BY THE POLICE WHAT TO DO. YOU SHOULD FIRST GO INDOORS, CLOSE ALL DOORS AND WINDOWS AND AWAIT FURTHER INSTRUCTIONS.

104

5

FREEING THE VOICES: A SCIENCE OF THE PEOPLE?

Communities need to get involved. The other important thing that people need to remember . . . is that they probably know as much or maybe even more than some of the experts drafted in to view certain things. I know I get called into certain things . . . someone asks me about something they've been researching for a long time and they've put a lot of stuff together and quite often they know far more about it than I do, yet people will defer to me because I've done toxicology or something else. . . . I am increasingly impressed with what people can put together.[1]

Whatever skills and forms of knowledge lay people may lose, they remain skilful and knowledgeable in the contexts of action in which their activities take place and which, in some part, those activities continually reconstitute. Everyday skill and knowledgeability thus stands in dialectical connection to the expropriating effects of abstract systems, continually reshaping the very impact of such systems on day-to-day existence.[2]

In Chapter 4 we took a major step away from the conventional paradigm of 'science and citizenship'. Rather than charting the apparent lack of public understanding, we found a more complex picture of social and technical interactions as they have operated within one local context. In this chapter, we need to build on this specific case in order to see whether it is indicative of a wider pattern of citizen response. Is it possible – as Beck's analysis of the 'risk society' suggests[3] – that new relations of knowledge, science and citizenship are emerging within late modern society?

At least partly, we can consider that change is occurring as a consequence of the problematic application of science within areas such as environmental threat (and the wider applicability of the environmental context will be considered in Chapter 7). Citizen concerns and responses need to be seen against the background of problems, however, which go beyond matters of 'application' and into the very fabric of science as a knowledge system. To summarize the previous discussion, these problems include:

- *structural uncertainties* (discussed in Chapter 2) where science is asked to give simple and unambiguous responses to questions which are at the very limits of its understanding and competence – and also where no simple and unambiguous responses may *ever* be possible as we enter a world of uncertainty rather than control;
- the unavoidability of scientists operating with underlying *social assumptions and social models* (e.g., concerning evacuation procedure as discussed in Chapter 4). In offering technical advice about a risk situation, scientists are also offering social judgements about public response, the credibility of different information sources and the likelihood that various safety procedures will actually be practised. Scientific models of risk and the environment must, therefore, draw upon social models of how things work in the 'real world';
- these difficulties relate also to the problem of *closed system vs open system*. In areas of citizen concern such as environmental threat, we are operating not in the carefully contrived world of the laboratory but instead in a much more complex and constantly fluctuating universe. The success of many areas of science stems directly from the ability of scientists to manipulate and control extraneous variables – in the area of risk and the environment, such control is simply impossible.

In this context the notion of *experiment* changes radically – we are all now living in the 'environmental laboratory' or indeed, as one book on reproductive technology puts it, we are now 'living laboratories'.[4] Consequently, new relations are generated between experimental subjects and the experimenters: as, for example, when workers argue that they will no longer be human 'guinea pigs' for new chemical substances or when HIV/AIDS sufferers demand a greater involvement in the development of new drugs.[5]

These characteristics of science are all clear in the areas of major hazards, mad cow disease and 2,4,5–T where scientists have struggled to offer a unified and consensual account. This is often represented as a dilemma for decision-making; how can we make rational decisions on the basis of such uncertain knowledge?[6] At the same time, this situation is (as Beck argues) at least potentially liberating for citizens since it opens up the possibility of wider social debate and of an acceptance of a more pluralistic approach to decision-making.

Essential to this debate will be an acknowledgement of the limitations but also strengths of science. Unfortunately at present – and as the dominant form of the 'public understanding of science' discussion seems to reinforce – this kind of constructive reappraisal is often deemed 'anti-scientific'. Meanwhile, and despite the above characteristics, risk debates are regularly presented in a particularly reductionist form as if the facts somehow spoke for themselves.

Science provides the framework within which all debates must take place. In the examples so far we have seen the apparent *certainty* with which scientific accounts are presented. Nevertheless, as cases such as 2,4,5-T suggest, we may have reached the stage where that form of legitimation has worn decidedly thin.

In parallel with these structural aspects of the operation of science within decision-making, Chapter 4 began to offer a range of critical *public* responses to technical advice: from ignoring official guidance through to a perception of science as invariably 'interested' once it enters the public domain. In the kind of situation presented in the previous chapter, science is considered to be one source of knowledge among others – and, moreover, one which is generally allied to powerful social groups. Despite the regular claim of science to 'stand above' everyday social conflict, credibility judgements about science become inseparable from judgements about the institutions which actually offer scientific accounts. Thus, in the previous chapter we found widespread scepticism about the notion of science as 'objective knowledge' – whilst objectivity may exist in the abstract (suggesting a high status for science), within loaded social situations science was seen as above all serving social interests.

However, in any discussion of contemporary science we have to recognize that science is not homogeneous – either at the level of its own institutional and cognitive structures or at the level of social assessment. Thus, it is important for any critical analysis of science that we recognize both the diverse nature of contemporary science and also the range of social meanings and significances which it has acquired. As Giddens argues:

> Lay attitudes towards science, technology and other esoteric forms of expertise, in the age of high modernity, tend to express the same mixed attitudes of reverence and reserve, approval and disquiet, enthusiasm and antipathy, which philosophers and social scientists (themselves experts of sorts) express in their writings.[7]

Any serious discussion of science and its relationship to everyday life must, therefore, take full account of the, often contradictory, meanings that science has assumed within our society. As was suggested in the previous chapter, within debates over risk and the environment a number of such meanings can be identified. Thus, science is portrayed in the following ways amongst others:

- as independent and objective knowledge (for example, when industry or government attempts to 'reassure' public groups);
- as the servant to business and power (when public groups react with suspicion to science as it is offered);
- as the most rational basis for public and private assessments of threat (as scientific institutions would argue);
- as the source of hazard (when the products of scientific research become the focus of hazard debate);
- as an established set of theories and working hypotheses (as presented to downplay the limitations and uncertainties discussed here);
- as an everyday irrelevance (for those who cannot 'make sense' of science as it is made available to them);
- as the best route to progress (as the modernistic paradigm suggests);
- as a spiritual and moral dead-end (as the strongest critics of scientific rationality argue).

This list suggests the range of social meanings attributed to contemporary science – and also their overlap and entanglement. Science is not just 'one thing' but a diverse cultural phenomenon – and not least because of the variety of institutional locations within which it is conducted and utilized.

The key points about this in the current context can be summarized as follows:

- first, it should not be surprising that public groups often hold these meanings of science simultaneously despite their apparent contradictions. Science has a number of meanings and these different meanings seem to coexist. Thus, in interviews of the kind discussed in Chapter 4, cynicism about 'company experts' could rapidly give way to respect for 'university scientists' which could then move into anger about the damage which scientific development has done to the local environment and then unhappy memories of schoolroom science. Science is indirectly encountered in many different ways within everyday life;
- second, that debates about science often revolve around such differences of meaning and interpretation in such a way as to render discussion incommensurable (whilst one account stresses the spiritual vacuum created by science another simply cannot comprehend a future without the products of science). Equally, respect for the high ideals of academic science will not necessarily translate into respect for a university scientist who has been commissioned by local industry.

This phenomenon is evident, as Giddens has noted, both within everyday discussions of science and scientific issues and also within more academic debate over the same questions. Thus Beck, for example, tends to equate science with what Lash and Wynne term 'scientism':

> The culture of scientism has in effect imposed identity upon social actors by demanding their identification with particular social institutions and their ideologies, notably in constructions of risk, but also in definitions of sanity, proper sexual behaviour, and countless other 'rational' frames of modern social control.[8]

Meanwhile, the defenders of contemporary science tend to portray science as above all open-minded, sceptical and independent of institutional constraints;

- third, there is an intriguing congruity between citizen views of science and those which have emerged, for example, from the post-Kuhnian sociology of scientific knowledge. Both, for example, link the outputs of science to the institutional structures in which science is created. Thus, the regular shop-floor critique of 'bosses' science' is similar in its conclusions to sociological critiques of industrial toxicology and its dependence in Britain on private funding.[9]

Within this discussion we also need to recognize the range of institutional and disciplinary contexts in which science operates: an industrial consultancy is not the same as a research laboratory, particle physics is not the same as botany. Science is institutionally and culturally diverse. Of course, it is easier to offer a one-dimensional account of science (as 'rationality', as 'legitimation', as 'threat'), but the wider view is (to use Beck's language) more liberating since it offers – as the rest of this book will argue – the basis for a constructive renegotiation between science and the needs of citizens.

This discussion of the diverse social and cultural significances of science stands in stark contrast to the one-dimensional account offered by most enlightenment perspectives on science. However, in discussing these perspectives, it is important to emphasize that it is not only held by powerful social groups – but also by apparently more radical social movements. The 'science for the people' movement of the 1970s tended to view the problem as one of schism between 'science' and the 'people' – if only better technical information could be made available to ordinary citizens, then they could play an enhanced role in decision-making. Whilst elements within this movement called for the 'demystification of science' (often in extremely vague terms), the general analysis was of science as the key to social progress so that the task of 'progressive' scientists was to disseminate and serve, where necessary, as 'counter experts'.

In this, the radical science movement of the 1970s may have represented a step forward from the scientific socialists of the 1930s who believed in what Werskey calls 'scientific determinism'.[10] As with the 1970s proposal for a 'Community Research Council', the notion was instead to encourage greater citizen involvement in the activities of science. Nevertheless, this would not change the fundamentally uneven relationship between 'science' as the source of knowledge and 'citizens' as the recipients of that knowledge; a science for (but not *of*) the people. As we will see in Chapter 6, such assumptions are still intrinsic to most current attempts at widening citizen access to science and scientific institutions.

Against these different complexions of enlightenment perspective, we have the evidence of the last chapter which suggests a very critical and contextual treatment of scientific advice. Judgements of credibility and relative scepticism mean that science will not be accepted by citizen groups without considerable qualification and reshaping. Science must also 'make sense' to citizens within particular situations – a process which requires the active generation of everyday meaning. New information must be accommodated within an established framework developed often through direct and practical experience of the world – otherwise, it is simply meaningless.

It follows that it is important to consider more seriously the kinds of knowledges and understandings developed by citizens in the face of the truth claims of science. In the remainder of this chapter, we will address these possibilities for citizen knowledge and even citizen participation in scientific debate – an area which we can refer to as 'citizen science' in the latter sense outlined in the Preface. In what ways might groups of citizens play an active role in the process of knowledge dissemination and knowledge development? This will involve an assessment of the kinds of knowledges developed by citizen groups rather than by the institutional processes of science. We can begin by looking once again at the three main examples which have run through this book.

Citizen science and three stories of our time

2,4,5–T and the farmworkers

As presented in Chapter 1 and Chapter 3, the confrontation between the farmworkers and the Advisory Committee on Pesticides over 2,4,5–T can be analysed in a number of ways. From the conventional modernistic perspective, it can be portrayed as the technical experts desperately 'holding the line' against campaigning groups and trade union activists. Of course, this perspective is very evident in the advisory committee's comments on the trade union testimony – and not least with the apparent suggestion that public groups are incapable of assessing technical argumentation. As the ACP argued with regard to miscarriages and birth deformities:

> it can be relatively easy to select some product (or indeed some occupation, pastime, social group or locality) and without enquiring very closely, to assume some connection with these family misfortunes – especially if alleged connections are regularly publicised. Moreover there can be an understandable desire to identify some outside agent as the cause of what has in practice been an unhappy but not unnatural fact of life throughout the ages.[11]

111

For the ACP, only an 'independent' body such as the ACP (and its scientific subcommittee) is in a position to sift through evidence in the necessarily cool and analytical fashion.

> The Advisory Committee lays no claim to absolute mastery of everything concerning pesticides. What it can claim is that its own knowledge and experience is backed up by a valuable body of medical and scientific expertise within and beyond the machinery of Government. And, of course, it draws strength from its independence.[12]

However, the 2,4,5-T case strongly suggests the inadequacy of portraying such an encounter as being between 'experts' and 'concerned parties'. Instead, we can see the farmworkers as demonstrating various types of expertise – even if their testimony was generally not regarded in this fashion. In terms of this chapter and its concern with 'new knowledge relationships', a number of elements are especially important. In general, these suggest the willingness of 'lay' participants to challenge the assumptions and conclusions of 'experts'. Going further, they indicate the role which lay groups can play not only in criticizing expert knowledge but also in *generating* forms of knowledge and understanding – in serving as 'living laboratories' in an active as well as passive fashion. It can be argued that in cases such as this, citizen knowledges can be at least as robust and well-informed as those of experts – despite the steep differential in status and power.

Thus, a regular theme of this debate (at least from the farmworkers' perspective) was that the ACP's stress on 'recommended way' and 'recommended purposes' revealed extraordinary ignorance of the realities of pesticide spraying. This reinforces one major difficulty encountered by the enlightenment perspective – that expert statements will be met with scepticism – especially if they are seen to be emerging from institutions with perceived links to interested parties (in this case, and despite the advisory committee's regular denials, the committee was linked by the farmworkers to the agro-business).

Equally, this case suggests the impoverishment of expert accounts which do not draw upon the knowledges of participants. As one farmworker is quoted by the farmworkers' union: 'They (the "experts") may know the risks of 2,4,5-T. They may handle the stuff properly. They tell us we'll be alright if we use the spray normally. But have they any idea what "normally" means in the fields?'[13] Or, put more bluntly: 'It's like working in a laundry and being told to keep out of the steam!'[14]

Farmworkers involved in the 2,4,5–T campaign repeatedly ridiculed the ACP's notion of 'recommended' working conditions – basing their ridicule on specific cases where such conditions had been clearly breached. More pointedly, their whole argument was that such breaches are not just occasional lapses but are inevitable consequences of 'risk and the real world' (to borrow a chapter heading from one account of the 2,4,5–T story).[15]

> Users, too, are often simply unaware of the directions for use or, if they are aware of them, find that they are working under so much pressure that it is easier to ignore them. This is all a long way from the laboratory conditions in which tests may be conducted.[16]

In particular, the farmworkers could draw upon a knowledge of possible *spraying conditions* (through thick undergrowth, in high winds, at the top of a ladder, in hot weather). The variety of these conditions seems to suggest that there is no such thing as 'normal operation' nor any procedures which can apply in every condition. The farmworkers could also identify a similar variety in *circumstances of operation* (with inadequate equipment, long distances away from toilet and washing facilities, being uninformed about the actual substances involved, with pesticide drifting onto other fields, with others inevitably exposed, with possibly inadequate facilities for the cleaning and disposal of containers). The farmworkers also operated within a rather different *social model of farmworking* than the advisory committee. The farmworkers' notion of the social organization of the technology was based on isolated workers with little access to trade union support and often highly dependent upon one employer for wages and housing.

The argument for a ban on the pesticide was, therefore, constructed in terms of an inherently uncontrollable technology and of a messy and heterogeneous 'real world'. The advisory committee's insistence on 'recommended' conditions made little sense within this social and technical model of pesticide administration. Instead, the workers' understanding of pesticide usage was swept aside by the apparent requirement for scientifically established 'proof'.

Of course, for the farmworkers, no demarcation could be made between 'technical' argumentation and the conditions of application and use – the two were simply inseparable. For the advisory committee, an intellectual line could be drawn – with the farm-workers' insights considered irrelevant. However, critics of the advisory committee saw this line as a largely ideological device – reflecting above all the social commitments of the regulatory process.

Technical decisions of this sort are also inevitably caught up with the required criteria of proof. The advisory committee seemed to consider that guilt should be established 'beyond all reasonable doubt' before the substance was banned. The farmworkers, how-ever, tended to employ a 'balance of probabilities' approach to the evidence – given the amount of doubt, isn't it more cautious to ban? Here again, we seem to have an area where citizen insights may be as valuable as those of supposed experts.

Finally, one important theme which runs through this case is that of 'popular epidemiology', i.e., an assessment of the level of risk which builds from direct experience but also from more systematic data and external analysis. In this case, the popular epidemiology drew upon the experience of workers in other countries and upon international campaigns as well as upon the evidence of British workers. Interestingly in this case, the workers' assessment was also developed in a very specific form through a questionnaire prepared by the farmworkers' union. This methodology and its reception by the ACP goes to the heart of many citizen-science issues.

As noted in Chapter 1, the farmworkers' union attempted to organize its own database by requesting information on the health effects of 2,4,5–T directly from its membership. The responses were then put together not in statistical form but as a series of case-studies for submission to the advisory committee. For the farm-workers, this represented a reasonable attempt to synthesize in-formation in a suitably persuasive manner. The advisory committee response was dismissive of such 'anecdotal' evidence. However, the farmworkers' attempts at expropriating knowledge for themselves both permitted and served as the basis of a wider campaign about pesticide safety and the regulatory processes involved.

Whilst the experience of dealing with the advisory committee was obviously frustrating for the farmworkers, a realization of the knowledges and expertise at their own disposal was also ultimately empowering. In terms of more effective regulatory structures, we are left to ask whether it is sensible for the understandings of such highly involved parties as the workers themselves to be excluded from decision-making.

Now at this point it must be noted that the story of 2,4,5–T may have been as frustrating for the advisory committee as for the farmworkers. Such a tale of non-communication might also feed 'deficit' theories and further encourage the orthodox 'public understanding of science' framework. The value of social science in this context may precisely be to challenge assumptions on both sides and so facilitate a more informed dialogue.

Equally, our improved sense of the limitations of science in a case like this should not lead to an uncritical (and perhaps romantic) espousal of all forms of contextual understanding as necessarily superior to more 'scientific' accounts. We have already begun to note that these different forms of knowledge may have different characteristics. For example, we may consider science's drive to *universalism* (statements which apply across contexts) as opposed to the farmworkers' concern for the *local* situations in which they operate. Which of these perspectives may be more applicable in specific situations cannot be determined in advance.

The point of discussion here is not to privilege either 'citizen' or 'scientific' understandings but rather to note the diversity of knowledges which seem relevant to risk/environmental issues. Certainly, it is not my intention to advocate some new form of reductionism. The very simple hypothesis at this stage is that decision processes would benefit from an awareness of this plurality rather than attempting to impose one cognitive framework.

BSE and the consumers

In the case of 'mad cow disease', similar patterns of diverse (and divergent) knowledge, experience and expertise can be identified. Thus, the 'official' claim to authority with its expert legitimation came under challenge from a range of social groups and individual scientists. Certainly, it is important to note that scientists and public groups are not inevitably in opposition to one another. In both the case of BSE and 2,4,5–T, scientists formed alliances with concerned public groups. The diversity of scientific opinions can overlap and inform public assessments – even if, as Chapter 6 will discuss, that overlap can also be problematic.

Typically however, and in line with the case of 2,4,5–T, the statements of government and industrial representatives offered an apparent scientific consensus. Oppositional groups were attempting to portray food safety as an area of everyday concern and everyday experience (hence the naming of organizations such as 'Parents for Safe Food') – whilst government and industry statements tended to identify appropriate expertise in only one institutional location.

In terms of this chapter's concern with science and changing knowledge relationships, choices over food safety represent an area of considerable significance. Once again, judgements over food require a range of assessments which move across and beyond the officially defined 'expert' domain. Thus, in a case such as BSE, groups of citizens enquired about:

- the *credibility* of various authorities – and, particularly, the possibility that social interests are being served within official statements (in this case, the possibility of a coalition between government and the meat industry created much public hostility and scepticism). Credibility judgements will also inter-connect with previous experience of food safety messages – especially when apparently authoritative statements are rapidly contradicted without obvious explanation or loss of official confidence. Thus, the language of certainty may not convey strength and authority (as is presumably intended) but rather arrogance and even ignorance – especially when judged against the previous history of official health statements regarding diet (for example, debates over butter vs margarine in terms of coronary protection);
- the *social practices* at stake – what, for example, are the likely conditions in the abattoir? Will various precautions actually be effectively enforced? Discussion here centred on whether meat production was seen as a carefully controlled and standardized social system (as official statements suggested) or a more disorganized and random environment where 'mistakes' would inevitably occur. The link to the 2,4,5–T debate is quite clear here;
- very importantly, the *alternatives* which exist and the relative costs involved – food must be provided and choices must be made but these choices will inevitably be constrained by budgetary and lifestyle factors;
- the compatibility of official statements and *personal experience* – obviously this is problematic for such a hypothetical yet potentially devastating disease as BSE. However, more routine episodes of food poisoning and dietary related health problems will be taken into account – and also other (often contradictory) health promotion messages such as the need to cut intake of fatty foods.

All of this suggests a considerably more complex process of public response and evaluation than is implied by most official statements (and also by routine criticisms of public hysteria and over-reaction). Whilst the kind of consumer response considered here is less organized than the trade union based strategies discussed above, it nevertheless suggests – as evidenced by public debate around this topic – the richness of responses to hazard issues. In such a situation, the language of the official announcement is unlikely to provide reassurance and comfort since it typically fails to recognize the legitimacy of consumer experiences and expertise in the area of food safety.

Major hazards and local communities

The case of community response to major accident hazards was discussed extensively in Chapter 4 – that discussion suggests a similar pattern to that presented with regard to 2,4,5-T and BSE. Certainly, both popular epidemiologies and social judgements of trust, credibility and choice can be identified in that area.

In particular, public assessments and knowledges tend to draw upon a detailed experience of specific major hazard sites whereas scientific assessments (e.g., in the form of probabilistic risk analysis) must operate with a more general set of assumptions (e.g., about normal working practices and levels of professional competence). Thus, the well-established context to popular assessments can lead to a rich understanding of persistent areas of organizational weakness, previous propensity to environmental damage and hence hazard potential.

At present, official inquiry processes seem to down-grade local understandings due to the latter's possibly circumscribed, heavily contextual and non-transferable status.[17] In this situation, citizen understandings generally possess much less influence than those of the official bodies – as the next section will emphasize. However, this criticism of 'popular epidemiology' (or 'citizen science') only has weight if one accepts that all knowledge must (or must claim to) be 'universal' in character – a modernistic assumption which seems inappropriate to matters of environmental response where situations may be more than specific instances of some well-developed scientific framework.

This debate over the intrinsic merits of 'universalism' is indeed very important for any discussion of science and the environment.

On the one hand, forms of knowledge developed by citizens do not typically make such a claim. Their very strength is in the observation of specific areas of everyday reality. On the other hand, the claims for the superiority of scientific knowledge rest especially on notions of universalism. Scientific knowledge claims to be replicable (or falsifiable) in any location and not just in the place of its original development.

However, the specific contexts offered by our 'three stories' seem remote from the world of scientific experimentation. They are inherently messy and uncontrollable since so may variables are at flux. From a scientific perspective, they seem unlikely to generate or falsify universalistic claims. Accordingly, they are frequently re- duced to the status of 'sites of implementation' where science is *applied* but not developed. Meanwhile, citizen understandings – which typically see the local environment not as a 'special' case but as *the* case – fail to engage with wider scientific debate. In that sense, scientists are denied access to what might represent a substantial body of socio-technical data.

At one level, this lack of engagement may be inevitable – the farmers were not, for example, concerned to attend scientific conferences nor to publish in journals. The *difficulty* in such cases, however, is that scientific accounts can come to be seen not just as remote but as an obstacle to citizen concerns. At the same time, the legitimate questions and knowledges of citizens fail to be granted the significance they may deserve. Once again, this is not to suggest that such knowledges are inevitably superior to those of science but rather to advocate a more symmetrical form of analysis and policy debate.

Lay understandings and contextual knowledges

The production and dumping of toxic waste

Further evidence of 'citizen science' in action can be taken from various community campaigns around local exposure to toxic chemicals. Typically, such campaigns have involved opposition either to waste disposal sites (typically, incinerators or landfill) or to toxic pollution from the chemical industry. Very often, the beginnings of such campaigns have been informal public know- ledges of health effects. Thus, for example, in Robert Allen's account of local community campaigns against waste disposal[18] there are numerous examples of local knowledges stimulating oppositional activity. Such knowledges take many forms:

- direct observation of working practice, e.g., of smoke plumes emanating from disposal sites, of smells and vapours, of the condition of emission stacks. Local knowledge can also be built upon crucial information concerning, for example, the kinds of delivery made to disposal sites. In one case, the claims of a company were directly countered by the itemizing of the trucks which arrived at the site displaying certain HazChem signs. It is also commonly observed that emissions are more severe at night when formal inspection tends to be limited – the local community is well-placed to make such observations;
- evidence that health has been directly affected – as when workers at a neighbouring site claimed they were suffering from incinerator emissions or members of a community noted unusual patterns of illness (typically, problems relating to the eyes, nose and throat, respiratory system or to nausea, headaches, birth deformity or miscarriage);
- observations of animal health disorders – either involving family pets or farm animals;
- understandings of the relative efficiency and management competence of key organizations – these can be important in suggesting bad safety or pollution practice (e.g., with regard to the average temperature of waste incineration);
- comparisons with other sites – generally, those run by the same company or where similar industrial processes are in operation. This can involve the establishment of community networks where groups build upon the experience of others elsewhere;
- the testimony of workers (or former workers) about conditions of operation and associated hazard. Workers may also be local citizens and, as such, become an important source of information about a site's operation and management;
- systematic data collection – in one case, through a round the clock 'toxic watch' recording activities and pollution levels. This could also involve the study of published accounts of hazard.

Evidence of this active knowledge generation fits well with the patterns of local knowledge discussed in this and the previous chapter. In a case-study of one other planned waste disposal site in North-East England, Hooper observed how the local community in question was particularly successful in generating two main forms of evidence.[19]

First, direct contact was made between groups living in the area of the proposed Sunderland site and those living in the area of an existing facility run in the Midlands by the same company. Residents in the Midlands gave evidence of smells, noise and disruption, an explosion at the site and a tanker leak. This severely dented the company's claim to pollution-free operation. Second, since the planned site had been a coal mine, it was possible to draw on local practical expertise of the rock formation and its characteristics. Thus, a former mine worker gave evidence that there had been a history of flooding within the mine – suggesting the strong possibility of toxic leakage and contamination. Prior to this intervention, the technical assurance had been that the site was secure.

In all these cases, locally generated testimonies have suffered from the accusation of being 'anecdotal'. However, it is also clear that they have offered well-grounded accounts of hazard which standardized scientific evaluations have generally failed to draw upon or even acknowledge. Thus, outside scientists have found it impossible to offer a historical perspective on previous experience of hazard, to consider local variations or to deal with failures of operation and safety organization. Instead, such 'decontextualized' accounts are generally built on the idealized social models and sets of assumptions which were seen to operate in cases such as the 2,4,5–T controversy. This gives rise to two particular points.

First, there is, as noted at the end of the previous section, a general reluctance from official bodies to accommodate citizen knowledges within decision-making processes. The common experience of citizen groups is that their testimony is disregarded despite what has been suggested here about its possible significance. As Allen quotes one campaigner:

It has been suggested that ordinary mortals keep out of this debate – let's leave it to the experts to make the right decision. This underestimates our intelligence and the ability of people to research into a subject that affects them deeply. Moreover, 'experts' can sometimes have vested interests! Our vested interests are our own health and that of the natural environment.[20]

Second, and linked to this, there is the problematic relationship between 'local' and 'scientific' knowledge. Whilst local knowledge may form the heart of any campaign, protesters are often wary of presenting evidence which may be seen as circumstantial and unconvincing (once again, as suggested in the previous chapter, the dominant form of discourse can serve to stifle other knowledge and concerns). However, the inevitable resource imbalance leaves them weakly placed to offer 'expert' testimony – there is also a distinct shortage of scientists willing to go to the assistance of campaign groups without payment or technical resources.

Furthermore, for a scientist to 'mediate' between oppositional groups and policy-makers can create real difficulties – the risk is that the scientist will then be seen to have lost 'neutrality'. The institutional and professional pressure is for the scientist not to 'get involved'. In this situation, local groups are effectively disenfranchised from the 'science-centred' decision-making process.

Down's syndrome, domestic energy, methane and Sellafield

We can turn now to an academic account – presented by Layton, Jenkins, Macgill and Davey – which has compiled further evidence of the complex relationship between science and its publics and, in particular, of positive citizen responses in this domain. These authors put their general case in terms broadly sympathetic to the argument in this book:

> It is easy to romanticize 'folk science' and it often can be erroneous. Nevertheless, the indigenous knowledge of the laity can at times represent a valid challenge to the scientific knowledge offered by 'experts'. Awareness and identification of problems is one area where non-expert observations and judgements may be significant. Similarly, traditional knowledge, validated by trial and error over long periods of time, may embody understandings which could enrich science.[21]

As an immediate example of this, Layton et al. offer the Himalayan 'Chipko Audolan' movement dedicated to a holistic analysis of deforestation. Whilst 'scientific' forestry tends to advocate the replacement of traditional forests by commercially valuable teak and pine, this movement stresses the importance of self-reliance (and hence 'sustainability') in 'food, fodder, fuel, fertilizer and fibre'.

In this specific case, we see the tension between 'scientific' and 'citizen' perspectives – but also the manner in which citizen knowledges complement a given lifestyle and cultural appreciation. The latter form of knowledge would not claim 'universality' since this would be to detract from local ways of living with and understanding the social and natural world. For these citizens, as in the other cases in this book, 'knowing' cannot be disembedded from 'living'.

The Leeds University-based authors select four case-studies as the basis for empirical analysis. In the first, concerning the parents of Down's children, we witness the incommensurability of medical accounts of Down's with the immediate needs of everyday life. In what follows, particular attention will be paid to this example.

As the Leeds authors relate it, Down's syndrome is a genetic condition linked to mental retardation and various physical symptoms – including certain facial characteristics, poor muscular development and restricted height. At present, there is no cure. Layton *et al.* effectively convey the deep shock often experienced by parents upon being given a first medical diagnosis after birth. This shock might be accompanied by fear and uncertainty about the future. As one father put it:

> I shut my eyes and I could see a grossly obese mongoloid woman of twenty. And I could see a little wizened old . . . (wife) worn to a shadow by this . . . daughter. And I could see . . . (wife) lugging her upstairs to sit on the lavatory.[22]

Nevertheless, most parents seem to have developed strategies for dealing with their new family situation. However, of particular significance here is the relationship between these parents and scientific understanding. To what extent was scientific knowledge a helpful resource in such a pressured context?

In the first place, the Leeds authors note the 'fragility' of genetic knowledge regarding the manifestations of Down's syndrome. The calculation of recurrence risk (would my next child also have the syndrome?) is, for example, fraught with uncertainties. In terms of parents' reaction to scientific information, a number of responses seemed to occur. Some parents spoke with bitterness about the categorical advice being offered. Bleak prognoses were sometimes provided by the medical profession – 'a virtual cabbage', 'incontinent', 'unlikely to live long'. Such advice could lead to temporary rejection of a child.

In other cases, technical information was provided about the causes of the syndrome in terms of its chromosomal origins. Such information was often seen as irrelevant or of limited practical value

– especially since it had little to offer in terms of 'getting on with things'. However, for one group of parents this information could be useful in terms of allaying guilt. Unfortunately, the same information might also be construed as attributing guilt to one of the parents.

The relationship between the parents and medical expertise is described as follows:

> What these parents were reacting to was the offer of 'insider's science', knowledge generated, validated and standardized by a community whose prime motivation is curiosity about the natural world and whose long term goal is generalized understandings. What the parents were seeking was knowledge which articulated with their perceptions of what needed to be done, short term, immediately, within their own particular setting.[23]

Whilst various medical experts operated within the familiar 'downward transmission' mode of knowledge flow, parents set about the construction of an expertise of their own. The bleak message offered by the medical profession (as one parent put it 'I suppose their fear is they might give you hope, but hope is all you've got'), provoked the development of more constructive knowledges (at least from the parents' perspective). Typically, these knowledges combined 'technical' matters (e.g., the design of drinking cups with a curved edge so as to keep the child's tongue in place) with emotional and social support. Typically also, they avoided the generalities of science – often based on historical experience of children in institutionalized care – and built around the unique potentialities of each individual child. As a mother asserted: 'There's just as much a difference in Down's syndrome children as in the general population. I'm sure there must be as much a spread of intellect and whatever as there is within the population as a whole'.[24]

This claim specifically stresses the diversity of the Down's population as opposed to offering a single, standardized account of the syndrome. It stresses local variation rather than constructing a 'typical' case.

This case-study concludes:

> The body of practical knowledge which parents had themselves constructed was a powerful alternative to the 'high

science' of Down's syndrome available from medical and other 'experts'. Too often, it seemed, parents had received from such 'experts' a message of despair when they were desperate for one of hope. Knowledge was offered in the wrong form, reflecting priorities different from those of practical action; in the wrong way, discounting understandings which parents had wrought from experience; and, often, at the wrong time, serving the convenience of donors, ignoring emotional traumas which parents might be undergoing, and undiscerning of the moment of need.[25]

Meanwhile, as this Leeds case-study suggests: 'for most parents their most important resource was not formal science, the medical profession, ancillary services, or even voluntary organisations. It was themselves.'[26]

A similar pattern of incommensurability in the relationship between science and groups of citizens emerges in the case study of domestic energy and the elderly. Here, the 'scientific' approach to domestic energy management is based on such principles as cost-effectiveness, insulation, energy efficiency and careful monitoring. Thus, the scientific outlook may clash with the social significance of heating and also traditional practices such as opening a window to 'air' a room or heating a 'best' room before visitors arrive.

In particular, concepts such as 'heat' serve as the basis of technical discussion. By contrast, most citizens rely on the notion of 'keeping the cold out' but also follow everyday practices based on personal comfort, hygiene and social decorum. One elderly lady having heated her house would leave a door or two open so that her Yorkshire terrier could get in and out. Once again – as with the emergency planning example – we see the artificially limited statements of technical experts failing to grasp the everyday complexities within which technical advice is actively understood and reconstructed so as to make sense in specific social situations.

The management of energy thus involves far more than a consideration of the nature of energy itself. As one writer is quoted:

People may get warmth from their fires (which is what energy theorists believe fires are for), but in practice they *use* fires for other purposes – a feeling of well-being, or security, or a focal point . . . so fires have a place in a person's life which is very different from the heating engineer's view of a fire.[27]

'Rational' scientific information may simply not 'make sense' within such contexts.

The final two case-studies provided by Layton and his colleagues deal with the management of methane gas by a local authority and the local response to new information about the Sellafield nuclear reprocessing plant. In the former case we see a division between expert accounts and those of local people claiming to be affected by the methane problem – with councillors struggling to achieve some consensus. In such a situation, issues of *trust* come to the fore – if councillors stop trusting their advisors (especially local government officers) then their job would become virtually impossible. As this case-study concludes:

> For the experts, persuading councillors of the 'safety' of a proposal for waste disposal involved explicating technical evidence, derived from a body of tested and self-standing scientific knowledge in which they had confidence, and which had meaning and significance for them as professionals. For the councils and the residents confident of their own concerns and experiences, risk was assessed not on narrow technical grounds but by reference to a complex of knowledge that was specific to the problem that they sought to address and which rejected the notion that technical information is context-free. It is thus hardly surprising that an accommodation of these two perspectives could not be reached.[28]

The Sellafield case-study explores the outcome of one official inquiry into the incidence of leukaemia among children who live near the site. In particular, we see the complexities involved in making sense of science within such long-standing controversies. Professional science struggled once again to achieve effective communication with local people.

In overall conclusion to their four case-studies, Layton *et al.* reject the 'cognitive deficit' model of the public understanding of science and outline what they describe as an 'interactive model'. Within this latter model, the following characteristics are prominent – as indeed they are also in the other examples discussed in this chapter:

- the boundaries of science are problematic;
- 'science' is usually seen by lay persons as inseparable from its social and institutional connections;
- 'ignorance' may be functional and defensible. What is taken as

'ignorance' by outsiders may actually represent a robust understanding. This is very different from the absence of knowledge;
- people 'engage in the opportunistic construction of syncretic
bodies of practical knowledge'. This fits well with the previous
examples in this book. Contextual knowledges are put together
piecemeal by 'learning through doing' (or *bricolage*);
- '"everyday thinking" and "knowledge in action" are more complex and less well understood than "scientific thinking"'.

We are now in a position to pursue further that final point
through the rapid presentation of other examples. Since the point
is to convey the richness of these examples no attempt will be made
to structure or interlink them.

Sheep farmers, health, safe sex and the workplace

Particularly significant support (and also stimulus) for our discussion of science and citizens has been provided by Brian Wynne's
study of Cumbrian sheep farmers and their response to official
advice regarding radioactive fall-out following the Chernobyl disaster. The sheep farmers under study found themselves facing a ban
on the movement and slaughter of sheep – a ban which became
extended despite initial assurances that it would last only a few
weeks. In keeping with the discussion in this book, Wynne presents
an account of the hill farmers' own knowledges and experience
coming into conflict with the 'official stance' (sanctioned by scientific evidence) of Ministry of Agriculture scientists – a conflict which
was regularly exacerbated by the apparent reluctance of the authorities to listen to the farmers' assessments of sheep behaviour and
local grazing conditions:

> the farmers felt that their whole identity was under threat
> from outside interventions based upon what they saw as
> ignorant but arrogant experts who did not recognize what was
> the central currency of the farmers' social identity, namely their
> specialist hill farming expertise. This expertise was not codified
> anywhere: it was passed down orally and by apprenticeship
> from one generation to the next, as a craft tradition, re-
> inforced in the culture of the area.[29]

According to Wynne's account, the scientists regularly failed to
draw upon the local knowledge of sheep farming – so that official

126

advice was repeatedly found to be mistaken and to be inappropriate to the local conditions (the initial optimism about the dispersion of radioactive pollution was based on analysis of the wrong soil type for the upland areas). The confidence of official assertion also led to credibility loss since such assertions were so often found to be incorrect. Meanwhile, the farmers' own knowledge was implicitly downgraded: 'The farmers had expressed valid and useful specialist knowledge for the conduct and development of science, but this was ignored'.[30]

In terms of the farmers' approach to science, Wynne argues that two models were in operation – the 'conspiracy theory' of science ('they knew all along that the high levels would last much longer than they admitted') and the 'arrogance theory' (which implies unadmitted ignorance within science). However, these apparently anomalous social models sprang from the same incommensurability between the scientists' perspective and that of the hill farmers and from the same credibility gap.

Of course, this credibility gap was experienced by both sides. The farmers' sense of having their social identity denied was matched by the scientists' commitment to their own intellectual and cultural premises:

> The scientists were expressing and reproducing their intellectual-administrative framework of prediction, standardization and control, in which uncertainties were 'naturally' deleted, and contextual objects, such as the farmers and their farms, were standardized and 'black-boxed' in ways consistent with this cultural idiom. Whatever private awareness they may or may not have had of the cultural limits and precommitments of their science, they successfully suppressed these.[31]

This argument about the 'certainty' of official science has of course already emerged clearly in Chapter 4 (especially in the discussion of emergency response) and in this chapter regarding 2,4,5–T and BSE. As Wynne suggests, lay knowledges may actually be more reflexive and self-aware in this respect than scientific expertises: 'it is interesting that those who would be regarded as the representatives of traditional society showed this reflexive capability, whilst the putative representatives of enlightened modernity, namely the scientists, did not'.[32]

Thus, lay accounts may be more open to changing circumstances and new information than the accounts offered by official science –

which seems impervious to renegotiation and revision on the basis of locally generated evidence. Any mismatch is seen as a problem of *application* rather than of the knowledge base itself. For Wynne, the implication of this analysis is that we need to look again at the institutional structures of science – an argument which will be taken up later in this book.

The analysis so far of contextually generated knowledges also fits well with (and once again has been influenced by) current research and discussion in the area of health and sexuality. In a study of the 'ethnography of fatalism', Davison, Frankel and Davey-Smith examine public responses to the risk of coronary heart disease. Their analysis stresses the nature of what they term 'lay epidemiology' – a notion which we have already encountered in the case histories of hazard and environmental threat:

> where cases of illness and death from personal observation, histories known through personal and kin networks, media reports etc. are discussed and analysed. Part of this process is involved with the collection of 'evidence' or 'data' which can be used to support or challenge suspected aetiological processes.[33]

This study focuses particularly on the relationship between official advice on 'looking after your heart' (with, again, its language of authority and certainty) and the everyday experience of the patterning of heart disease (so that some who engage in 'risky' activity survive to old age whilst others with a 'healthy' lifestyle nevertheless suffer or die from coronary ailments). Public responses and conceptualizations of risk typically offer a well-developed cultural system of accountability and explanation which deal both with the general misfortune (why does it happen?) but also with the classic existential issue of 'why does it happen to this particular person at this particular time?' Thus:

> Accounting for the randomness and scatter that exist around epidemiological trends is not a central issue for public health professionals. Rather, they deal with the trends themselves and concern themselves with taking action directed at amending a probabilistic future. Popular health culture, on the other hand, cannot turn its back on any illness or death. Those which violate general principles must also be explained. It is within this context that an ethnography of fatalism is import-

ant, as it seeks to throw light on the cultural structures within which common, but apparently anomalous, events can be accommodated.[34]

In this case, we see the development of 'lay epidemiologies' which run parallel to health orthodoxies but which combine 'technical' assessments with social judgements of the credibility and utility of various health care messages. Once again, we find a robust conceptual model in operation – but one which is considerably broader than that employed by officially sanctioned experts.

Of course, the existence of such models can also create resistances to health care messages – especially when official advice can be undermined by everyday experience of morbidity/mortality and by personal judgements of the need to alter current lifestyles and practices. Thus, for example, the popular notion of 'everything in moderation' (or 'a little of what you fancy does you good') acts as a brake on sudden lifestyle shifts in order to meet the latest official advice. This links also to widespread cynicism about those regular shifts in advice – shifts which, in accordance with the sheep farmer case, are rarely accompanied by any apology or apparent loss of certainty in expert pronouncements.

As Davison *et al.* also note, there is loss of credibility in official advice which focuses constantly on individual and lifestyle changes but says little about environmental degradation or industrial safety. A similar argument has been put forward in the context of cancer prevention where the generally individualistic ideology of medical advice ignores the existence of industrial and environmental carcinogens.[35] Thus, the narrowly focused and selective nature of official health advice creates problems of public reception since citizens operate with a wider conceptual framework of everyday health practice.

This case also stresses that 'contextual knowledges' of the kind developed by citizens do not necessarily reject technical information – although we have seen considerable evidence in these two chapters of scepticism, on the one hand, and perceived irrelevance, on the other. However, such information will be incorporated in specific contexts in an *ad hoc* and selective fashion.

We should avoid automatically placing 'scientific' and 'contextual' knowledges in opposition to each other for at least two reasons. First, because the latter variety may indeed incorporate elements of the former as appropriate (although this may be considerably less than science communicators might prefer). Second, because science is itself a form of contextualized knowledge as the SSK literature so strongly suggests. Put in that form, the problem under discussion is one of working across different contexts of operation but without a recognition of the difficulties created by such a move.

These arguments and issues have also been found in the area of HIV/AIDS and 'safe sex' where the official message has often assumed an ill-informed and '*tabula rasa*' public (this neatly summarized by the message 'don't die of ignorance'). In sharp contrast, a number of studies[36] have examined the social and cultural context in which, for example, condom usage is negotiated. There may be other reasons than ignorance why safe sex is not practised – including a powerlessness within sexual relationships and also a culture of fatalism due to diminished life opportunities.

As in the other cases discussed here, differentials of power and control will form an essential part of everyday knowledges and understandings. Once again also, externally generated messages which depend for their authority on generalized notions of individual behaviour and which fail to recognize the actual context of, in this case, sexual encounters will be regarded with cynicism and ultimate dismissal.

As a final illustration of citizen knowledges and popular epidemiology we should note the activities of workplace-oriented groups and trade unions. The case of 2,4,5-T suggests one example of this. However, Watterson, in a discussion of occupational health in the gas industry traces an earlier example of popular epidemiology which he defines as: 'the process by which lay persons gather statistics and other information and also direct and marshal the knowledge and resources of experts in order to understand the epidemiology of disease'.[37]

Watterson's account describes not only the hazardous working conditions of the gas industry in the late nineteenth and early twentieth centuries but also efforts on the part of gas workers to gain recognition for those hazards. In a detailed chronology of 'gas workers' knowledge' and 'scientific' evidence, the identification of hazard by the workers themselves is highlighted: 'Recognition of hazards and potential hazards was not restricted to "expert" researchers in the field but came much earlier through workers and, in some instances, their representatives too'.[38]

As Watterson notes, the emergence of such worker evidence is hardly special to this case but can be found in numerous areas of occupational health:

> The story is not unique: similar tales exist for asbestos workers, plastics workers, textile workers – mule spinners with cancer and byssinosis, welders and foundry workers with respiratory diseases, engineering workers with vibration-induced white finger and shipbuilders with occupational disease.[39]

These cases suggest the struggle of citizens to have their knowledges substantiated by expert testimony and then acted upon. In this, Watterson's account of the gas workers sounds very similar to Wynne's account of the sheep farmers or the other examples offered in this chapter.

Science and citizenship: freeing the voices

> The formal language of science, however, was a language of certainty. The formal language of science was a language of mastery and domination. The formal language of science was a language which denied its social origins and its human limitations. These basic features of scientific culture were dangerous . . . because they were exported beyond the realm of laboratory practice and applied inappropriately in the attempt to conquer the unique, ever-changing, immeasurably complex and interconnected events of the everyday world.[40]

All of the examples in this and the previous chapter suggest a problematic relationship between the formalized knowledges of science and the local understandings generated within everyday life. Put at its weakest, the discussion in this and the previous chapters suggests the inappropriateness of most enlightenment assumptions about the public understanding of science. These cases suggest not a failure of scientific dissemination but a more fundamental social gap between different forms of understanding and expertise.

Put more positively, we can discern the existence of lay knowledges which might enrich decision-making processes and the general knowledge of hazard and health issues – but which are currently excluded due to their supposed 'irrationality' and anecdotal nature. From the perspective of a concerned citizen, this does indeed seem insulting, provocative and detrimental to notions of self-identity and citizenship – it also offers little hope of a socially sustainable process of societal and technological development (as we will explore in Chapter 7).

The local and contextual knowledges which we have examined are (by definition) very different from each other in form and focus. The examples discussed so far also raise many different questions and issues – to which we will return in the final chapters of this book. At this stage, and by way of preliminary summary, it is possible to identify certain general characteristics.

In the first place, we have seen the social and cultural 'groundedness' of such knowledges – in that sense, local knowledges typically offer well-tested models of complex areas of reality. This is not necessarily to privilege such knowledges or to downgrade science. Such an assertion would simply replace one dominant knowledge system with another. The contemporary challenge is to move away from such a rigid framework – to free the voices.

Nevertheless, as the quotation from Mulkay at the beginning of this section argues strongly, scientific forms of understanding may struggle to grasp this contextual knowledge – and, moreover, may deliberately seek to label it as anecdotal and merely experiential in order to protect the privileged status of science. Scientific failure at the local level will generally be diagnosed as a minor matter of inappropriate application or variance from the norm – rather than as a major area of cognitive and institutional challenge for the activities of science.

Equally, the notion that untrained members of the public can offer valid understandings of technical issues is heretical to science – it undermines much of the institutional separation of science from other social activities. This separation has historically been essential to the activities of science. Such a separation – and the underlying model of rationality on which it is based – also seems central to 'modernity' as a wider social structure.

Our discussion so far has highlighted the existence of 'popular epidemiologies' – of lay groups and individuals as active as well as passive participants in the 'living laboratory'. At one level, the existence of such knowledges seems unremarkable – as Watterson puts it succinctly: 'the gas workers recognized the polluted nature of their environment because they worked there'.[41]

What this apparently simple observation omits (and as Watterson recognizes) is the difficulty for lay groups of gaining recognition for their highly relevant expertise. As we have seen, official channels of advice and decision-making currently exclude public understandings from the status of 'expertise'.

One aspect of this difficulty is that such knowledges typically engage simultaneously with questions which conventional science tries to keep apart (e.g., knowledge of hazard and judgements of the credibility of various sources of hazard information). Within this form of understanding, issues of risk *analysis* do not separate from those of *evaluation*. In that sense, it may be sensible to consider the existence of popular *epistemologies* as well as epidemiologies, i.e., forms of knowledge which are considerably wider in their focus than the analyses of scientists and which rest on rather different premises (although one also needs to be careful lest this should imply acceptance of the scientists' own account of their epistemological framework, e.g., their claims to offer 'decontextualized knowledge'). As Layton *et al.* put this: 'The relationship between scientific knowledge and other forms of local and particular knowledges amounts to a challenge to an epistemology of science that rests on the belief that the world is separate from the scientific observer'.[42]

Thus, for the farmworkers it was simply nonsensical to separate the assessment of pesticide safety from its social conditions of use or from an evaluation of the trustworthiness of the regulatory authority. Contextual knowledges also make little claim to definitive status – they are admittedly constructed by bricolage and, as Wynne argues,[43] are open to regular rethinking and alteration.

Typically also in the cases we have examined they are 'knowledges for doing' – they are highly practical, case-specific and instrumental in orientation with no necessary claim to general theory or application elsewhere. All this contrasts sharply with the statements of science and is, once again, deeply challenging to science which depends for its authority on the notion of impartial judgement and generalized (or 'universalistic') objectivity.

Finally, in this chapter we need to link these very empirical studies to the analysis of modernity, late modernity and the 'risk society'. Certainly, the cases presented here fit very well with a 'late modern' analysis – especially one which portrays such citizen groups as struggling against the knowledge-authority structures of modernity. At the same time, however, there may be a hint of the 'traditional' or 'pre-modern' in many of these cases – of citizen groups struggling to express values and understandings which may have preceded the discourses of science. As Zonabend puts it in an illuminating study of one French community (at la Hague in Normandy) and its complex interaction with the nearby nuclear fuel reprocessing plant: 'Modernity has not swept tradition away. The fact is tradition has a surprising way of re-emerging where we least expect it'.[44]

In that sense, discussion of the late modern may also necessitate a discussion of values and community networks which may be suggestive of the pre-modern (as cases such as the sheep farmers also suggest).

So far, these chapters have counterposed the knowledge structures of 'citizens' and 'scientists' in rather stark fashion. However, it also seems important to our discussion that we recognize and consider the various attempts which have been made to bridge these institutional and cognitive categories. Such cases may be less typical of science–citizen interactions (and 'counter expertise' may well, as we have already noted, simply recycle science-centred notions in an apparently 'alternative' format). Nevertheless they may both highlight issues of 'citizen science' but also suggest constructive ways forward for science, citizenship and sustainable development. That at least is the rationale for Chapter 6.

6

BUILDING SUSTAINABLE FUTURES: SCIENCE SHOPS AND SOCIAL EXPERIMENTS

The discussion (about social and technological development) that has begun in the offices of scientific consultants to government agencies basically has to be transferred to the broader political forum of the general public. The same holds for the dialogue now going on between scientists and politicians about the formulation of a long-term research policy.

(Habermas)[1]

How do we combine the benefits of specialized knowledge and expertise with life in a sector where no group is unduly dominant, no group unduly pressed upon by another? . . . It is a problem which neither Habermas nor anyone else has even begun to solve, even at the level of theory. It could indeed be that the problem is an insoluble one.[2]

It's the first time anybody bothered asking us how we felt.
(Native spokesperson at the Mackenzie Valley Pipeline Inquiry)[3]

The previous two chapters have stood conventional models of science–citizen interactions on their head; rather than simply problematizing public ignorance, we have asked questions about science and the limits to its application within real-world situations. As was argued in Chapter 3, however, prevailing approaches to policy-making have characteristically been based on a set of assumptions which place science at their very core. The public are seated ringside but certainly not at the centre of the environmental action – at least so far as 'official' decision-making processes are concerned.

Of course, important international documents like the Brundtland Report (or *Our Common Future* which sought to provide a new

135

international framework for development and the environment) have already made the case for greater social democracy in this area:

> Making the difficult choices involved in sustainable develop-ment will depend on the widespread support and involvement of an informed public and of non-governmental organizations, the scientific community and industry. Their rights, roles and participation in development planning, decision making and project implementation should be expanded.[4]

This emphasis on social equity and citizen participation is gener-ally swept away whenever national governments begin to tackle 'sustainability' – once again policy becomes government-led and naturalistic. The environmental agenda is somehow set by 'Nature' (as unproblematically defined by scientific institutions) and the contribution of citizens is diminished to that of responding 'pos-itively' to that agenda. Whilst recent statements of government policy build upon the rhetoric of 'our' common future, the sug-gested citizen actions are generally individualistic in character and show little concern to attack underlying questions of power and equity:

> Although the Government has to be in the lead, responsibility for the environment is shared by all of us; it is not a duty for Government alone. Businesses, central and local government, schools and voluntary bodies and individuals must all work together to take good care of our common inheritance. *That is a job for us all.*[5]

Within this ideological framework, the 'responsibility' falls to us all but only once we follow the government's lead. Equally, and as might be expected, there is little attempt to build upon the citizen knowledges and epistemologies discussed in the last two chapters. Characteristically, these currently marginalized expertises define the 'environment' as part of a wider set of issues and as linked to everyday life and the construction of self-identity.

Seen from the dominant environmental paradigm, this difference in epistemology and understanding renders citizen views weak and poorly articulated. However, it can also be argued that citizen voices provide a useful antidote to prevailing notions of scientific and technological determinism. Typically also they stress the com-plexity of locally identified environmental problems rather than regarding these as minor difficulties. This will in turn have consequences for our understanding of the *causes* of environmental harm. As Beck expresses this:

> From the outset, techno-economic innovations as a motor for permanent social change have been excluded from the possibility of democratic consultation, monitoring and resistance. Therefore a number of contradictions are built into the design of the innovation process, and these are opening up today.[6]

It is possible, therefore, that a constructive dialogue between these diverse knowledges and epistemologies can 'install brakes and a steering wheel into the "non-steering" of the racing techno-scientific development'.[7] As this whole book suggests, a reappraisal of the relationship between science and citizenship is essential to such processes. In particular, it may follow that the necessary level of social and cognitive change cannot be achieved by government-led and science-centred strategies. In such a situation, contextual understandings may be at the heart of a sustainable pattern of socio-economic development.

Now, in developing a 'symmetrical' analysis of science, citizenship and social sustainability, it is also essential that we consider those attempts that have already been made to deal creatively and constructively with the social dislocations described so far. Certainly, it is important that we review previous initiatives (or perhaps 'social experiments' from the perspective of *Citizen Science*[8]) in this area if we are to offer anything more than merely programmatic statements.

In so doing, the concept of 'social learning' will be especially significant – defined here in terms of the wider implications for science, citizenship and sustainability which can be drawn from individual examples or 'experiments'. On that basis, this chapter's main objective is to offer a brief review of attempts since the 1970s aimed at straddling the current divide between 'science/technology' and 'citizens'. What policy and analytical lessons can we draw from this important area of experience?

Some notion of the difficulties within current science–citizen relations can be gauged from what we can term the *participatory dilemma*; put simply, should citizen groups participate in science-centred decision-making processes (such as those discussed in Chapter 3) which appear heavily stacked against them or stay clear and be effectively disenfranchised?

In one illustration of this dilemma, Smith examined the use of quantitative risk analysis within British public inquiries (notably at Canvey Island and Ellesmere Port) and noted its consequence of excluding the kinds of concern discussed in Chapter 4 and, consequently, downgrading public involvement in decision-making.[9] In such circumstances, and as we have already suggested, citizen groups appear almost overwhelmingly disadvantaged in the face of the greater resources of government and industry. Scientific resources become ammunition for the defence of certain social positions – is it wise then for citizen groups even to go into battle? As Nelkin has put the argument with regard to attempts at enhanced 'public participation':

> Such efforts can serve several objectives; they may increase direct public influence on the formation of policy, or merely inform policy makers about public concerns. More often, they are a means to win acceptance and facilitate the implementation of decisions already made.[10]

These issues can be readily illustrated with reference to the 1977 Windscale Inquiry in Britain.[11] The Inquiry concerned the plans by British Nuclear Fuels Ltd (BNFL) to build a thermal oxide reprocessing plant (THORP) in West Cumbria. It was chaired by a High Court Judge (Mr Justice Parker) and run on a semi-legal and adversarial basis. Moreover, the burden of proof was placed on the *objectors* rather than the proponents (i.e., it was for them to disprove BNFL's case rather than for the nuclear industry to prove it). A number of further characteristics of the Inquiry placed the objectors at a disadvantage:

- the emphasis placed by Mr Justice Parker on 'the *facts* of government policy not its merits';
- the imbalance in resources between BNFL and its opponents – no government support was given to the objectors despite the need for legal counsel and technical witnesses;
- the organization of the Inquiry by a sequence of witnesses rather than by issues – this caused problems of co-ordination for groups whose strategy was evolving over the course of the Inquiry;
- uncertainty amongst oppositional groups over the correct tactics to adopt in the face of such an inquiry process – and also competition between the groups – led to fragmentation and a lack of co-ordination. Should they adopt a conventionally 'technical' argument in order to beat BNFL scientists at their own game or

should they simply call for the abolition of nuclear energy on ethical and explicitly value-oriented grounds?[12]

These characteristics were strongly reinforced by the eventual conclusion of the Inquiry as presented by Mr Justice Parker in early 1978. The report recommended full-scale development of THORP and swept aside the arguments of the objectors. Whilst this conclusion was obviously controversial, it is the rejection of oppositional evidence which is particularly significant for our discussion. As *Nature* noted at the time:

> Parker was there to decide, not to illuminate controversy. . . . Once (he) had decided that the decision should go in BNFL's favour he went out of his way to find for them on almost every issue – rather as a judge confronted by a bunch of witnesses prepared to testify to a man's innocence, might dismiss their evidence *in toto* once satisfied that the man was guilty.[13]

Certainly, the Parker Report left many oppositional groups convinced that their testimony had been misunderstood and misportrayed – leaving them to doubt the value of their own participation. Whilst the Inquiry was useful for the environmentalist lobby in some ways (e.g., by making data available which might otherwise have remained secret), as an exercise in science–citizen interaction (and in citizen–legal interaction) it seems to have failed. The very structure of the Inquiry – and especially its legalistic and scientistic base – militated against a wider exchange of views and understandings. The outcome of the Inquiry left oppositional groups wondering particularly whether it would be worthwhile to participate in future nuclear inquiries. Such an approach to decision-making is very reminiscent of the encounters over BSE, major hazards or 2,4,5–T.

Of course, and as we will discuss, this brief discussion of the Windscale Inquiry does not suggest that all forms of public participation will inevitably fail in the same fashion. Nor, and this point needs full emphasis, does it suggest that *science* (whether as an institution or as an epistemology) is solely to blame for such situations. However, we are presented with a clear example of how current procedures work against the expression of a broader range of voices and understandings.

Certainly, and although the brief account above fits well with the analysis offered in the previous two chapters, it does not imply that all science–citizen encounters will follow the same pattern. In particular, it serves to remind us that mere 'participation' is not enough, since such attempts can be designed to serve a number of purposes and will necessarily embody assumptions about the relative authority to be granted to different social actors and bodies of expertise. These assumptions have most typically been science-centred in character. Accordingly, participation may well be designed to achieve legitimation rather than social dialogue.

In order to deal with these issues, we need to clarify the kinds of requirement for 'science–citizen dialogue' which have so far been implicit in the discussion.

In studying the practice of these initiatives, we will have certain criteria of evaluation in mind which follow from our analysis so far. These can best be represented as a series of questions:

- Does the 'social experiment' permit the expression and development of wider social judgements, e.g., concerning the credibility and trustworthiness of institutions?
- Do practical initiatives offer the possibility for enhancing rather than downgrading citizen knowledge? In particular, is it possible for public groups to be seen as knowledge generators as well as receptors?
- What model of science is assumed by such initiatives? In particular, are they based on the notion of science as consensual, homogeneous and apart from social and technical controversy?
- Do various forms of public participation and science–citizen interaction permit real policy change (e.g., at the level of governmental or industrial practice)? More particularly, can there be identified a longer-term implication for future research directions and for the organization of scientific practices? The concept of 'social learning' implies that this level of institutional change may be one of the most valuable outcomes of science–citizen encounters.

These questions are only indicative and certainly not comprehensive. However, they do illustrate the kinds of practical re-examination which are required once a citizen-oriented rather than enlightenment perspective is adopted. Clearly also, these questions go beyond the specific focus of policy decisions and address social and technical progress at a wider level.

Nevertheless, and very fundamentally, there is an assumption underlying all of these questions that 'science' and 'citizen needs' can indeed prove compatible and mutually beneficial. The very basis of social experimentation in this area is that citizens can benefit from exposure to science (and vice versa) – even if current social and institutional processes (of the kind discussed in Chapter 4, for example) are somehow obstructing this flow of information and mutual understanding. This important point provides the major analytical perspective to this chapter. It will be explicitly developed here through one specific 'ideal type' of science–citizen mediation – the Science Shop.

These lines of enquiry will be considered first of all with regard to one important document – the 1979 OECD report significantly entitled *Technology on Trial*. During the following account, special emphasis will be placed on initiatives which would appear to offer (or at least have the capacity to offer) an approach which goes beyond 'downward' dissemination.

Technology on Trial: early efforts at participation

The report in question was produced by the Organization for Economic Co-operation and Development (OECD) as part of a general initiative aimed at devising 'effective means of informing the public of the implications of new technological developments, soliciting their reactions, and engaging them in decision-making processes'. In many ways, this publication is quite distinct from the aims and objectives of *Citizen Science*:

> This study attempts to address . . . how governments have responded to the demand for greater participation on the part of the public in decisions concerning science and technology. It looks at the process of public participation largely from the *point of view of government, not from the perspective of citizens or citizen groups.*[14]

Despite this, *Technology on Trial* offers an excellent representation of the 'state of the art' with regard to 'public participation' as of the late 1970s. Moreover, the 1970s were something of a high water-mark for these issues so that the broad framework established by the OECD report is still valid today.

The OECD report identifies four main categories of government response to 'public pressures for more direct participation in decision-making on issues related to science and technology':

informing the public, informing policy-makers, reconciling conflicting interests, collaborative decision-making. In this summary,
the first two will be given special prominence.

Informing the public

This category includes 'public access to information' (e.g., the US
Freedom of Information Act) and 'information on the nature, scope
and timing of decision-making' (as provided, for example, by the
Federal Register). However, of greatest relevance here is the third
item within this category: 'government efforts aimed at improving
(sic) public understanding on scientific and technologically-related
matters'. The OECD stresses the range of activities which fit within
this category. This range encompasses both 'highly centralized' and
'decentralized' initiatives, e.g., government-coordinated vs local and
non-governmental programmes (although government funding does
not necessarily lead to centralization). It also covers a broad scope
in terms of topics (from the US National Aeronautical and Space
Administration (NASA) programme specifically aimed at informing
the public about space and space investigation through to very
general campaigns). The activities vary too in terms of the extent to
which 'they are purposefully aimed at encouraging broad-scale
public discussion and debate' rather than 'disseminating the facts'.

In addition, therefore, to the questions posed above, we have the
emergence of other (albeit linked) evaluative criteria: degree of
centralization, topic coverage, linkage to discussion/debate (as
opposed to simply 'dissemination'). On this basis, we can now
examine the actual practical efforts in the area of 'public understanding' considered by the OECD. These include:

Study circle mechanisms   For example, the Swedish system of small
study groups – largely *ad hoc*, decentralized and funded by the State
– were established to initiate discussion and understanding of the
civil nuclear power programme. As described by the OECD, the
Swedish government had two central objectives in undertaking its
overall 'energy public education programme' – broadening the base
of decision-making and establishing a consensus on energy policy.
The study circle mechanism (which has origins in Sweden going
back at least a century) had the capacity to meet both of these.
However, the Swedish experience can be seen as offering 'decidedly
mixed results':

On the one hand, the reports from the study groups suggest continued and sometimes increased uncertainty and confusion. Moreover, subsequent surveys on the direct effect of the study circles on public attitudes, showed only slight differences in opinion between participants and non-participants. On the other hand, inquiries into the impact on attitudes of the four public hearings held in late 1974 and early 1975 indicated some shift in terms of enhanced public sympathy for the government position.[15]

Thus, initiatives such as the study circles do not necessarily lead to consensus – but can instead cause polarization. As has been noted in a separate study of public attitudes to nuclear power: 'knowledge does not foster positive attitudes; on the contrary, those with negative attitudes are motivated to acquire knowledge and to construe it in support of their case'.[16]

Public information campaigns The 1979 OECD report examined the experience of several countries in this area. Austria, Canada, Denmark, France and Germany had all experimented with such campaigns. In Germany, for example, the government initiated a publicity campaign from 1975 onwards aimed largely at explaining government views with respect to nuclear energy. The campaign covered public advertisements and the dissemination of technical reports, public seminars and discussions, the stimulation of seminars and activities aimed at 'target population groups', the preparation of 'energy information packages' for schools and adult education centres, efforts to engage with political parties and the large employer and trade union organizations. The OECD estimates that some $6 million were spent on these activities during the three-year period 1976–8.

The OECD make a number of observations about this German programme. First of all, that it was largely opposed by anti-nuclear groups as 'nuclear propaganda' – an observation which fits in well with the previous analysis in this book. Second, that such an information campaign did little to impede or prevent the growth of a strong nuclear protest movement. Third, that it is difficult to detect any discernible effect on public opinion more widely. However, the German initiative can also be compared with the experience of other countries – in which case, a series of further points emerge.

143

First, that initiatives must reflect wider culture and national traditions – thus the 'study circle' mechanism, for example, may not be easily (if at all) transportable to other countries. This is clearly an important point when attempting to draw lessons from international experience.

Second, that national experience of public information campaigns tends to be rather *ad hoc* and fragmented so that governments have typically not taken a long-term role in this area.

Third, and very importantly for our discussion, that the objectives of, for example, governments in this area may vary substantially (even, one might add, within a single country over time). However, 'education' does not in general appear to have been such an objective:

> the education of the public, in the narrow classical sense, does not appear to have been the single or primary aim of these activities. In many cases, the main motivations behind decisions to initiate public information campaigns appear to have been to defuse controversy, gain time and thus avoid having to take quick decisions that might have politically divisive repercussions. In some instances, the purpose of such campaigns has included the legitimising function of seeking to lend credibility and legitimacy to governmental decisions, past and pending.[17]

Finally, the OECD report notes that public 'education' needs to go beyond points of technical detail and instead embrace wider social, economic and political aspects of scientific and technological developments. Thus, in an argument which again fits with the analysis offered in previous chapters, it is suggested that national experiences such as the above indicate that the general public is not especially interested in the technical detail of, for example, nuclear energy generation. Instead, broader issues of reactor safety, fuel reprocessing and waste disposal are seen as much more important to public groups. The public treatment of these issues will in turn relate to matters of trust and credibility: 'Acceptance on the part of the public of certain risks appears to be heavily dependent both upon its government's ability to weigh all of these factors and on public trust in government institutions, their legitimacy and credibility'.[18]

Seen in this broader perspective, government initiatives in this area may have served a most useful purpose:

Though they may not have resulted in a higher level of citizen technical expertise in these matters, they have contributed toward making a large section of the general public more aware of the broader set of factors surrounding, for instance, the nuclear debate; a debate previously dominated by industrial interests and by exclusively scientific and technological considerations, capacities and expertise.[19]

Science education programmes As defined by the OECD, initiatives in this area are designed to promote 'public understanding' in general. The United States and The Netherlands are singled out by the OECD for their activity in this area.

Within the United States, for example, the National Science Foundation's (NSF) efforts in promoting the public understanding of science are noted. Special attention is paid to decentralized activities within this programme such as state and local discussions, conferences and workshops. Within the 'Science for Citizens' programme attempts had been made to develop mechanisms which would provide citizens with the technical information necessary for effective participation in decision-making. One attempt at this was through 'Public Service Science Residencies' and 'Internships' whereby individual scientists and engineers could lend their expertise to citizen organizations.

However, the OECD also reports that in the US (as elsewhere) controversy had developed over financial assistance to citizen groups – just how far should the government go in supporting opposition to what would often be its own plans and initiatives?

Science, technology and the media Finally, within the discussion of 'informing the public' the OECD noted the relationship between media reports and public attitudes towards science.

The media have brought government decision-making processes under closer public scrutiny and have provided citizens with more timely information on all aspects of daily life than ever before. . . . However, media coverage of issues related to science and technology is often uneven, incomplete and highly selective.[20]

It must also be noted that the mass media have played only a minor role in the cases discussed in this book. Almost by definition, such media seem remote from the knowledges and problem definitions of differentiated publics.

In overall conclusion to this section, the OECD offers a number of comments which still remain important – including the significance of institutional credibility and issues of 'public ignorance':

> Finally, and most importantly, one must place the problem of public information and understanding (or the alleged lack thereof) in the proper perspective. . . . Many of those who oppose certain scientific or technological programmes are extremely well-informed as to their details and associated risks. Nor can attitudes of public scepticism be explained by one reason alone. Often they result from a broad panoply of public concerns and misgivings about the social goals to be pursued, the protective measures to be taken, and the way costs and benefits are to be distributed in society-at-large.[21]

The OECD report also addresses the relationship between knowledge and action:

> access to information without effective means for its use is like possessing a lever without a fulcrum. Public demands for information are, therefore, closely associated with demands for broader and more direct opportunities for public participation in government decision-making.[22]

Informing policy-makers

In this chapter of *Technology on Trial*, the relationship between policy-making and citizen groups is considered. Thus, advisory bodies (a category which would include the Advisory Committee on Pesticides) are seen to be very limited in this respect: 'Advisory mechanisms are . . . only of limited utility as a mechanism for broad-scale public participation. Most citizens lack the time, expertise or interest required'.[23]

Legislative and parliamentary hearings are discussed also. The main attention, however, is given to 'commissions of inquiry'. Two examples of these are considered in some detail – the Windscale Inquiry (discussed earlier) and the Mackenzie Valley Pipeline Inquiry held in Canada during the mid-1970s. Since the latter inquiry has been one of the most discussed examples of attempted 'public participation' (and because it presents a sharp contrast to the conduct of the Windscale Inquiry) it is worth a brief overview here. The OECD report summarized the difference between the two inquiries in the following terms:

> If the Windscale Inquiry can be partially characterized as a trial between competing facts and competing logics, then the Mackenzie Valley Pipeline Inquiry was a consciousness-raising teach-in. One was to the other like a courtroom to a school.[24]

The official purpose of the inquiry concerned the social, economic and environmental impact of a proposed natural gas pipeline in the Northwest Territories and the Yukon. Formal hearings began in March 1975 and ended in November 1976. However, one major contrast with the Windscale Inquiry can be established if we consider the diversity of hearings which were conducted and the attempt which they suggest to draw in as wide a range of views (including values and knowledges) as possible:

- **preliminary** hearings which highlighted the issues and, for example, expanded the inquiry so as to cover all potential activities relating to the Mackenzie Valley corridor;
- **formal** hearings which were organized on the basis of full disclosure and availability of all relevant information;
- **special** hearings which received evidence from potential gas producers;
- **Southern** hearings: these were held in large cities across Canada and had the effect of bringing these issues to the attention of the larger Canadian population;
- very importantly for our discussion, **community** hearings: these were held in twenty-eight cities, towns, villages and settlements in Northern Canada and were informal in style;
- In particular, witnesses were not cross-examined – they simply (as the OECD report nicely puts it) 'spoke what was on their mind'.

As the OECD explains this, there were two main consequences of such public participation and accessibility. First of all, underlying values could emerge in a manner which would simply be impossible within the framework of a Windscale Inquiry or advisory committee based and incremental approach adopted by industry. The disagreement over the very notion of 'land' symbolized this basic value dispute. As one spokesperson made the point at a community hearing:

The land belongs not only to the people presently living, but it belongs to past generations and the future generations that are yet to be born. Past and future generations are as much a part of the tribal entity as the living generation. Not only that, but the land belongs not only to human beings but also to other living things; they too have an interest.[25]

Second, and equally important for the general argument of this book, different forms of knowledge (and, especially, contextually generated knowledge) could emerge without fear of expert demolition. As the OECD puts this very tellingly:

Testimony at the community hearings from non-technical persons also demonstrated the fallibility of the conventional belief that only people with specialised technical knowledge should make decisions about technological matters. Time and again it was the so-called 'non-experts' who provided important insights and information concerning such natural phenomena as, for example the vulnerability of the Beaufort Sea, seabed ice scour, and native hunting and trapping practices. This 'non-expert' testimony provided the elements of a more comprehensive understanding of both quantitative and qualitative impacts of the proposed development project.[26]

Thus, the Mackenzie Valley Pipeline Inquiry and the Windscale Inquiry appeared to embody very different sets of assumptions about *values* and the importance of their expression, about *knowledge and expertise* and the possession of this by different social groups, and about *citizenship* and the intrinsic merits of achieving a broad base of involvement and participation. The two inquiries clearly operated on different notions of the very nature of social and technical development – with the latter seemingly attempting to find the 'rational' way forward whilst the former openly embraced a diversity of scenarios and social assumptions.

Whilst the Mackenzie Valley model has problems of its own – not least at the levels of cost, time delay and the ultimate necessity of imposing a decision – it does suggest one approximate model for More particularly, the Inquiry also suggests that large-scale decision-making structures are not necessarily insensitive to citizen values and understandings.

148

Reconciling conflicting interests

This section of the OECD report considers governmental efforts aimed at responding to 'new participatory demands'. Such efforts cover administrative decision-making, regulatory decision-making and citizen recourse to the legal system through administrative and judicial appeal. As Jasanoff has since noted, there is considerable potential for citizen challenge to decision-making through such legal processes.[27]

Collaborative decision-making

> What distinguishes more collaborative modes of participation is the inclusion of representatives of the general public, not just as informants but as partners in negotiation, with some power to ensure that decisions taken will reflect public concerns.[28]

As the above quotation makes clear, this important category is concerned with social experiments aimed at incorporating the public within the actual decision-making process. The referendum offers one rather controversial model of this – such national, state and local referenda have been employed in a small number of countries with regard to nuclear issues (e.g., in California or, to a limited degree, in parts of Western Europe).

New initiatives have also been proposed in this area as a means of resolving technically related disputes in an open and accountable fashion. One such possibility – which was originally proposed in the 1960s – is the Science Court concept. This can take a number of forms but has basically been conceived as a forum whereby members of the public, representatives of government (whether local or national) and scientists could discuss and confront each other in a relatively structured fashion. 'Such a discussion could contribute to the clarification of the nature of technical disagreements and their relationship to political concerns and values.'[29]

In the overall conclusion to *Technology on Trial*, a number of further points are made about public participation, information and understanding.[30] One important issue for the OECD study concerns the *timing* of information provision – the public needs to be informed 'not just after issues have become politicised and opinions polarised, but at the stage when policy goals and objectives are being formulated'.[31]

This implies, as the quotation from Habermas at the beginning of this chapter also suggests, that public discussion should not just be an 'end-point' activity, i.e., to be initiated after the processes of technology development have run their course. This seems an important point for any discussion of 'sustainable futures'. The report also calls for 'more pluralistic sources of information' – a point made in Chapter 4 with regard to communities facing hazard issues. However, information and action must be interlinked:

> as we have attempted to show in this report, information and the promotion of a more informed citizenry is but one facet of public participation. Equally important is the possibility and opportunity for citizens to express themselves in decision-making processes and forums. Public demand for such forms of participation pose (sic) a new challenge to representative government.[32]

Science and Technology on Trial: discussion and development

As can already be gathered from discussion here and in the previous chapters, the agenda and framework presented by the OECD in 1979 still has considerable validity today. This, of course, reflects partly the perspicacious nature of *Technology on Trial* but also the comparatively little progress that was made on these issues through the 1980s. Furthermore, some of the initiatives described above have actually lost government support and funding. Thus, Layton *et al.* note the termination in 1981 of the NSF Science for Citizens Programme – which was seen as being of lower priority than basic scientific research.[33] This example, of course, raises many questions about the relative significance of this whole area within science budgets.

Rather than moving further into this descriptive mode, however, it is worth pausing to consider some of the questions, issues and points of tension that have been revealed in the brief account above. Earlier in this chapter, a list of general evaluative criteria for assessing 'citizen–science experiments' was proposed. The examples relate to these criteria – and also the underlying questions which must be considered. These issues and questions relate back in turn to the 'participatory dilemma' raised above.

If we work through the above questions, we can see first of all that these experiments vary considerably in the extent to which they 'permit the expression and development of social judgements'. Thus, the Windscale Inquiry with its legalistic and scientist basis offered only very limited scope for such expressions – and then reinforced this with its final report which went even further in terms of excluding 'irrelevant' argumentation. Such a situation seems to be a consequence of the science-centredness of decision-making processes as presented in Chapter 3. In contrast, the Mackenzie Valley Pipeline Inquiry made real efforts at 'listening to the voices'. However, the obvious conclusion is that the mere existence of 'public participation' does not guarantee that broad discussion will be permitted – nor even when it is allowed that such discussion will actually have an impact on decision-making processes. 'Participation' without a willingness to broaden the scope of discussion and to establish appropriate social processes and procedures for the representation of views will remain reductionist in approach.

This point links closely with the notion of public groups as knowledge generators as well as receptors – do participatory mechanisms enhance or downgrade such understandings? There is a clear potential in the above cases for 'downgrading' to occur due to the 'enlightenment' model discussed extensively in this book. Certainly, there does seem to be a general 'top-down' assumption embedded within most participatory mechanisms – at least on the evidence as presented so far. Enlightenment notions appear strong in most – if not all – these examples. Thus, the Swedish study centre experience seems to have disappointed due to its failure to create consensus. However, there is no guarantee that public debate will lead to consensus even if it does generate an improved level of understanding and policy legitimation. Indeed, the analysis in this book suggests that public exposure to scientific arguments will lead to greater awareness – but that this awareness may heighten uncertainties and awaken controversial issues rather than eliminate them. This seems an inevitable characteristic of contemporary society – the old certainties and possibilities of consensus may no longer hold sway.

The above evaluative questions also raise issues of the policy changes and research implications which emerge from these cases. As the OECD report argues, without the possibility of such change there will be little motivation for involvement and knowledge-seeking – a point made also in Chapter 4. The above cases suggest that many of these initiatives may be designed for legitimatory purposes rather than attempting to achieve change. Differences in the motivation for 'social experiments' will have major consequences in terms of their capacity for social and institutional learning.

A number of key points therefore emerge from this discussion:

• the significance of not just *whether* such initiatives take place but also their objectives and underlying assumptions;
• the significance of the link to practical action. As has already been argued here, citizen participation will not be taken seriously (unless as part of an institutional attempt at legitimation) unless it has the potential for achieving change (whether in terms of political and industrial decisions or the establishment of research priorities). Change requires considerable sensitivity to the timing of debate – typically, matters of social consequence are only raised *after* the innovation process has run its course.[34] This is a severe impediment to citizen participation;
• the significance of three sets of assumptions within these initiatives: assumptions about the place of wider *values* within debate (a dimension which is typically stressed by citizen groups); assumptions about *knowledge* and who possesses that knowledge; assumptions about *citizenship* and the role of democratic involvement.

These issues can be further illustrated by considering other initiatives. Thus, for example, a major public debate in The Netherlands concerned with energy policy began in 1981 and continued until 1985.[35] The 'broad national debate' (known as 'BMD') had a series of objectives which marked it apart from many other initiatives. In particular, it was designed to stimulate wide discussion, create a favourable climate to public participation, and to provide 'well-balanced' (but not 'objective' or 'neutral') information on energy issues. Discussion meetings were organized across The Netherlands on the basis that every Dutch citizen could attend a meeting within 7 km of their home. TV, radio and schools also played a part within the debate. As a genuine exercise in participation, this initiative seems to meet a number of important criteria. However, it suffered from a government reaction to the report which one of BMD's prime organizers has described as 'very disappointing' (a fate which also befell the Mackenzie Valley Pipeline Inquiry). This in turn 'deepened the credibility gap between citizens and politics, people and power' – suggesting again the significance of practical response if such initiatives are not to become devalued.

It is also important to note the relevance of worker participation in technological decision-making. Of course, trade unions represent one important manifestation of citizenship – even if, as with environmentalist groups, they may also operate predominantly within enlightenment assumptions about science and expertise.

The most discussed example of worker-led action in this context must be the 'alternative plans' of Lucas Aerospace workers in the mid-1970s. Lucas Aerospace was at that time a major British defence contractor. In response to management plans for redundancies and factory closures, the Lucas Aerospace Combine Shop Stewards Committee launched an 'alternative corporate plan' in January 1976. The 'plan' drew on the technical skills of workers in order to put forward a concrete and practical set of proposals for the redeployment of the workforce. The plan was considered 'socially useful' by the Combine since it promoted health and safety, the conservation of energy and the 'humanization' of work. Specific proposals included heat pumps, kidney machines and a road/rail vehicle. Neither management nor the government supported this venture – illustrating not just the significance of knowledge but also the need for the organizational power to put this into practice.[36]

Nevertheless, as Loet Leydesdorff and Peter van den Besselaar have noted in a useful review,[37] it has stimulated such plans elsewhere – including some twenty-nine cases in The Netherlands by the mid-1980s. However, such plans have typically not engaged at the level of R&D, nor do they seem to have served as an input to scientific research institutes – suggesting a singular lack of interaction between workers and scientists.

> The evaluations reported above stand in sharp contrast to the increase in the ability of management in knowledge-intensive industries to direct technological developments in a way which suits the interests of their company. Even when resources are made available and R&D personnel in the public service are willing to do research on labour-oriented questions, the workers' point of view does not seem to penetrate to the level of longer-term scientific and technological development.[38]

Of course, this difficulty for even such a relatively well-organized public group as trade unionists suggests the greater difficulty for other citizen groups in gaining influence over the processes of scientific and technological development.

The results are even more depressing – from a point of view of participation of labour in the knowledge society – than we had expected them to be. They are depressing, because we cannot think of a science policy of the national states – or even of the European Community – if there is no basis in society to counterbalance the economic integration of science and technology in our system. If the unions . . . have rarely been successful in that . . . then there is not much room for hope that other organizations will have access to these types of decisions. The implications for our Western European mixed types of economy are immense: we lose political control on major developments in our societies.[39]

In considering this example, we must also be aware that not every trade union is committed to change of the kind advocated by Leydesdorff and Van den Besselaar. In that sense, trade unions may operate on the boundaries between modernism and a late modern style of activity. The point as expressed in the above quotation also links very closely to Beck's argument that control over the direction of science and technology is a key factor in shaping the direction of society – and yet this domain is impervious to democratic intervention.[40] The authors argue that the only way to achieve this wider change is through greater state intervention and the provision of information on technological alternatives to the public on a regular basis: 'Good information is a first prerequisite for the development of an effective interface with R&D facilities'.[41]

However, 'greater state intervention' may be a classic strategy of modernity and, as we have argued, 'good information' is a distinctly problematic category.

One further proposal which has attempted to deal with these problems of anticipation and intervention is 'Constructive Technology Assessment' as pioneered in The Netherlands.

The aim of Constructive Technology Assessment (CTA) is to tailor technical change to societal needs and objectives, like high employment and quality of labour, reduction of pollution, safety, reduction of costs, privacy and other ethical considerations. Whereas traditional TA focuses more on external effects of technologies and early warning, CTA shifts attention to the steering of technical change itself. CTA tries to broaden design, development and implementation processes. . . . This could also work between organizations and social groups. Thus, a societal learning process can be started up, which anticipates future impacts, while producing better technologies and practices.[42]

CTA – which is still at a relatively early stage of development – draws explicitly on recent work in the sociology of technology which stresses the socially contingent and socially negotiated nature of technological development. According to this perspective, technologies emerge from a series of decisions made by human actors. They embody social as well as technical factors. They possess a certain flexibility, i.e., there is 'room for manoeuvre (or choice)' in the final form of a technology. However, they can be extremely *in*flexible once they have been introduced. The task of CTA, therefore, is to try to 'positively shape' technology prior to its innovation.[43]

Accordingly, attention should focus on the design phase of a technology and on the anticipation of adverse social consequences at a very early stage. It follows also that these stages of technology development need the input and participation of a wider group of social actors – a proposal which takes us back to the central concerns of this book with citizen science.

However, all of these specific points and examples link back to the basic question of whether science can meet the needs of citizens within loaded social situations such as those dealt with in this book. The implication of the previous two chapters is that this 'inter-change' is deeply problematic – we have seen the same tension in all the above cases (including those which appear most positive and progressive). As the OECD report repeatedly observes, science has not led to consensus but instead to greater confusion and doubt. This seems to suggest a 'gap' between science and citizens in such cases (always remembering that there will also be such 'gaps' between different citizens) – a gap which appears structural rather than simply a consequence of insufficient activity and effort in this area. This issue is indeed fundamental to public participation and to our whole discussion of science–citizen interactions. We can begin to address it by considering one 'ideal type' of science–citizen interaction – the 'Science Shop'.

Science–citizen mediation: the Science Shop example

Within its discussion of 'new mediation procedures', the 1979 OECD report makes brief reference to a 'pilot' scheme funded by the Dutch government at five of its universities. The intention was to 'mediate' between university researchers and potential client groups:

> The aim of these so-called 'Science Shop' mechanisms is to promote socially-relevant Research and Development ('action research') on behalf of under-privileged groups. . . . This 'Science Shop' experiment is, of course, relatively modest, depending as it does largely upon the voluntary contribution of researcher-staff time and energy. Nevertheless, it has served to encourage the growth of new communication links between university researchers and community groups, stimulate researcher awareness of community problems, and promote closer interactions between scientific and technical specialists and the general public.[44]

In fact, Science Shops have become one of the more conspicuously successful experiments in this whole area (at least in Western Europe) – although that does not imply that there are not significant problems and issues which confront Science Shops, as the remainder of this chapter will discuss. However, Science Shops have now been established at all Dutch universities (which often have more than one) and related initiatives have taken place in at least Germany, Belgium, France, Denmark and the United Kingdom. Put simply, a Science Shop provides the means whereby members of the public who need information or technical assistance – but do not have the means to pay for it or collect it for themselves – can gain access to the necessary resources. As such it provides a key example of the kind of mediation between citizens and science with which this book is concerned. Thus, it is precisely because Science Shops have been relatively effective in operating within this area that they deserve special discussion here.

The term 'Science Shop' is an approximate translation of the Dutch 'wetenschapswinkel' and it is in The Netherlands that Science Shops have become best established. By one estimate, the Dutch Science Shops had together received some 11,000 information requests by January 1987. In terms of topics, questions received by the Amsterdam Science Shop (one of the Dutch pioneers in this area) have covered in descending frequency: environmental matters, health, occupational health and safety, education and child care, housing, workplace, law, social services, Third World issues. Client groups are similarly varied, including: environmental groups, urban organizations, trade unions, welfare workers, women's groups, tenants' organizations, Third World organizations. However, it is important to note (especially given the usual connotation of 'shop') that there are three generally held criteria for Science Shop involvement in any particular project:

- that the client group has no money to pay for research;
- that it has no commercial motives;
- that it is in a position to implement the results for some practical purpose.

It should also be noted that the term 'science' here is potentially misleading – Science Shops cover social science and humanities issues as well as 'scientific' questions (although Science Shops in The Netherlands may also specialize in certain questions, e.g., a 'Chemistry Shop' or a 'History Shop'). Of course, this broad coverage should be helpful in terms of grasping the wider social significance of specific technical issues.

Typical examples of Science Shop enquiries include: (from the Northern Ireland Science Shop) a community group wishing to discover whether local soil poses any health risk as a consequence of previous gas storage on the site of a proposed housing development; (from the Nijmegen Science Shop) a village group concerned about the consequences of large-scale tourist development in their area and requesting help and advice; (from the French Science Shop network) a tenants' group concerned about the cost of heating in their block of council flats ask for an independent assessment of an 'expert report'.

Dealing with such enquiries in a thoughtful and constructive fashion has provided much of the excitement (and also sheer hard work) for Science Shop operation. As such, Science Shops offer an important means of addressing in a highly practical manner many of the issues raised in this book. Thus, and this point could be supported with numerous examples, Science Shops are in a position to provide technical advice but also to serve as an important actor within a 'self-help network' – putting groups in touch with others with similar experiences and problems, drawing science students and researchers into an awareness of social problems, influencing research agenda through the suggestion of important questions for investigation, assisting groups to develop and enhance their own expertise, enabling various groups to 'put science into perspective' (i.e., getting away from the notion of science as the universal problem-solver). At its best, therefore, Science Shop operation offers the kind of innovative and imaginative treatment of citizen needs which on the basis of the various examples in this book seems to be required.

Quite clearly, however, public requests to 'science' for advice and assistance are far from straightforward for the local Science Shop – as Science Shop workers have generally recognized for themselves, leading to a highly reflexive and self-aware mode of Science Shop management. In the following discussion I want to consider the nature of these complexities and difficulties *not* in terms of important but immediate issues (e.g., is there a local Science Shop in existence? Might it adopt an enlightenment perspective? Can it cope with the level of external demand?) but in terms of an ideal-typical Science Shop, i.e., one which has appropriate resources, wide access to appropriate institutions (e.g., a local university with a broad disciplinary coverage), enthusiastic staff and dedication to a citizen-oriented perspective. Even when such difficult matters as arranging funding and staffing for a Science Shop have been tackled, what structural difficulties are inherent in the operation of this example of science–citizen interaction? What follows is not a critique of Science Shops but instead an attempt to examine the practicalities of citizen–science interactions through one very promising example.

Some immediate sense of the complexity and difficulty of making a Science Shop work can be gathered if (again, ideal-typically) we take the operation as involving a number of stages:

• generating appropriate and useful questions;
• Science Shop mediation;
• linkage to the larger institution;
• linkage to the research base;
• feeding back into the wider community.

If we take the first of these stages, then the formulation of 'appropriate questions' is obviously not straightforward. As Stewart puts this in a rather pessimistic account of Science Shops in France: 'Typically, the clients had no idea what to ask, because they had no way of knowing what science might or might not have to offer'.[45]

Based on our discussion in Chapter 4, it follows that many of these requests for help – rather than taking the form of a specific and precisely formulated information request – will form part of a wider call for action and change. Stewart refers to these as 'problem situations'. Examples might include the case of community hazards discussed in Chapter 4; what is required is not scientific detail but a wider and more practically-oriented response.

In such a situation, the task of the Science Shop is less to 'mediate' between the Science Shop client and the scientific community than to reformulate the 'problem situation' in terms which a scientist might recognize. Given the point that scientific information may only represent one small part of a wider call for practical action (i.e., 'getting something done'), this reformulation is likely to prove difficult. More particularly, if groups are committed to changing a situation then it is highly likely that they will already have decided that a problem exists. In that sense, a call for the testing of possibly contaminated ground or for the reassessment of an expert report will represent a call for scientific authentication of a problem rather than a 'curiosity-driven' information request.

Such 'problem situations' will cause difficulties not just for the Science Shop but also for the wider institution on which it depends. Thus, scientists may be reluctant to cross disciplinary boundaries or to delve into issues with a social as well as technical component:

> I have said that the French Science Shops were quite successful in recruiting consultant scientists; and this was true, but with one enormous caveat. Scientists were willing to collaborate, but *on condition* that they remained strictly within the role of providing scientific answers to scientific questions in their specialty. If we had required them to take part in dealing with the social/political context from which the inquiry came (as of course we would have liked to do), I doubt whether we would have found a single consultant.[46]

In such circumstances, it becomes even harder to imagine how citizen-generated requests might feed back into the research direction of scientists. Thus, Leydesdorff and Van den Besselaar in a study of 'what we have learned from the Amsterdam Science Shop' reach fairly negative conclusions about the possibility of trade unions influencing research direction through their involvement in Science Shops – largely because the position of trade unions within corporations does not allow them to gain the necessary overview of R&D policy.[47] However, in a separate paper on the experience of the Amsterdam Science Shop, Zaal and Leydesdorff do note some effect on research output:

Our results indicate that one can transform social problems into scientific problems through active reformulation of the questions of under-privileged groups. Such reformulation, with the help of some creativity and scientific skill, can be done without harm to the knowledge interests of the science shop clients.[48]

Difficulties, of course, also surround the feeding of scientific research into the community – not only might the language of such research be alien and incomprehensible, its narrowness may not be of much assistance to the client groups when dealing with their 'problem situations'. Put simply, such information may simply 'legitimate' what they already knew – and hence be useful albeit unilluminating. Alternatively, it may contradict or even undermine their public position – in which case it might be suppressed or otherwise hidden. Neither way does science contribute conspicuously to 'improved understanding'.

In presenting his very critical account of French Science Shops, Stewart notes difficulties at the levels of scientific inflexibility, Science Shop mediation and public disappointment at what science can provide – constituting a three-way 'negative synergy':

> The fact that the communication gap between scientists and the public is even worse than we had imagined could be taken as actually reinforcing the need for something like Science Shops if science is ever to become a part of culture in anything other than a totally alienated sense. But in the event, the negative synergy between these three difficulties was just too much.[49]

Of course, demonstration that there is a high public demand for Science Shops does not negate this point. For Stewart, the demand is for scientifically-generated solutions to specific 'problem situations' which are simply impossible to achieve. As Stewart summarizes this experience: 'I came to feel that I was trying to convince all parties concerned – the public, scientists and institutions – of the credibility of something that none of them wanted. All in all, not a bad version of hell'.[50]

The broad conclusion from this is as follows:

> To my mind, the major issue is indeed the gap between 'scientific expertise' and the needs of people. . . . In other words, the problem is that 'scientific knowledge' as currently

constituted is not sufficiently relevant to the needs of people.
... I think that the Science Shops experience shows that
'demystifying' – which we did, by and large, do – is not
enough; people won't even really accept being 'demystified'
unless they have something to put in its place. So I feel that
nothing much can happen unless and until we start producing
knowledge which is positively relevant.[51]

From this perspective, science–citizen relations founder not simply
because of the lack of appropriate mediating structures but because of a deeper incongruity (or structural incompatibility) between the needs of citizens and the cognitive and institutional
structure of contemporary science. Put bluntly, social experiments
to bring together scientific and public groups have failed due to
the impossibility of achieving a workable dialogue. Science dismisses externally-generated issues, questions and understandings
as irrelevance and ignorance. Public groups find science in-
accessible. However, when even that barrier has been crossed such
groups are likely to find science as of only limited assistance within
everyday life and particular problem situations – a point argued
in different ways in Chapters 2 and 4. Meanwhile, scientists
struggle to make scientific sense out of the concerns and demands
expressed by public groups – such involvement can then appear
not only as a distraction from 'real' scientific work but also as
counter to the neutral discourse and ostensibly disinterested
nature of science.

Although this scenario is highly persuasive, at least some account
must also be taken of occasions when 'dialogue' has been achieved
(albeit in a limited manner) – for example, in the Mackenzie Valley
Pipeline case or indeed the many positive examples of Science Shop
operation (at least from the perspective of the citizen groups
involved). In such cases, a genuine 'citizen science' seems to have
been created – or at least its precursor. The existence of a 'gap' does
not, therefore, mean that it is insurmountable. However, it does
seem to necessitate a willingness to reappraisal and change which
extends beyond those directly involved in social experimentation.
We thus need to recognize the existing barriers but also those
constructive experiments which have already begun and the importance of learning from these.

The Northern Ireland Science Shop

As one illustration of the positive demand which can exist for an improved science–citizen dialogue, we can consider the example of the Science Shop in Northern Ireland.[52] The Northern Ireland Science Shop (from here simply the 'Science Shop') officially opened in January 1989. With financial support from the Nuffield Foundation, the shop was attached to both the universities in Northern Ireland. The Science Shop as it was operating in 1992 had two part-time staff and a voluntary working group to co-ordinate its activities (this included a mix of representatives from the higher education and voluntary sectors across Northern Ireland).

By the beginning of 1992, over a hundred requests to the Science Shop had been generated by sixty-seven different organizations. The majority of these requests (over 60) emanated from community groups. Significant numbers also emerged from 'environmental' groups (15 requests), and groups specifically concerned with issues of homelessness (12 requests), welfare (7), youth and education (7), disability (5), arts (4) and women (4). Of course, there is a degree of overlap in these categories but they do convey a sense of the Science Shop's clientele.

It follows from the previous analysis in this book, that client groups could be expected to display a strong practical motivation for seeking information from the Science Shop. A classification of the topics of enquiry produces the following major headings: health/environment (39), community development (25), welfare (15), work/training (11), homelessness (9). It is in the nature of Science Shop work that groups of citizens should be seeking 'knowledge for action's sake'.

If we take client groups' comments on the Science Shop itself then these appear overwhelmingly positive – with the only criticism being of the time-delays involved. What were client groups hoping to get from the Shop? Responses here formed a standard pattern: 'access to expertise', 'help with research', 'advice', 'assistance', 'technical help'. The sense of 'instrumental knowledge' took on a particular *legitimatory* orientation in the Northern Ireland setting. As one community group put this:

> To a large extent, research often proves what you already know or have a good idea about. However, if you want to get funding – or lobby statutory agencies etc., to do something about the problem, you must prove, through research, the

nature and the extent of the problem. The actual value of our information was significant as the results were taken seriously and we have already attracted funding.

The notion that research is expected to 'prove what you already know' follows from the previous discussion in this book about contextual knowledges. Community requests for research will often be made against the background of a strong pattern of expectations. Indeed, the request may only make sense because of those expectations (why else bother unless you feel there is a problem?). This will in turn mean that academic involvement will take place within a 'loaded' situation – to the possible discomfort of researchers familiar with a less pressured environment. Equally, community interest and involvement could also encourage and facilitate new research ideas. Unsurprisingly, therefore, one academic respondent described Science Shop work as 'high risk' – with potentially great pay-offs but also a greater-than-usual degree of responsibility and pressure.

If we now break these topics down by academic discipline, then an interesting pattern emerges. In this breakdown, I have taken forty-nine 'completed' requests to the Science Shop (i.e., excluding those 'withdrawn' or 'in mediation'):

Table 6.1: Completed requests to the Northern Ireland Science Shop

Social Studies*	20
Business and Public Administration	6
Building and Housing	6
Science (incl. Chemistry, Biology, Mathematics)	4
Technology (incl. Mech. Eng., Transport, Design, Computer Studies)	4
Arts (incl. History and Fine Art)	3
Other	6

*incl. Sociology, Social Anthropology, Psychology, European Studies
Source: Author's original research

It follows from the table that, despite the 'science' title, citizen groups have an equal or greater demand for *social* scientific expertise and assistance (typically in the form of a community survey or assessment of some area of need). Not surprisingly, the distinction between 'social' and 'natural' sciences seems less rigidly applied outside academic institutions than it is within. This seems an important point for 'Citizen Science'; internally developed academic boundaries may not be relevant to public needs and demands. Furthermore, if 'knowledge' is required for its relevance to particular social contexts then even the much reinforced science/social science divide loses significance.

Of course, two other possibilities should also be considered. First of all, that social science may be more 'accessible' to public groups (it is easier to incorporate citizen views in the design of a questionnaire than in the analysis of a soil sample). Second, that the public expectation of social science (e.g., to 'survey' a community) is more clear than it is of science (what exactly does a mathematician do?). Both of these possibilities are open to question from an academic viewpoint (social science often resists the problem definitions of groups under study and can indeed be as arcane as any area of mathematics). However, it is also possible that science can learn from social science in terms of working with community groups in this area.

As an illustration of these processes of 'working with' community groups, we can take an example from the Science Shop. A group of women at one community centre were keen to conduct a 'child care survey' – basically to assess the provision of family support in their area. This formed part of a sustained campaign to bring more public resources into their community. The survey was conducted with the assistance of a group of university students. However, rather than following the usual academic model, the survey contents were very much the subject of negotiation between community representatives and the students. We see here the emergence of a new style of 'scientific' enquiry – one which attempts to negotiate with the concerns and problem definitions of the concerned groups.

In particular, lively debate developed over whether it was desirable to ask smoking-related questions within the survey. The university group generally felt that smoking patterns were relevant to child care. The community view tended to see this as irrelevant to their needs and likely to lead to the community being 'blamed' for any health or child care problems. In the end, the community view prevailed. The survey itself was then carried out by local people with student assistance.

This style of 'research partnership' clearly has potential in terms of encouraging an open and constructive dialogue between citizen groups and those with technical expertise. However, experience suggests that it has its problems – not least in terms of challenging traditional notions of academic control and independence. The question becomes one of how far 'dialogue' can be established without undermining the integrity of expert analysis. Of course, this form of 'partnership' is quite familiar in the setting of industrial and governmental sponsorship – so that the 'integrity' concern should not be exaggerated. Nevertheless, it seems unavoidable that Science Shop-type work will involve the transfer of 'ownership' of research at least partly in the direction of non-scientific groups.

As significant as matters of 'integrity' for those academics who have been involved with the Science Shop, is the kind of *incentive* which exists for involvement. Whilst conventional academic work leads to publication and research awards, and industrial consultancy generates recognition and research income, Science Shop involvement has a distinctly less glamorous aura. Especially if the research spin-offs from involvement are unclear, the benefits may not be apparent. To quote one academic: 'Apart from altruism, it is difficult to see how individual members of staff derive any benefits from involvement'.

It seems that greater institutional recognition and support for citizen-oriented activities is essential in this area. This extends both to financial support for Science Shops and similar ventures (which typically struggle to survive) and to recognition of the professional contribution of those scientists who are active in this area. If issues of 'science and its publics' are to be taken at all seriously, then it is not possible for such initiatives to operate only at the margins of the academic system.

The Northern Ireland Science Shop illustrates the need which can exist for a science which is at least partly citizen-oriented. Sometimes this need reflects a 'legitimatory' requirement – official groups take a 'scientific' report more seriously than a community assessment (suggesting the power of modernist institutions in such local contexts). At other times, the pattern can be closer to that found in Chapter 4 – groups are seeking an 'independent' account in order to compare views. As one Northern Ireland group put this concerning a dispute over contaminated land: 'It is difficult for local people and potential workers on the site to know if it is safe or not since independent information is so hard to come by'.[53] Or, as the same group also put it: 'Official versions may be accurate, but when people are concerned for their health, the community should be able to monitor developments for themselves'.[54]

Science Shops seem to have the capacity both to offer 'independence' and to enable communities to 'monitor for themselves'. As this chapter has suggested, this task is far from easy but neither does it appear impossible.

Towards a citizen science?

Discussion in this chapter has considered various models and 'social experiments' intended to produce a more effective and open relationship between science, technology and citizen concerns. At times, the excitement of actually making this interaction work has been very tangible – what Stewart calls the 'magic' of Science Shop work.[55] This magic and excitement should not be dismissed – they suggest at least the possibility of a more positive relationship between science and citizens (and also provide an important motivation for even attempting this).

We have stressed the structural problems which bedevil this area – of which the most fundamental concerns the gap between scientific and citizen perspectives on social issues and concerns. Of course, this rather pessimistic conclusion follows closely from the analyses presented in Chapters 4 and 5 where, for example, locally-generated understandings of a hazard situation sat uneasily alongside, and were often confrontational with, 'official' and scientifically legitimated forms of knowledge.

This is not to argue that these different forms of understanding are necessarily incommensurable – although this conclusion can be tempting when considering the failures of past communication. We have also seen that the 'Science Shop' model has at least the potential to engage constructively with 'science' and 'citizens'. Equally, the CTA approach has possibilities in this area – although it must somehow deal with the issues of this book if it is to be 'constructive' in the sense advocated here.

As a final note in this chapter, it would be useful to consider the bare elements of what a 'citizen science' might involve. Such a term in this context implies a 'meeting point' between different forms of knowledge and understanding. It also implies the possibility of cross-fertilization within a diverse area of different knowledges. Especially for the institutions of science, it will involve change but also a reflexivity in the face of social pressures. 'Citizen science' thus implies the recognition of new social and knowledge relations which:

- are willing to engage with non-scientifically generated understandings and expertises. As the Science Shop case suggests, this
may involve difficult negotiations about project design and
methodology in order to incorporate the knowledges but also
sensitivities of external groups;
- are heterogeneous in form rather than trying to impose a unitary
consensus. It seems to follow from all the examples in this book
that no single 'knowledge' exists regarding risk and environmental issues but rather a plurality of knowledge forms which
need to be acknowledged and built upon;
- are prepared to engage with the 'problem situations' which give
rise to citizen concerns rather than merely attempting to filter out
science from non-science (or 'science' from 'social science').
Citizen concerns will not fall easily within established academic
categories;
- are reflexive in terms of the uncertainties and limitations but also
the constructive possibilities for science within everyday life;
- are institutionally flexible and open to change. Progress cannot
be made without the support of powerful institutions – but they
must also be prepared to reconsider their own practices.

Quite obviously, the creation of such a 'citizen science' is a major
challenge – although it might be argued that some of the more
positive examples of social experimentation represent an already
developing response. Clearly also, this is a challenge not just to
science but also to wider society. However, the alternatives are
either to argue that the current relationship between science and
citizens is unproblematic and therefore does not require modi-
fication (a conclusion which is disputed by all the evidence in this
book) or to deny that science should have everyday relevance
(which will inevitably lead to an even greater public onslaught
on science).

7

SCIENCE, CITIZENSHIP AND TROUBLED MODERNITY

Environmental problems are *not* problems of our surroundings, but – in their origins and through their consequences – are thoroughly *social* problems, *problems of people*, their history, their living conditions, their relation to the world and reality, their social, cultural and living conditions. . . . At the end of the twentieth century nature *is* society and society is also *'nature'*.[1]

Modernity reaches that new stage . . . when it is able to face up to the fact that science, for all one knows and can know, is one story among many. 'To face up' means to accept that certainty is not to be, and yet persevere in the pursuit of knowledge. . . . 'To face up' to this fact means to know that the journey has no clear destination – and yet persevere in the travel.[2]

This final chapter intends – as final chapters generally do – to bring together the underlying themes and issues of *Citizen Science*. However, and after several unsuccessful attempts at this, it is quite clear that there is no easy synthesis on offer which can replace enlightenment/modernist thinking.

What should also have been immediately obvious to this author is that such a conclusion follows directly from the whole argument of this book. The very notion of 'freeing the voices' (as suggested in Chapter 5) implies an openness to diverse understandings and knowledges. It also suggests the need for reflexivity and the sceptical analysis of knowledge claims. In that sense, this account has offered 'one story among many'. For it now to claim priority over all alternative stories would be dishonest. Equally, this book is not designed as an exercise in ventriloquism – the point is to establish a

168

framework where diverse expertises are given legitimate status rather than to speak on behalf of those who can speak more eloquently for themselves.

However, the lack of an easy synthesis and a denial of sociological ventriloquism does not end – but should rather open – the discussion of expertise, citizens and sustainability. As Bauman suggests, 'facing up' to the limits and uncertainties of our knowledge systems does not mean 'giving up'.[3] Instead, the evidence and argumentation of this book should be read as presenting a substantial challenge to scientific institutions and to citizens.

Thus, the reconstitution and reintegration of science within everyday life may prove painful for institutions which would prefer a less reflexive mode of existence – and which have often been sheltered from the more critical commentaries found in this book. However, it seems vital both for the practice of science and for sustainable development that this emerging context should be seen as a challenge and an opportunity. This book should not be interpreted, therefore, as an assault on science but rather as an argument for its reformation within the contexts of everyday life. Equally, as will be suggested, social science must reconsider its own contribution to these issues of science, citizenship and sustainability.

In this conclusion, therefore, I am going to suggest how we might now move on in terms of social and technical responses to the specific matter of environmental threats. The journey may indeed possess no clear destination – or, perhaps, the route of the journey may only be clear when we look back.[4] However, the loss of such certainties should serve as a stimulus to that journey. It may well be that – at least in formal institutional terms – we have been standing still for too long.

This discussion should begin with the knowledges and institutions of science which have been so important throughout this account. In particular, Beck and Giddens typically present a very 'essentialist' view of science – as if it was indeed a single enterprise following one set of goals and practices. By contrast, the Sociology of Scientific Knowledge-based analysis here has acknowledged that there is a substantial diversity and difference within contemporary scientific practice. It may, therefore, be that this heterogeneity offers a more sustainable foundation for knowledge relations than is assumed by externalist accounts of science.

In particular, the 'science-centredness' of decision-making (see

Chapter 3) does not necessitate the *reductionist* form of scientific assessment encountered in cases such as BSE or 2,4,5–T (where, for example, a very narrow range of evidence is taken into account). The question, therefore, becomes not *whether* science should be applied to environmental (and, of course, other) questions but rather *which form* of science is most appropriate and in *what relationship* to other forms of knowledge and understanding.

As we will shortly discuss, a move away from essentialism opens up more productive possibilities in the relationship between science, citizens and the environment. As Barnes has expressed this, our focus should not solely be on a critique of science in itself but also on the current framework of knowledge relations which gives ascendancy to some knowledge forms over others: 'the power to determine *which* expert is believed is the important form of power . . . not the power of experts themselves'.[5]

In what ways might the institutional frameworks for the development and selection of expertise be altered so as to accommodate the evidence of this book?

Science and sustainability

If we now move directly to the discussion of new possibilities for scientific intervention in environmental questions, then one immediate point concerns the desirability of a 'precautionary' approach. One regular theme of the cases discussed here has been the struggle of public and environmentalist groups to have risk concerns taken seriously. Until 'sufficient proof' is offered, existing practice continues. The burden then lies with citizen and environmentalist groups – with 'evidence' being viewed in a particularly narrow fashion. Wynne and Mayer have labelled British policy in this area as indeed reductionist in character:

> that is, breaking down an area into its smallest components in the belief that only these directly observable and measurable paths matter. It often takes the view that factors have no significance unless they can be traced directly into a cause-and-effect relationship. The consequence is that research with a high degree of control over the system being studied . . . becomes equated with 'good science'.[6]

Wynne and Mayer, in contrast, stress the uncertainty and ignorance within scientific understanding of the environment. Current notions of 'good science', however, struggle to deal with such unavoidable characteristics:

> What is needed is a different, 'greener' culture of good science. As well as giving a greater value to areas of science such as ecology which consider the environment in its broader context, it would value the usefulness of observation and, crucially, embody a wider responsibility which incorporated the recognition of ignorance.[7]

The 'greener science' for which they call would oppose reductionism with an open acknowledgement of the limitations and uncertainties of science. It would also permit open debate rather than allowing the dominance of one definition of 'good science'. Equally, it would serve as a check on powerful institutions which currently sponsor the bulk of 'relevant' research. For individual scientists, this would allow the expression of doubts and legitimate concerns. Thus, a scientistic and reductionist policy culture could give way to a more mature and all-encompassing assessment of the relationship between science and the environment. In that way too, scientific expertise could work towards sustainability rather than standing as an impediment to change: 'It is irresponsible to dismiss this attempt to recognise science in its wider context as unscientific as it accords science a necessary but redefined role in a wider challenge it has yet to fully recognize'.[8]

The call from Wynne and Mayer for a more productive form of scientific intervention – especially in terms of the shift away from reductionism – fits well with the analysis in this book. However, it follows very closely from the previous discussion that this new role must also recognize a place for citizen knowledges and understandings. A 'greener' science may nevertheless be unable to connect with non-scientific expertises and with socially sustainable ways of life. Funtowicz and Ravetz have attempted to incorporate this dimension in their discussion of 'post-normal' science:

> This emerging science fosters a new methodology. . . . In this, uncertainty is not banished but is managed, and values are not presupposed but are made explicit. The model for scientific argument is not a formalized deduction but an interactive dialogue. The paradigmatic science is no longer one in which location . . . and process are irrelevant to explanation. The historical dimension, including reflection on

humanity's past and future, is becoming an integral part of the scientific characterisation of Nature.[9]

Particularly important to this discussion is Funtowicz and Ravetz's treatment of 'extended peer communities'. As they express this in terms redolent of 'citizen science' (or, as they prefer, 'popular epidemiology'):

> persons directly affected by an environmental problem will have a keener awareness of its symptoms, and a more pressing concern with the quality of official reassurances, than those in any other role. Thus they perform a function analogous to that of professional colleagues in the peer review or refereeing process in traditional science, which otherwise might not occur in these new contexts.[10]

This concept of 'extended peer review' works at a complementary level to Wynne and Mayer's case for more open debate within the 'greening of science'. In particular, Funtowicz and Ravetz see the 'creative conflict' between 'popular' and 'expert' epidemiologies as serving to improve scientific knowledge (and also scientifically informed decision-making). Thus, in the terms of this book, the current impasse within the relations of science, citizens and sustainable development becomes transformed into a source of improved understanding and sustainable environmental response.

> When problems lack neat solutions, when environmental and ethical aspects of the issues are prominent, when the phenomena themselves are ambiguous, and when all research techniques are open to methodological criticism, then the debates on quality are not enhanced by the exclusion of all but the specialist researchers and official experts. The extension of the peer community is then not merely an ethical or political act; it can possibly enrich the processes of scientific investigation.[11]

One major negative characteristic of orthodox 'deficit' theories is that they operate on precisely the opposite principle. Ultimately, however, Funtowicz and Ravetz's argument is for an enhanced *quality* of scientific understanding – a quality which is undermined by current 'enlightenment' assumptions and the accompanying insulation of scientific institutions from broader scrutiny and enquiry.

Let us be quite clear about this; we are not arguing for the democratization of science on the basis of a generalized wish for the greatest possible extension of democracy in society. The epistemological analysis of post-normal science, rooted in the practical tasks of quality assurance, shows that such an extension of peer communities, with the corresponding extension of facts, is necessary for the effectiveness of science in meeting the new challenges of global environmental problems.[12]

The task is not to remove science from decision-making nor to erode its significance. Instead, questions of citizen science and sustainability present a challenge to integrate scientific expertise with other assessments, problem definitions and expertises; to acknowledge diversity as a positive element within sustainable development and to appreciate the inter-connectedness of 'social', 'environmental' and 'technical' issues and concerns. Such a challenge once again suggests the new agenda and new possibilities created by our current stage of social and technological development. As Beck puts this:

> The other side of the uncertainty that the risk society brings upon tormented humanity is the *opportunity* to find and activate the increase of equality, freedom and self-expression promised by modernity, *against* the limitations, the functional imperatives and the fatalism of progress in industrial society.[13]

It also follows from our discussion that no single framework or blueprint will meet this important social and technical challenge. The call for a reassessment of science's contribution to environmental questions, for a wider social debate, and for the acknowledgement of emerging forms of peer review should all be seen as necessary – but necessarily partial – elements of a broader sociotechnical response. The challenge is to achieve a flexible and responsive set of institutional structures for the development and scrutiny of expert knowledges of different kinds. As has already been stressed, the point is not to sweep aside one knowledge form and to replace it with another. Instead, we need to recognize the contextual and partial nature of all the forms of understanding discussed in this book.

Simply to state this as an institutional and cognitive challenge may be the very easiest part of the exercise – although an acknowledgement of even this is not currently widespread (as the various case-histories in this book strongly suggest). However, and as an indication of more positive responses which are already occurring, we can point to certain contemporary initiatives. The Science Shop may be one such example. As discussed in the previous chapter, the difficulties of this model do at least clarify the nature of the challenges involved. There is also some sign for optimism that scientists and citizen groups can enter into dialogue – although the legitimacy of that dialogue may not be accepted by formal institutions. As a social experiment, however, the Science Shop offers one focal point for learning and debate.

In this discussion of 'science and sustainability', it is possible to include other initiatives which are attempting not to offer a direct critique of existing policy (although this may be implied) but to build new ways of living, knowing and working. Typically, such initiatives take the form of localized, small-scale and citizen-led developments which aim to move away from the traditionally obstructive role of public groups ('either accept a technology or block it') and attempt instead to facilitate new social and technological possibilities for living in a broadly sustainable fashion.

These initiatives take a number of forms: they may focus on the development of a particular technology (windmills, waste recycling, even the domestic toilet) or, more broadly, on living in a sustainable manner (ecological villages or the urban ecology movement in countries such as Denmark). They may also seek to find ways of redefining the 'marketplace' in which technologies are developed and sold (by, for example, entering into co-operative arrangements with consumers or by helping to create new forms of demand for 'green' products). Rather than accepting governmental notions of the 'path to sustainability', the attempt has been for citizens to develop their own means of living within the local environment.

Thus, as opposed to accepting externally developed technical 'solutions' to urban environmental problems, urban ecology aims to minimize waste at its household source typically by altering everyday practice (i.e., changing the ways of living which produce waste in the first place).[14] Efforts are also being made in, for example, Denmark, Sweden and Germany, to move beyond recycling activities and to establish ecological neighbourhoods or communities. Once again, these initiatives do not separate the 'technical', the 'environmental' and the 'social' but work in a manner compatible with specific needs and requirements. Such initiatives are not without their difficulties – and not least at the level of accessing external expertise. However, they do offer a means of responding to citizen demand at an immediate, local and contextually appropriate level. We see here also an approach to sustainable development which builds positively upon citizen experiences rather than seeking to enforce change from above.[15]

One other characteristic of initiatives such as these is that they do not represent a wholesale rejection of science (or of Beck's broad 'scientific rationality').[16] Instead, the emerging practical experience is of a much more measured and case-specific evaluation by citizen groups of different ways of knowing and living. Accusations of 'anti-science' profoundly misrepresent current developments. Only once the easy comfort of such accusations has been abandoned can the real institutional challenges be faced.

Thus, from the perspective of certain scientists and scientific institutions such initiatives and suggestions may evoke scepticism and even hostility. Attempts at establishing ecological communities, urban ecology schemes or Science Shops stand – at least in many Western countries – apart from the mainstream of science–public interactions. Their suggestion of a new, and more humble, role for science fits awkwardly with the rhetoric of groups such as the Royal Society. Their requirement that scientists should be reflexive in the face of public demands sits uneasily with the defiant rhetoric of modernity. Attention to the sites of scientific implementation and social practice transgresses current scientific norms and procedures. Recognition of professional service in such areas seems a long way from current institutional practice.

All of these challenges offer both a threat and an opportunity to scientific institutions. I would prefer at this stage to stress the opportunities which are being created within the particular area of sustainable development – the challenges have been dealt with sufficiently in the previous chapters.

In the first place, and as Funtowicz and Ravetz have argued, the opening up of science to a wider set of knowledges and sources of enquiry can only be beneficial to the growth of knowledge regarding environmental response.[17] This follows from the social and technical complexity of building sustainable futures. Put simply, we need to develop and extend our critical antennae if we are to cope with this order of complexity. The challenge of sustainability offers new avenues for self-critical and self-aware forms of knowledge and understanding. Science should play an important role in this development.

Going further, the 'deficit' notion typically distances such institutions from their publics and precludes the possibility of more constructive inter-linkages. Meanwhile, it is quite clear that scientific assumptions about the public and everyday behaviour are unavoidable – as numerous cases within this book have explored (for example, assumptions about the local public in the event of a petrochemical accident or about farmworkers operating 'in the recommended way' with pesticides). If everyday life is the 'laboratory' in which risk and environmental threat is evaluated, then assumptions about human as well as 'natural' variables must be made (and indeed it becomes impossible to separate the two).

The basis on which these assumptions are made seems nevertheless unclear – they are implicit and generally undefended. We have also seen the apparent inflexibility of such assumptions in the face of public critique. The prevalent notion of 'good science' shields scientific assessments from the contexts of application including, crucially, the social arrangements within which application occurs. The opportunity now – both in analytical and practical terms – is to open up these constructions of the public to critical scrutiny – including, of course, that of the public itself. Such a move implies new possibilities for scientific practice – and also for the social scientific appraisal of science–public relations.

The suggestion for extended peer review may offer a partial way forward here. It seems unavoidable, however, that the wider practice of scientific institutions needs to be made more transparent so that implicit social models as they function within science can be considered. Such a move would not be without its difficulties – but it would also suggest an important development of the relationship between science, citizens and sustainable development.

There are a number of specific and general forms which this transparency might take: the greater inclusion of public groups in scientific priority-setting (e.g., at the level of science policy-making); the creation of new fora for discussing the scientific understanding of the public as this operates within scientific and technological development (e.g., with regard to the innovation process); support from scientific and related institutions for public debate which goes beyond the rigid and defensive parameters of the 'public understanding of science'; support for local and citizen-defined initiatives which seek to 'make sense' of science within the conditions of everyday life (e.g., the Science Shop model); the education of scientists in the wider dimensions of the relationship between science and the social structure.

The central point, however, is that questions of the public understanding of science lead back to the social and technical processes which produce new sciences and technologies. At the analytical level, we need to know more about how and at what level assumptions about 'the public' influence the form and direction of these processes. In more policy terms, the need is to open these up to wider scrutiny. There seems every possibility that such scrutiny would benefit scientific institutions – as well as assisting the social and scientific relations of sustainability.

Whilst the wider challenges of sustainability contain both threats and opportunities for science, the implications for citizenship must also be considered. In particular, where does this discussion of science and sustainability take our underlying notions of 'environmental citizenship'?

Citizenship and sustainability

At one level, the traditional concerns of citizenship have been central to this account. Thus, many of our cases have touched upon matters of inequality, relative power (or powerlessness) and social class. As one of the respondents noted in Chapter 4, high-level technical skills (in that case, a PhD in Chemistry) are useless without the capacity to change the local situation. Hazardous environments and social powerlessness do indeed seem to coexist.

In that sense, Beck's 'boomerang effect' claim that in the 'risk society' even the rich and powerful are not safe may be correct but also misleading. Whilst it is difficult to buy immunity from the effects of ozone depletion, not every class in society is equally exposed to local environmental pollution or workplace hazards. Money can indeed buy at least partial immunity – it comes as no surprise that wealth should also have its environmental privileges. Equally, the worldwide effects of global environmental disaster are likely to affect the poor of the earth before the rich.

In an important fashion, therefore, environmental citizenship raises many familiar questions of power and equality in a relatively new setting. In that sense also, the late modern claim that a transformation has taken place in the central questions and concerns of everyday life must surely be mistaken.

At another level, however, citizenship has indeed taken on new meanings in the environmental context. Thus, one fundamental expression of citizenship has been in parliamentary democracy and political parties – and yet their role here has been marginal. Equally, the regulatory activities of the State have appeared remote from citizen demands and typically something to be struggled with rather than relied upon.

Most importantly for this book, traditional treatments of citizenship have concerned themselves very little with questions of knowledge and expertise. While such questions overlap with matters of empowerment and democracy, they also bring a new element into focus: the linkage between ways of knowing and of acting. Meanwhile, discussions of science and citizenship (e.g., in the 'science for the people' mode) have seen 'knowledge' as an obstacle to citizen demands – but without challenging the enlightenment assumptions upon which such a problem formulation is based.

More positively, as we saw in Chapter 5, citizens have become their own resource – including of course the expertises and understandings which they can generate. One powerful aspect of environmental response has been its connection with the actions of citizens at the most immediate level – involving everyday behaviour as consumers, workers and residents as well as with self-consciously global initiatives. Practical action becomes possible at levels removed from the 'mainstream' concerns of what is usually defined as 'politics'.

Perhaps the key point about this expression of citizenship is that environmental response functions within the terms and conditions of citizens themselves rather than being framed by State-led activities. We can thus (following, for example, Turner) portray environmental citizenship as representing pressure 'from below' rather than conforming with the framework decided 'above' (i.e., the State).[18]

If sustainability is to build upon evolving patterns of everyday life, then this point seems essential. At least to some generally unacknowledged degree, the social and technological arrangements upon which sustainability depends are being created far from the global conferences and international wrangling over that topic. Indeed, many of the citizen groups may never have heard of the term 'sustainable development'. Particular care is needed lest this naturalistic and inter-governmental discourse becomes a constraint on local initiative rather than a stimulus. The challenge now is to find more positive means to draw upon such local initiative rather than to see it as an unfortunate distraction from the 'global agenda'.

The other point about this 'bottom up' notion of environmental citizenship is that it permits the expression of needs and concerns in a positive fashion. Put differently, it works at the level of demand rather than as a response to the available supply of centrally co-ordinated options and possibilities. In that way also, it will stimulate institutions to respond to the new climate of environmental action.

Drawing also upon Turner's discussion of citizenship, the form of citizenship under discussion here deals simultaneously with the 'public space' and the 'private space'. Quite clearly, issues of risk and the environment involve public matters of regulation and control – in that sense, the environment is an 'external' threat which engages us at a collective level. However, the issues discussed here are also deeply private in character. They force us as individuals to reconsider our view of the world, to challenge the trust we accord to institutions and key individuals, to assess our personal lifestyle and consumer decisions.

The environment, therefore, sits in both public and private space; it challenges us in terms of public policy but also raises personal questions of a profound and ethical kind. At the same time, and as the first quotation at the beginning of this chapter reminds us, 'environmental problems ... are thoroughly *social* problems'. Citizenship issues are therefore central rather than peripheral to sustainable development.

In this, risk and environmental questions pose substantial challenges to prevailing notions of citizenship – which often separate the public from the private (voting behaviour is then understood at the society-wide level rather than being seen as the outcome of personal and ethical choices). This important characteristic again suggests that conventional top-down political responses are unlikely to be sufficient.

Crucially also, citizenship in this area has begun to concern itself with the direction of scientific and technological change. Questions, for example, of the safety of 2,4,5–T can lead to a further questioning of chemical pesticides and the possibility of alternative approaches to weed control. The expression of risk concerns has thus led (albeit in a limited and indirect way) to a wider scrutiny of the knowledge forms and institutional processes which produce risk and environmental threat. This seems an avenue of citizenship which has long been shielded from discussion and debate. The contemporary attack on 'public irrationality' then appears as a last desperate effort at foreclosing this debate. It may already be too late for such a rearguard action.

Ultimately, the main significance of environmental citizenship is in providing a meeting point for a number of current dichotomies: bringing together the 'social' and the 'natural', the 'local' and the 'global', the 'personal' and the 'public', the 'technical' and the 'everyday'. In so doing, we can see the possibility of an approach to sustainable development which is rooted in the preferred living practices and social arrangements of citizens rather than in accepted institutional arrangements and unchallenged relations of knowledge and power.

It may well be that the 'environmental citizen' is not a totally new phenomenon. The inter-relations and dichotomies opened up by this notion of environmental citizenship are also and by nature problematic. Thus, for example, at the level of sloganizing, the 'local' and the 'global' may be connected. The precise nature of this connection within everyday life is, however, far from straightforward. Nevertheless, the issue for policy responses is to facilitate rather than obstruct these dialectic and creative processes of enquiry.

Science, citizen science and social science

Finally, as I hope to have already made apparent, one of the most exciting aspects of the developing context for science, citizenship and sustainability concerns the new possibilities created for a constructive, challenging and forward-looking relationship between science, public groups and the social sciences. Issues of citizen science inevitably draw upon all three as has been extensively discussed. For social science, this will pose a challenge as great as that to the other two categories.

The call is for a social scientific analysis which is theoretically and empirically sophisticated and, because of this, is able to deal symmetrically with both scientific and public statements. Notions of late modernity and the risk society serve an important purpose in stimulating the sociological imagination – even if they also offer an overblown portrayal of radical transformation and change. Meanwhile, SSK and its emphasis on the particular conditions of knowledge generation and transmission serve to stress that the 'local' is not simply a validation of the epochal changes identified by social theorists. It is instead the context within which change is brought about.

In that way too, the relationship between the 'local' and the 'global' is as much a matter for social scientific analysis as it is for citizen and scientific groups. This book's attempt has been to portray the relationship as dialectic in nature. We have indeed been 'following the actors'[19] as methodological situationism directs. Equally, the critique of modernity as discussed in this book has consequences for the grand narratives of sociology as well as for those of science (Beck and Giddens place themselves in an obviously paradoxical situation in this regard). However, none of this is an argument for ignoring the wider inter-connections and consequences of local actions. The sociological imagination is precisely about the interplay between the local and the global, between the biographical and the broadly historical.[20]

Equally, as Mulkay has expressed it:

> I have come to see sociology's ultimate task, not as that of reporting neutrally the facts about an objective social world, but as that of engaging actively in the world in order to create the possibilities of alternative forms of social life.[21]

This is clearly a task for the sociologist which is every bit as fraught as that presented to the scientist. In particular, 'engaging actively' will involve social scientists reappraising their knowledge structures and relationships to 'external' groups in exactly the same way that this book has suggested for other scientists. Nevertheless, the goal of a development path which is socially sustainable requires that this be undertaken and indeed makes the task worthwhile. More particularly, the need is for a sociological account which is 'situated' within the contexts of everyday life rather than seeking to impose itself from the outside. At the same time, 'engaging actively' involves a willingness to question and challenge rather than simply obey the acknowledged framework of understanding and interpretation.

It may also be that the collapse of the Society/Nature barrier and the recognition of 'citizen science' have even more radical implications for the relationship between the social and natural sciences. Certainly, the enlightenment worldview which created these categories is, as we have seen, under substantial assault. If sociology was created through the separation of the 'social' and the 'natural' (and likewise for the natural sciences), then a reconsideration is now required. The same is true for the distinction between 'citizen' and 'technical' knowledges.

Put in this way, the various case-histories and initiatives described in this book do indeed become the experimental testing ground for knowing and living in the future. The challenge is then not just to find a mode of sustainable development but also of sustainable knowledge. The challenge to both 'social' and 'natural' science should not be underestimated. In particular, it seems essential that we abandon the prevailing separation of the 'social' and the 'technical' dimensions of environmental response. If nothing else, this book has suggested that in the new context of sustainability, the existing institutional structures of knowledge generation will need to be revisited and restructured.

It is not simply that environmental concerns will be channelled through the current relations between science, citizenship and modernity – those relations also shape and construct our environmental awareness. Equally, environmental threat does not sit apart from a wider range of threats to our sense of identity and security. The crisis of the environment is unavoidably and simultaneously a wider challenge to our ways of knowing and acting in the world – including the relationship between various forms of expert knowledge and understanding. Our ability to cope with the threats and challenges of the environment will also be a wider test (if such were needed) of our ability to sustain current relations of knowledge and social action.

NOTES

INTRODUCTION

1 For an excellent review of Weberian thinking on science and technology see Schroeder, R., 'Disenchantment and its discontents: Weberian perspectives on science and technology' in *Sociological Review*, May 1995.
2 Hill, S., *The Tragedy of Technology: human liberation versus domination in the late twentieth century* (London: Pluto Press, 1988).
3 ibid.
4 ibid., p.23.
5 Perutz, for example, traces an average life expectancy in Western Europe of 40 years in 1830 climbing steadily to over 70 by 1980. A similar average increase has occurred in developing countries since 1940. Perutz, M., *Is Science Necessary?* (Oxford and New York: Oxford University Press, 1989) p.38.
6 ibid., p.5.
7 Williams, R., *Resources of Hope*. Collection of writings edited by Gable, R. (London and New York: Verso, 1989) p.8.
8 ibid., p.305.
9 Nelkin, D., 'The political impact of technical expertise', *Social Studies of Science*, 5 (1975), 37.
10 Stewart, J., 'Science Shops in France: a personal view', *Science as Culture*, 2 (1988) 73–4.
11 The World Commission on Environment and Development, *Our Common Future* (Oxford and New York: Oxford University Press, 1987) p.43.
12 ibid., p.49.
13 ibid., p.8.

1 SCIENCE AND CITIZENSHIP

1 Dickens, C., *Hard Times* (Harmondsworth: Penguin, 1985 reprint) p.47.
2 ibid., p.92.

3 Nehru, J., quoted in Perutz, M., *Is Science Necessary? Essays on science and scientists* (Oxford and New York: Oxford University Press, 1991) p.vii.
4 See, for example, Charles Babbage, *Reflections on the Decline of Science in England and of Some of its Causes* (London, 1830).
5 Werskey, G., *The Visible College* (London: Allen Lane 1978).
6 Haldane, J.B.S., *Science and Everyday Life* (Harmondsworth: Pelican Books, 1939 – reprinted 1943) p.8.
7 Members of the Association of Scientific Workers, *Science and the Nation* (Harmondsworth: Penguin, 1947) p.30.
8 ibid., p.205.
9 For example, Haldane produced a stream of articles for the *Daily Worker* on such topics as 'Why bananas have no pips', 'Is there life on the planets?', 'Occupational mortality' or 'How British science is organised'. Typically, these articles had a political orientation towards the critique of contemporary capitalism.
10 Association of Scientific Workers, op. cit., p.249.
11 ibid., p.16.
12 Royal Society, *The Public Understanding of Science* (London: Royal Society, 1985) p.9.
13 ibid.
14 Berg, M., *The Machinery Question and the Making of Political Economy 1815–1848* (Cambridge: Cambridge University Press, 1980).
15 For example, Habermas, J., *Towards a Rational Society: student protest, science and politics* (London: Heinemann, 1971) Chapter 6.
16 Marcuse, H., *One Dimensional Man* (London: Sphere Books, 1970) p.46.
17 Marx, K., *The Grundrisse* (Harmondsworth: Penguin, 1983) p.693, quoted in Hill, S., *The Tragedy of Technology* (London: Pluto, 1988) p.52.
18 Hill, S., op. cit., p.38.
19 Advisory Committee on Pesticides, *Further Review of the Safety for Use in the UK of Herbicide 2,4,5-T* (London: MAFF, 1980) p.26.
20 National Union of Agricultural and Allied Workers, *Not One Minute Longer!* Submission to Minister of Agriculture, Fisheries and Food, July 1980, p.3.
21 According to the Pesticide Action Network, the 'dirty dozen' campaign identifies twelve 'extremely hazardous pesticides that should be banned, phased out, or carefully controlled everywhere in the world'.
22 NUAAW, op. cit.
23 *Landworker*, June 1980, pp.6–7.
24 NUAAW, op. cit., p.20.
25 Advisory Committee on Pesticides, op. cit.
26 ibid., p. 35.
27 ibid., p. 13.
28 Boddy, J., quoted in Cook, J. and Kaufman, C., *Portrait of a Poison – the 2,4,5-T story* (London: Pluto Press, 1982) p.71.
29 Gummer, J., quoted in *The Times*, May 18, 1990.
30 Advertisement in *The Times*, May 18, 1990.

31 Quoted in the *Guardian*, July 13, 1990.
32 Southwood, R., quoted in Food Safety Advisory Centre leaflet, *The Facts about BSE*. The Food Safety Advisory Centre is sponsored by Asda, Gateway, Morrisons, Safeway, Sainsbury's and Tesco.
33 *Guardian*, July 16, 1990.
34 ibid.
35 Gummer, J., quoted in *The Times*, May 18, 1990.
36 The Royal Society and The Association of British Science Writers, *Bovine Spongiform Encephalopathy: A Briefing Document*, April 1990.
37 *Guardian*, July 13, 1991.
38 Leaflet distributed to the residents of Carrington and Partington, Greater Manchester.
39 Jones, T., *Corporate Killing: Bhopals will happen* (London: Free Association Books, 1988) p.246.
40 Council Directive, June 24, 1982 on the major accident hazards of certain industrial activities, 82/501/EC, *Official Journal of the European Communities* L230, 25, August 5, 1982.
41 See Jupp, A. and Irwin, A., 'Emergency response and the provision of public information under CIMAH – a case study', *Disaster Management* 1: 4 (1989), 33–7. For a more complete account, see Jupp, A., 'The provision of public information on major hazards'. Dissertation submitted to the Department of Science and Technology Policy, University of Manchester, January 1988.
42 *The Times*, May 18, 1990.
43 Quoted in the *Guardian*, July 13, 1990.
44 Habermas, J., op. cit., Chapter 5.
45 Jones, T., op. cit., pp.245–6.
46 For a starting point to this influential literature, see: Barnes, B. and Edge, D. (eds), *Science in Context* (Milton Keynes: Open University Press, 1982); Latour, B. and Woolgar, S., *Laboratory Life* (Beverly Hills and London: Sage, 1979); Mulkay, M., *Science and the Sociology of Knowledge* (London: Allen and Unwin, 1979); idem, *Sociology of Science* (Milton Keynes and Philadelphia: Open University Press, 1991); Woolgar, S., *Science: the very idea* (Chichester and London: Ellis Horwood and Tavistock, 1988).
47 Wynne, B., 'Frameworks of rationality in risk management: towards the testing of naive sociology' in Brown, J. (ed.) *Environmental Threats; perception analysis and management* (London and New York: Belhaven Press, 1989), p.37.
48 Bauman, Z., *Postmodern Ethics* (Oxford and Cambridge, Mass.: Blackwell, 1993) p.203.
49 Wynne, B., op. cit., p.43.
50 Kauffman, C., '2,4,5-T: Britain out on a limb', in Goldsmith, E. and Hildyard, N., *Green Britain or Industrial Wasteland?* (Cambridge: Polity Press, 1986) p.169.
51 On this issue, see: Collingridge, D. and Reeve, C., *Science Speaks to Power: the role of experts in policy making* (London: Frances Pinter, 1986); Jasanoff, S., *The Fifth Branch: science advisers as policy makers* (Cambridge, Mass. and London: Harvard University Press, 1990).

52 As I write this, one newspaper is running a science-writing competition under the slogan 'Enlighten the public with science'.
53 The World Commission on Environment and Development, *Our Common Future* (Oxford and New York: Oxford University Press, 1987).

2 SCIENCE, CITIZENS AND ENVIRONMENTAL THREAT

1 Royal Society, *The Public Understanding of Science* (London: Royal Society, 1985) p.10.
2 Beck, U., *Risk Society: towards a new modernity* (London, Newbury Park, New Delhi: Sage, 1992) p.70 (emphasis in original).
3 Two major speeches on this subject were given by Margaret Thatcher – on September 27, 1988 (to the Royal Society) and on October 14, 1988 (to the Conservative Party Conference).
4 For a full discussion, see: Hansen, A. (ed.) *The Mass Media and Environmental Issues* (Leicester, London and New York: Leicester University Press, 1993).
5 See, for example, various publications by John Elkington, including Elkington, J. and Hailes, J., *The Green Consumer Guide* (London: Victor Gollancz, 1988).
6 See, for example, Irwin, A., Georg, S. and Vergragt, P., 'The social management of environmental change', *Futures* 26:3 (1994), 323–34.
7 Beck. U., op. cit.
8 See, for example, Brown, J. (ed.) *Environmental Threats: perception, analysis and management* (London and New York: Belhaven Press, 1989); Irwin, A., *Risk and the Control of Technology* (Manchester: Manchester University Press, 1985).
9 Douglas, M., 'Environments at Risk' in Dowie, J. and Lefrere, P., *Risk and Chance* (Milton Keynes: Open University Press, 1980) p.289.
10 Diski, J. *Rainforest* (London: Methuen, 1987) pp.54–5.
11 Cotgrove, S., *Catastrophe or Cornucopia: the environment, politics and the future* (Chichester: John Wiley and Sons, 1982).
12 Schwarz, M. and Thompson, M., *Divided We Stand: redefining politics, technology and social choice* (Hemel Hempstead: Harvester Wheatsheaf, 1990).
13 Douglas, M. and Wildavsky, A., *Risk and Culture: an essay on the selection of technological and environmental dangers* (Berkeley, Los Angeles and London: University of California Press, 1982).
14 Yearley, S., *The Green Case* (London: HarperCollins, 1991).
15 Dickens, P., *Society and Nature: towards a green social theory* (Hemel Hempstead: Harvester Wheatsheaf, 1992) pp.3–4.
16 Beck, U., op. cit. pp.9–10 (emphasis in original).
17 Giddens, A., *Modernity and Self-Identity: self and society in the late modern age* (Cambridge: Polity Press, 1991) p.21.
18 ibid., p.30.
19 Lash, S. and Wynne, B., 'Introduction' in Beck, U., op. cit., p.4.

NOTES

20 As an example of this, see Latour, B. and Woolgar, S., *Laboratory Life: the social construction of scientific facts* (Beverly Hills and London: Sage, 1979).

21 For a useful discussion of this, see: Woolgar, S., *Science – the very idea* (London: Tavistock, 1988).

22 Kuhn, T.S., *The Structure of Scientific Revolutions* (Chicago: University of Chicago Press, 1987).

23 As examples, see: Latour and Woolgar, op. cit.; Mulkay, M., *Sociology of Science: a sociological pilgrimage* (Milton Keynes and Philadelphia: Open University Press, 1991); Latour, B., *Science in Action* (Milton Keynes: Open University Press, 1987).

24 For a very useful introduction to sociology of science and technology, see Webster, A., *Science, Technology and Society* (Basingstoke and London: Macmillan, 1991).

25 See, for example, Gilbert, G.N. and Mulkay, M.J., *Opening Pandora's Box* (Cambridge: Cambridge University Press, 1984).

26 I am grateful to Steve Woolgar for formulating these questions. This does not, of course, implicate Steve in my description of SSK.

27 For a discussion of this, see Harding, S. and O'Barr, J.F. (eds) *Sex and Scientific Inquiry* (Chicago: Chicago University Press, 1987).

28 Advertisement in *The Times*, May 18, 1990.

29 The following discussion draws upon Irwin, A., 'Acid pollution and public policy: the changing climate of environmental decision-making' in Radojevic, M. and Harrison, R.M. (eds) *Atmospheric Acidity: sources, consequences and abatement* (London and New York: Elsevier, 1992) pp.549–76.

30 Beck, U., op. cit.

31 Further references to this sociological literature are available in Irwin, A., 'Technical expertise and risk conflict: an institutional study of the British compulsory seat belt debate', *Policy Sciences*, 20 (1987), 339–64.

32 Cramer, J., *Mission-orientation in Ecology: the case of Dutch freshwater ecology* (Amsterdam: Rodopi, 1987) pp.49–52.

33 Kuhn, T.S., op. cit.

34 Yearley, S., op. cit.

35 Collingridge, D. and Reeve, C., *Science Speaks to Power: the role of experts in policy making* (London: Frances Pinter, 1986).

36 Graham, J.D., Green, L.C. and Roberts, M.J., *In Search of Safety: chemical and cancer risk* (Cambridge, Mass. and London: Harvard University Press, 1988) pp.185–6.

37 Wynne, B., 'Frameworks of rationality in risk management: towards the testing of naive sociology' in Brown, J., op. cit., p.44.

38 Beck, U., 'From industrial society to the risk society: questions of survival, social structure and ecological enlightenment' in Featherstone, M., (ed.) *Cultural Theory and Cultural Change* (London: Sage, 1992) p.109.

39 Ravetz, J., 'Usable knowledge, usable ignorance: incomplete science with policy implications' in Clark, W.C. and Munn, R.E. (eds)

Sustainable Development of the Biosphere (Cambridge: Cambridge University Press/IIASA, 1986) p.417.

40 Ezrahi, Y., *The Descent of Icarus: science and the transformation of contemporary democracy* (Cambridge, Mass. and London: Harvard University Press, 1990) p.34.

41 Beck, U., op. cit. in Featherstone, M., p.108.

42 Douglas, M. and Wildavsky, A., op. cit., p.10.

3 SCIENCE AND THE POLICY PROCESS

1 Jasanoff, S., *The Fifth Branch: science advisers as policy makers* (Cambridge, Mass. and London: Harvard University Press, 1990) p.1.

2 Habermas, J., *Towards a Rational Society: student protest, science and politics* (London: Heinemann, 1971) pp.112–13 (original emphasis).

3 Bauman, Z., *Postmodern Ethics* (Oxford and Cambridge, Mass.: Blackwell, 1993) pp.203–4.

4 Jasanoff, S., op. cit., p.1.

5 McGinty, L. and Atherley, G., 'Acceptability versus democracy', *New Scientist*, May 12, 1977, pp.323–5.

6 Advisory Committee on Pesticides, *'Further review of the safety for use in the UK of the herbicide 2,4,5-T'* (London: MAFF, 1980) p.1.

7 Jasanoff, S., op. cit.

8 Irwin, A. and Green, K., 'The British control of chemical carcinogens', *Policy and Politics* (1983), 439–59.

9 Ezrahi, Y., *The Descent of Icarus: science and the transformation of contemporary democracy* (Cambridge, Mass. and London: Harvard University Press, 1990) p.13.

10 Beck, U., *Risk Society: towards a new modernity* (London, Newbury Park, New Delhi: Sage, 1992).

11 Graham, J.D., Green, L.C. and Roberts, M.J., *In Search of Safety: chemicals and cancer risk* (Cambridge, Mass. and London: Harvard University Press, 1988) p.198.

12 Council for Science and Society, *The Acceptability of Risks* (London: CSS and Barry Rose, 1977) p.54.

13 See Irwin, A. and Lloyd, D., 'Pragmatism, effectiveness and institutional judgement in the British control of major accident hazards', *Technology Analysis and Strategic Management*, 4:2 (1992), 115–32.

14 For example, Vogel, D., *National Styles of Regulation: environmental policy in Great Britain and the United States* (Ithaca and London: Cornell University Press, 1986).

15 Wynne, B., *Rationality or Ritual? Nuclear decision-making and the Windscale Inquiry* (Chalfont St Giles: British Society for the History of Science Monographs, 1982).

16 Smith, D., 'Corporate power, risk assessment and the control of major hazards: a study of Canvey Island and Ellesmere Port'. Unpublished PhD thesis, Department of Science and Technology Policy, University of Manchester, March 1988.

17 For example, Vogel, D., op. cit.; Brickman, R., Jasanoff, S. and

Ilgen, T., *Controlling Chemicals: the politics of regulation in Europe and the United States* (Ithaca: Cornell University Press, 1985).

18 Mendeloff, M.J., *The Dilemma of Toxic Substance Regulation: how overregulation causes underregulation at OSHA* (Cambridge, Mass.: MIT Press, 1988).

19 Jasanoff, S., op. cit., p.8.

20 ibid., p.250.

21 Collingridge, D. and Reeve, C., *Science Speaks to Power: the role of experts in policy making* (London: Frances Pinter, 1986).

22 For a detailed account of this example, see Irwin, A., *Risk and the Control of Technology: public policies for road traffic safety in Britain and the United States* (Manchester: Manchester University Press, 1985).

23 See Irwin, A., 'Technical expertise and risk conflict: an institutional study of the British compulsory seat belt debate', *Policy Sciences*, 20 (1987), 339–64.

24 Meehan, R.L., *The Atom and the Fault: experts, earthquakes, and nuclear power* (Cambridge, Mass. and London: MIT Press, 1984).

25 For a larger discussion of this, see Vogel, op. cit.

26 For a fuller account of this case-study, see Irwin, A. and Lloyd, D., op. cit. See also, Lloyd, D.J., 'The role of risk analysis in the control of major hazards'. Unpublished PhD thesis, Faculty of Science, University of Manchester, March 1988.

27 Foot, M., *House of Commons Debates* 880: written answers, col.74, November 7, 1974.

28 Ryder, E.A. 'Discussion session'. Proceedings of the OYEZ European Major Hazards Conference, London, May 22–3, 1984, p.8.

29 Bulmer, A., private interview, November 20, 1986.

30 ibid.

31 See, for example, Lloyd, D.J., op. cit.

32 Jones, T., *Corporate Killing* (London: Free Association, 1988) p.275. For a fuller exposition of this argument, see Perrow, C., *Normal Accidents – living with high risk technology* (New York: Basic Books, 1984).

33 Bauman, Z., op. cit.

34 See, for example, Schwarz, M. and Thompson, M., *Divided We Stand – redefining politics, technology and social choice* (Hemel Hempstead: Harvester Wheatsheaf, 1990).

4 WITNESSES, PARTICIPANTS AND MAJOR ACCIDENT HAZARDS

1 Berger, J. and Mohr, J., *A Seventh Man: the story of the migrant worker in Europe* (Harmondsworth: Penguin, 1975) pp.92–4.

2 Royal Society, *The Public Understanding of Science* (London: Royal Society, 1985) p.24.

3 Durant, J., 'Thrilled by theories', *Marxism Today*, August 1991, pp.40–1.

4 The empirical data in this case-study is drawn from Jupp, A., 'The

provision of public information on major hazards'. Unpublished MSc dissertation, Department of Science and Technology Policy, University of Manchester, January 1988. See also Jupp, A. and Irwin, A., 'Emergency response and the provision of public information under CIMAH – a community case study', *Disaster Management*, 1:4 (1989), 33–8.

5 Council Directive of June 24, 1982 on the Major Accident Hazards of Certain Industrial Activities (82/501/EEC) *Official Journal of the European Communities*, L230 August 1–18, 1982.

6 None of this analysis should be read as imputing sinister motives (or malpractice) to the prime movers behind this information exercise. In fact, the Carrington example is a case of 'better-than-normal' British practice and, indeed, it was partly selected on this basis. Rather than challenging the good faith or competence behind the exercise, the intention is to debate the underlying model on which it implicitly operates.

7 Interestingly, Jupp notes that no written record of this incident could be traced – she sees this as highlighting difficulties over the availability of information. Nevertheless, it forms an important part of the local assessment of the site's safety – Jupp thus notes: 'Local residents remember the incident . . . and it is considered that the evidence from their experience is as valid as any "expert" record'. Jupp, A., op. cit., p.57.

8 See Beck, U., *Risk Society: towards a new modernity* (London, Newbury Park, New Delhi: Sage, 1992) and Giddens, A., *Modernity and Self-identity: self and society in the late modern age* (Cambridge: Polity Press, 1991).

9 Jupp, A., op. cit.

10 This case-study was conducted under an Economic and Social Research Council/Science Policy Support Group award. I am pleased to acknowledge this assistance and also the efforts of my co-workers Alison Dale and Denis Smith.

11 See, for example, Foucault, M., *Discipline and Punish: the birth of the prison* (New York: Pantheon, 1977).

12 Beck, U., op. cit., p. 69.

5 FREEING THE VOICES: A SCIENCE OF THE PEOPLE?

1 Alistair Hay quoted in Allen, R., *Waste Not, Want Not: the production and dumping of toxic waste* (London: Earthscan, 1992) p.ix.

2 Giddens, A., *Modernity and Self-identity: self and society in the late modern age* (Cambridge: Polity Press, 1991) p.138.

3 Beck, U., *Risk Society: towards a new modernity* (London, Newbury Park, New Delhi: Sage, 1992).

4 Rowland, R., *Living Laboratories: women and reproductive technology* (London: Lime Tree, 1992).

NOTES

5 Funtowicz, S.O. and Ravetz, J., 'Science for the post-normal age' in *Futures*, 25:7, September 1993, pp.739–55.
6 See, for example, Irwin, A., 'Acid pollution and public policy: the changing climate of environmental decision-making' in Radojevic, M. and Harrison, R.M., *Atmospheric Acidity* (London and New York: Elsevier, 1992) pp.549–76.
7 Giddens, A., op. cit., p.7.
8 Lash, S. and Wynne, B., 'Introduction' in Beck, U., op. cit., p.3.
9 See, for example, Gillespie, B., Eva, D. and Johnston, R., 'Carcinogenic risk assessment in the USA and UK: the case of aldrin/dieldrin' in Barnes, B. and Edge, D. (eds) *Science in Context: readings in the sociology of science* (Milton Keynes: Open University Press, 1982) pp.303–35.
10 According to Werskey, '[s]ocial development was seen as destined to run along tracks already laid down by past and present generations of rational scientists'. Werskey, G., *The Visible College – a collective biography of British scientists and socialists in the 1930s* (London: Free Association, 1988) p.99.
11 Advisory Committee on Pesticides, *Further Review of the Safety for Use in the UK of the Herbicide 2,4,5–T* (London: HMSO, 1980) p.13.
12 ibid., p.3.
13 NUAAW, *Not One Minute Longer!*, July 1980, p.4.
14 Cook, J. and Kaufman, C., *Portrait of a Poison – the 2,4,5–T story* (London: Pluto Press, 1982) p.53.
15 ibid.
16 ibid.
17 That is, understandings developed in one location would not claim to be equally applicable to other locations.
18 Allen, R., op. cit.
19 Hooper, P., 'The Silksworth Colliery Controversy: a case of un-democratic decision making?' Unpublished undergraduate dissertation, University of Manchester, 1986.
20 Allen, R., op. cit., p.4.
21 Layton, D., Jenkins, E., Macgill, S., Davey, A., *Inarticulate Science – perspectives in the public understanding of science and some implications for science education* (Driffield, W. Yorks: Studies in Education Ltd., 1993) pp.24–5.
22 ibid., pp.36–7.
23 ibid., p.45.
24 ibid., p.46.
25 ibid., pp.57–8.
26 ibid., p.57.
27 Williams, D., 'Understanding people's understanding of energy use in buildings' in Stafford, B. (ed.) *Consumers, Buildings and Energy* (Centre for Urban and Regional Studies, University of Birmingham) p.135 quoted in ibid., pp.73–4.
28 ibid., p.94.
29 Wynne, B., 'Misunderstood misunderstanding: social identities and

191

public uptake of science' in *Public Understanding of Science*, 1 (1992), p.295.

30 ibid., p.287.
31 ibid., p.298.
32 ibid., p.301.
33 Davison, C., Frankel, S., and Davey Smith, G. '"To hell with to-morrow": coronary heart disease risk and the ethnography of fatalism' in Scott, S., Williams, G., Platt, S. and Thomas, H. (eds) *Private Risks and Public Dangers* (Aldershot: Avebury, 1992) p.106.
34 ibid.
35 Doyal, L., Green, K., Irwin, A., Russell, D., Steward, F., Williams, R., Gee, D. and Epstein, S.S. *Cancer in Britain: the politics of prevention* (London: Pluto, 1983).
36 See, for example, Holland, J., Ramazanoglu, C., Scott, S., Sharpe, S. and Thomson, R., 'Don't die of ignorance – I nearly died of embarrassment – Condoms in context', Women Risk Aids Project (WRAP), Paper 2 (London: The Tufnell Press, 1990).
37 Watterson, A., 'Occupational health in the UK gas industry: a study of employer, worker and medical knowledge and action on health hazards in the late 19th and early 20th centuries'. Paper given to the British Sociological Association Annual Conference on 'Health and Society', Manchester, March 1991.
38 ibid., p.8.
39 ibid., p.18.
40 Mulkay, M., *Sociology of Science: a sociological pilgrimage* (Milton Keynes and Philadelphia: Open University Press, 1991) p.212.
41 Watterson, A., op. cit., p.7.
42 Layton, D. *et al.*, op. cit., p.139.
43 Wynne, B., op. cit.
44 Zonabend, F., *The Nuclear Peninsula* (Cambridge University Press/ Editions de la Maison des Sciences de l'Homme: Cambridge, 1993) p.125.

6 BUILDING SUSTAINABLE FUTURES: SCIENCE SHOPS AND SOCIAL EXPERIMENTS

1 Habermas, J., *Toward a Rational Society* (London: Heinemann, 1980 edition) p.79.
2 Barnes, B., *About Science* (Oxford and New York: Basil Blackwell, 1985) p.104.
3 OECD, *Technology on Trial: public participation in decision-making related to science and technology* (Paris: OECD, 1979) p.74.
4 The World Commission on Environment and Development, *Our Common Future* (Oxford and New York: Oxford University Press, 1990 report) p.21.
5 British Government, Summary of *This Common Inheritance* (London: HMSO, 1990) Cm.1200, p.3.
6 Beck, U., *Risk Society: towards a new modernity* (London, Newbury Park, New Delhi: Sage, 1992) p.228.

7 ibid., p.180.
8 The term 'social experiment' may be problematic. I simply use it here as a way of stressing the wider significance of specific initiatives as previously conducted. The term does not imply that these initiatives were carried out as a deliberate attempt to 'test out' the arguments of this book.
9 Smith, D., 'Corporate power, risk assessment and the control of major hazards: a study of Canvey Island and Ellesmere Port'. Unpublished Ph.D. thesis, Dept. of Science and Technology Policy, University of Manchester, March 1988.
10 Nelkin, D., *Technological Decisions and Democracy: European experiments in public participation* (Beverly Hills and London: Sage, 1977) p.15.
11 The best sociological source for this is: Wynne, B., *Rationality and Ritual: the Windscale Inquiry and nuclear decisions in Britain* (Chalfont St Giles: British Society for the History of Science, 1982).
12 OECD, op. cit., p.67.
13 *Nature*, March 23, 1978, p.297, quoted in ibid., p.68.
14 OECD, op. cit., p.12 (my emphasis).
15 ibid., pp.28–9.
16 Lee, T.R., 'Social attitudes and radioactive waste management in France' in *Radioactive Waste Management*, The 5th European Summer School, London, IBC Technical Services Ltd, 1989. Cited in Kemp, R., *The Politics of Radioactive Waste Disposal* (Manchester and New York: Manchester University Press, 1992) p.14.
17 OECD, op. cit., p.45.
18 ibid., p.46.
19 ibid., p.46.
20 ibid., p.50.
21 ibid., p.53.
22 ibid., p.53.
23 ibid., p.58.
24 ibid., p.68.
25 ibid., pp.72–3
26 ibid., p.73.
27 Jasanoff, S., *The Fifth Branch: science advisers as policy makers* (Cambridge, Mass. and London: Harvard University Press, 1990).
28 OECD, op. cit., p.97.
29 ibid., p.99.
30 ibid., p.111.
31 ibid., p.112.
32 ibid., p.113.
33 Layton, D., Davey, A. and Jenkins, E., 'Science for Specific Social Purposes (SSSP): perspectives on adult scientific literacy', *Studies in Science Education*, 13 (1986), p.45.
34 Irwin, A. and Vergragt, P., 'Rethinking the relationship between environmental regulation and industrial innovation: the social negotiation of technical change', *Technology Analysis and Strategic Management*, 1:1 (1989), pp.57–70.

35 See Jansen, L., 'Handling a debate on a source of severe tension' (unpublished mimeo).
36 See Elliott, D. and Wainwright, H. *The Lucas Plan; A new trade unionism in the making?* (London: Allison and Busby, 1982). Also see Steward, F., 'Lucas Aerospace: the politics of the corporate plan', *Marxism Today*, March 1979, pp.70–5.
37 Leydesdorff, L. and Van den Besselaar, P., 'Squeezed between Capital and Technology: on the participation of labour in the knowledge society', *Acta Sociologica*, 30 (1987), 339–53.
38 ibid., p.348.
39 ibid., p.349.
40 Beck, U., op. cit.
41 Leydesdorff, L. and Van den Besselaar, P., op. cit., p.350.
42 Rip, A., 'CTA: the next steps', August 1991 Background paper for International Workshop on CTA, University of Twente, Enschede, The Netherlands 20–2 September 1991.
43 See also, Schot, J., 'Constructive Technology Assessment and Technology Dynamics: the case of clean technologies' in *Science, Technology and Human Values* 17:1, Winter 1992, pp.36–56.
44 OECD, op. cit., p.102.
45 Stewart, J., 'Science Shops in France: a personal view', *Science as Culture*, 2 (1988), 56.
46 ibid., p.59.
47 Leydesdorff, L. and Van den Besselaar, P., 'What we have learned from the Amsterdam Science Shop' in Blume, S. *et al. The Social Direction of the Public Sciences. Sociology of the Sciences Yearbook*, 11 (1987), 135–60.
48 Zaal, R. and Leydesdorff, L., 'Amsterdam Science Shop and its influence on university research: the effects of ten years of dealing with non-academic questions', *Science and Public Policy*, 14:6 (1987), 315.
49 Stewart, op. cit., p.61.
50 ibid., p.62.
51 ibid., pp.73–4.
52 The data in this section are based on a survey of the Northern Ireland Science Shop and its clients conducted early in 1992. I am especially grateful to Eileen Martin for her support in this – and also to the Nuffield Foundation for their sponsorship.
53 Lower Ormeau Residents Action Group quoted in *South Belfast Herald and Post*, March 21, 1991, p.1.
54 *South Belfast Herald and Post*, March 22, 1991, p.9.
55 Stewart, J., op. cit.

7 SCIENCE, CITIZENSHIP AND TROUBLED MODERNITY

1 Beck, U., *Risk Society – towards a new modernity* (London, Newbury Park, New Delhi: Sage, 1992) p.81 (emphasis in original).
2 Bauman, Z., *Modernity and Ambivalence* (Cambridge: Polity, 1991) pp.243–4.

3 ibid.
4 I am grateful to Janet Rachel for planting this image in my head in her inimitable fashion.
5 Barnes, B., *About Science* (Oxford and New York: Basil Blackwell, 1985) p.110 (emphasis in original).
6 Wynne, B. and Mayer, S., 'How science fails the environment', *New Scientist*, June 5, 1993, pp.33–4.
7 ibid., p.34.
8 ibid., p.35.
9 Funtowicz, S.O. and Ravetz, J., 'Science for the post-normal age', *Futures*, 25:7, September 1993, p.740.
10 ibid., p.752.
11 ibid., pp.752–3.
12 ibid., pp.754–5.
13 Beck, U., op. cit., p.232.
14 See Irwin, A., Georg, S. and Vergragt, P., 'The social management of environmental change', *Futures*, 26:3 (1994), 323–34.
15 This area of the 'social management of environmental change' is the topic of a two-year research programme funded by the Commission of the European Communities (Research on social and economic aspects of the environment: DGXII/D/5). This programme is based at Brunel University, the Institute for Transport, Tourism and Regional Economics at the Copenhagen Business School and at Delft University of Technology. The study builds upon the experience of nine European countries.
16 Beck, U., op. cit.
17 Funtowicz, S.O. and Ravetz, J., op. cit.
18 Turner, B.S., 'Outline of a theory of citizenship', *Sociology*, 24:2, May 1990, pp.189–217.
19   There is an old sociological rule . . . that if we want to understand social life then we need to follow the actors wherever they may lead us. . . . This rule of method . . . asks us to take seriously the beliefs, projects and resources of those whom we wish to understand. It suggests that an analysis of social life depends upon such an understanding, and it implies that we make our best progress when we are sociologically humble.

Law, J. and Callon, M., 'Engineering and sociology in a military aircraft project: a network analysis of technological change' in *Social Problems*, 35:3, June 1988, p.84.
20 My text here is, of course, Mills, C.W., *The Sociological Imagination* (Harmondsworth: Penguin, 1973, originally 1959).
21 Mulkay, M., *Sociology of Science – a sociological pilgrimage* (Milton Keynes and Philadelphia: Open University Press, 1991) p.xix.

INDEX

Stewart, J. 160–1
study circles 142–3, 151
sustainable development 6–7, 33,
 36, 39, 64, 132, 134, 136, 137,
 150, 170–82

technology 8
toxic waste 118–21
trust and credibility 45, 66–9, 78,
 95–8, 107, 116, 126–8, 129,
 144
Turner, B.S. 178–9

ventriloquism 168–9

Watterson, A. 130–1, 132
Weber, M. 1, 3, 16
Werskey, G. 110

Williams, R. 4–5
Windscale Inquiry 69, 138–40,
 147–8, 151
Wordsworth, W. 1
World Commission on
 Environment and Development
 (Brundtland Report) 6–7, 36,
 64, 135–6; *see also* sustainable
 development
Wynne, B. 29–30, 47, 58, 69,
 126–8, 131, 133
Wynne, B. and Mayer, S. 170–1

Yearley, S. 43, 57–8

Zaal, R. and Leydesdorff, L. 160
Zonabend, F. 133–4